Prof. Dayanand is the Chief Instructor in the Institute of Palmistry. Having an experience of the subject extending over 30 years, Prof. Dayanand has explored the subject and made new discoveries, which have been tested and found correct.

Many of his books on psychology and on spiritual subjects have been published. Because of his deep knowledge of metaphysics and Yoga he was honoured with the YOGA RATNA by the World Conference on Yoga held in 1986.

This is a sequal to his earlier work on Palmistry ALL THE SECRETS OF PALMISTRY has been published under this series.

PALMISTRY

How to Master It ?

A gist of Indian and Western
System of Hand Reading

Prof. Dayanand
Institute of Palmistry (Regd.)

Books For All
Delhi-110052

First Published 1994
Third Reprint 2003
Fourth Reprint 2012

ISBN 81-7386-221-4
ISBN 978-81-7386-221-2

Published by

Books For All
(an imprint of Low Price Publications)
A-6, Nimri Commercial Centre,
Near Ashok Vihar Phase-IV,
Delhi-110052
Phones: 011-27302453
e-mail: info@Lppindia.com
website: www.Lppindia.com

Printed at
D K Fine Art Press P Ltd.
Delhi-110052

FOREWORD

In my earlier work ALL THE SECRETS OF PALMISTRY I dilated more on the Western concepts of palmistry. In other words that book dealt with the beliefs on this subject current in Europe, the USA and other countries of the west. References, though occasional, have been made to the ancient Indian science of palmistry -- the *Samudrika Shastra*. But, that does not suffice if a student wants to engage in advanced study of the subject. This science like all other branches of knowledge is limitless. One has to have knowledge of both the Indian and Western palmistry to grasp the subject in detail. This work, therefore, deals with some tested formulae from Indian and Western palmistry. The author has himself tested them and has included only those which he found to be the right ones.

Some of the readers might have a rudimentary knowledge of the subject before they chance upon this work and there might be others who are entering into this field of study for the first time. Keeping in mind the needs of both these categories of readers the work has been divided into four parts.

Part I includes the basic elements of palmistry so as to provide a grounding for those who want to understand this branch of science. After having gone into this part freshers can better understand the material provided further and others can refresh their knowledge.

Part II includes, in proper sequence tested formulae for reading the lines of the hand. In the earlier work ALL THE SECRETS OF PALMISTRY the lines, mounts and fingers have been dealt with in separate chapters. That is the proper method if one wants to understand the rudiments of palmistry. But a palmist's client come to consult him with specific questions in mind, like, when will his financial problems be solved? When would he marry? When would he regain health, or undertake travel to foreign lands or win in an ongoing litigation?

In Part II the author says that no question can be answered from a study of one or two lines. All the signs of the hand have to be studied. In the beginning of any course of training in the subject, the author tells his students that the Line of Life tells of the vital force of a person, the Head Line about his mental capacity, the Heart Line about his emotions and sentiments and the Line of Saturn about his worldly goods or wealth. Once the students have grasped these fundamental principles they are told that the Line of Life does not indicate only the state of an individual's health, but also speaks of his wealth, family and travels. Similarly questions with regard to marriage cannot be answered with reference to the lines of sexuality (marriage lines) alone, but a study of many other lines is vital to them. The same applies to other questions which a client might ask you. All the formulae which would help answer these questions are given in Part II. How to interpret the various lines is the keynote of the exercise so that the reader will not forget what the various lines signify.

In Part III remedies for dealing with the various faults of the lines have been given, because, palmistry would be of little value if it cannot suggest remedial action to deal with defective lines and the mounts of the hand.

In Part IV are given some handprints of clients who came to consult the author. They are interpreted so that a sort of exercise is undertaken about how the knowledge gained from the first three parts can be applied to actual cases. At the end we deal with the constant change that takes place in the handlines. Examples in support of the view have been provided.

The author hopes that the readers' curiosity about the mysteries of the hand would be satisfied from this work and those who want to take up palmistry as a profession would be able to gain not only wealth, but also fame.

W-21 Greater Kailash part I,
New Delhi-110048

Dayanand

CONTENTS

PART I

RECAP

Let us Recapitulate what we have learnt about Palmistry before we took up this work

CHAPTER I

AN INTRODUCTION TO THE HAND

Palmistry divides the hand into two :
(i) Thumb and the fingers
(ii) Palm and the Mounts on it

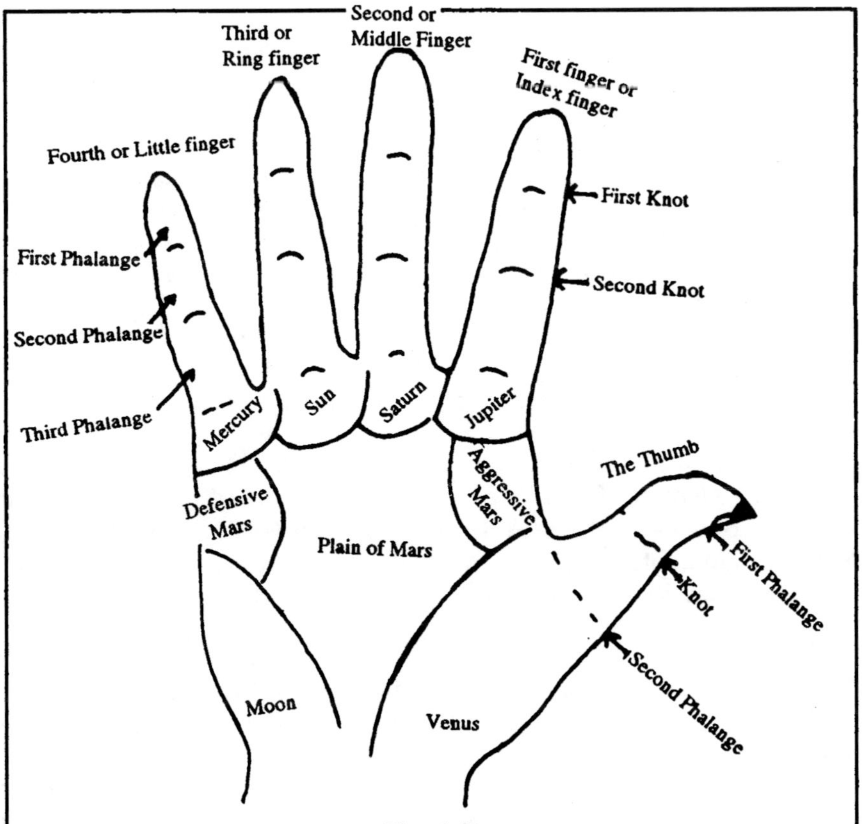

Fig. 1/1

The Thumb *(See Fig. 1/1)*

A long thumb signifies intelligence and discretion in its owner, whereas the short thumb is an indication of tendency towards haste. Its first phalange (on which the nail grows) is a measure of a person's resolve. Those with a long first phalange are men/women of action and the second phalange indicates the capacity for thought. Those with a longer second phalange have little inclination to action, but are always immersed in thought. Those with a short thumb are prone to act without thought.

The Fingers *(See again Fig. 1/1)*

Each finger has three phalanges : the one on which the nail grows is the first phalange, the next to it is the middle phalange and the one adjacent to the palm is the third phalange.

The finger next to the thumb is called the *Index* finger. It represents the ego of a person and his desire for recognition or prestige. If the index finger is longer than normal it is indicative of a person's desire to dominate others; smaller than normal it represents a lack of ambition. Such a person is only a follower, never a leader.

The finger next to the Index finger is called the *Middle* finger. It represents the balance of mind, sagacity and the love of solitude. It is, in most cases, longer than the rest of the digits or fingers. If it is equal in length to the index or the third, or *Ring* finger, it is supposed to be a small middle finger. A person with such a finger will be petty-minded and those having a very long middle finger shy away from human company.

The third or the *Ring* finger is indicative of a person's desire for ostentation and fame. A person with a small ring finger is totally devoid of the tendency towards ostentation. Nor do persons with such fingers take any risks. If the ring finger is longer than usual, i.e., if it is longer than the index finger, a person would be given to too much ostentation and would love to take risks. Those risks include speculation, gambling and other games of chance.

The fourth or the *Little* finger represents eloquence and wit. A little finger which extends to the end of the first phalange of the third finger is considered to be of average length. If it is longer, these qualities become more pronounced in a person. Converse is the case if the finger is of less than average length. A person with a small little finger suffers from an inferiority complex and he does not have the courage to speak out his mind.

Other Features of the Thumb and the Fingers

A thumb which extends upto the middle of the third phalange of the index finger is considered to be of an average length. Smaller than that, it is considered small and long if the converse is the case.

If the knots of the fingers are prominent, a person is given to too much thinking. He has more of an analytical bent of mind than emotions. If the fingers are soft and the knots are depressed or not prominent, a person has a highly developed imagination and is sentimental. His decisions are taken intuitively rather than as a result of thought.

Palms and the Mounts on the Hand *(See again Fig: 1/1)*

We now come to the palm. Palmistry divides the palm into nine divisions. They are called the *Mounts.*

The mount at the base of the index finger indicates a person's desire to lead others, his ambitions and his ego. Palmists call it the Mount of Jupiter. That is why the finger has the peculiarities of Jupiter.

The small area at the base of the middle finger is indicative of the placidity of character, the analytical power, the desire for worldly goods and the yen for solitude. It has been named after Saturn as the Mount of Saturn. The middle finger has all the peculiarities of Saturn.

The small area below the third or ring finger, is indicative of a person's zeal, desire for ostentation and the love of fine arts. It is called the Mount of the Sun or Apollo and the third finger has all the peculiarities of Sun.

The area below the little finger is indicative of a person's pragmatic bent of mind and eloquence. It is named as the Mount of Mercury and this finger has all the peculiarities of Mercury.

A small area below the Mount of Mercury is indicative of a person's patience. Western palmistry calls it the *Upper Mars.*

The area below the Mount of Jupiter is called the *Lower Mars* by Western palmists. It is indicative of the amount of courage a person has. The experience of the present author, however, shows that it is not easy for students of palmistry to remember the Upper and the Lower Mars. He has, therefore, taken the liberty of renaming these areas as Defensive Mars and the Aggressive Mars, on the basis of their peculiarities. It would be easier to remember them if you identify them by reference to their special qualities.

The area below the Defensive Mars, extending upto the edge of the palm in one direction and the wrist in the other represents the imagination and the desire for change in a person. This area is known as the Mount of the Moon.

The area under the Aggressive Mars which extends from the base of the thumb to the wrist shows the sex urge, the vitality and the amount of human sympathy in a person. It has been named as the Mount of Venus.

The area which lies within these mounts is known as the Plain of Mars. If it appears to be full, a person has excess of physical strength and he does not easily lose courage. If it is depressed, a person loses courage in the struggle for life.

If a mount in the palm is prominent, it is known as a developed mount. A person having a particular mount in a developed state is likely to have the qualities associated with that mount. Converse is the case if a mount is depressed or under-developed. The Mount of Saturn is generally found in a depressed state, but, because the finger associated with it, the Middle one, is longer than the rest, it offsets the deficiency of the depressed Mount of Saturn.

CHAPTER II

THE HAND -- SOME OTHER FEATURES

The Right Hand or the Left?

A palmist should study both the palms of all clients, whether men or women. If the lines on both the palms are similar, there are not many ups and downs in a person's life. If the lines are different, the palmist should study the hand which is more active. A hand which is used most often by a person to write with is called the more active hand. A majority of persons are right-handed. In a person who uses his left hand more often, the lines of the left hand should be studied first and than the other hand.

Types of Hand

If the skin of the hand is flexible, a person is more likely to have a flexible character. But, if the skin is thick and hard, a person is not likely to change his views in a hurry. He is a person with firmness of character. If the skin is flexible and the hand is hard it is known as a *Firm Hand.* Such a person is given to thinking and also action. His views are both firm and flexible. If the skin is flexible and the hand soft, it is known as a *Flabby Hand.* Such a person has an active mind, but less of physical strength or vitality.

Colour of the Palm

Pink is an auspicious colour. People with a skin the colour of wheat have a similar tinge in their palms. That is also thought to be auspicious. A red palm indicates an angry disposition. If a palm is yellow in colour it is an indication of the possibility of the person falling a prey to jaundice. People with a white palm always think of their own interests.

Nails

Fig. 2/1

If a nail is long, as well as broad, it is called a large nail. (*See Fig. 2/1*) Large nails are auspicious. People with such nails do not lose their balance of mind even under stress or shocks.

Fig. 2/2

Fig. 2/3

A person with long nails with small width is liable to fall prey to diseases of the throat. (*See Fig. 2/2*)

If a nail is of normal width, but less than average in length, it is called a small nail. (*See Fig. 2/3*) Such persons are devoid of tolerance. They are susceptible to stress and tension.

Let Us Now, in Brief, Talk About the Other Characteristics of the Palm

People with a broad palm tend to look at the practical aspect of things. Physically they are more active. A person with a long palm is, usually, a planner by nature.

People with a small hand have a tendency to look at things in a superficial manner and are wont to overlook the details. They do everything in a hurry. Similar is the case with people with small fingers. The latter are also quick workers.

Conversely, people with a large hand do things in detail. The pace of their work is slow. If the fingers are long, the standard of their performance goes up, but the speed is reduced.

Keep in mind the need to decide whether a hand is large or small. The height of women and the size of their hand is smaller as compared to men. A small hand in a woman is average. Do keep in view the height of a person while deciding whether he has a large or a small hand.

A heavy or a full hand indicates a man of action. Such a person would not easily admit defeat. He is apt to be frank. It is difficult to define what is going on in the mind of a person with thin hands.

Just as a doctor can understand the functioning of the internal organis of the body through a blood test or other tests, the palmist can study the lines on the palm and identify the latent possibilities in a person. Identifying the latent possibilities is the real reading of the past, the present and the future.

-- The Institute of Palmistry

CHAPTER III

LINES ON THE PALM -- AN INTRODUCTION

There are many lines on the palm. Those which are found on most hands are called the *Main Lines.* Those found on only some hands are known as *Secondary Lines.* Nomenclature of the main and secondary lines would be found in works on palmistry, but there are many other lines which have not been given any names. They are generally called the *Lines of Influence or Chance.* The part of the brain connected with a particular mount on which such a line starts is more active than others. The line or mount towards with a line of influence moves has more attraction in the life of that individual. These lines give rise to figures known as cross, star or island. These figures are called the signs of the palm. What these signs signify would be dealt with later under Recap. Let us first discuss the main and secondary lines and their characteristics.

THE MAIN LINES

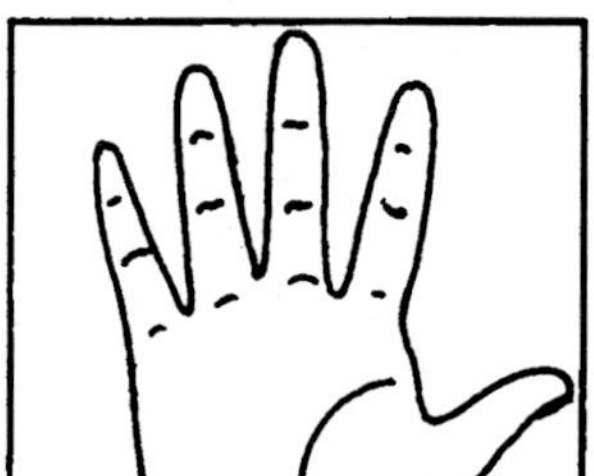

Fig. 3/1

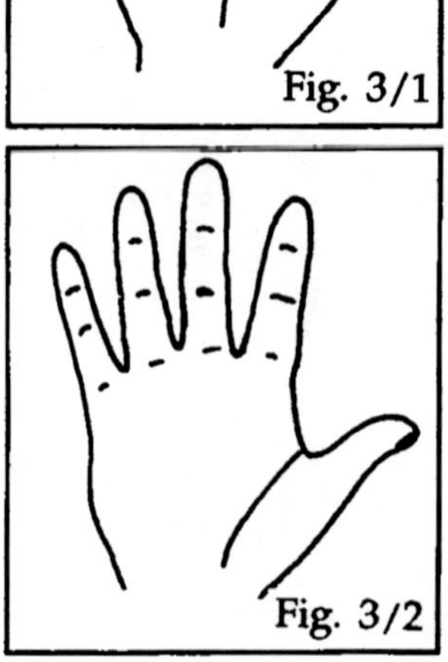

Fig. 3/2

The Line of Life *(See Fig. 3/1)*

According to the ancient science of India, the *Samudrika Shastra,* this line is called the *Gotra Rekha,* or the *Pitri Rekha* and represents the family. Western palmists, however, call it the line which indicates the physical capacity of a person. They judge a person's age, possibility of diseases etc. from this line, but the experience of the author is that it also indicates, health, wealth, change of residence, partnerships and the family too. If the Line of Life is semi-circular, thin and deep, it is an auspicious sign. A thick, shallow and straight line of life is not auspicious. A straight line of life is given in *Figure 3/2.*

This line starts from a place between the Aggressive Mars and the Mount of Jupiter and ends near centre of wrist line The Bracelet. Sometimes it is found originating from the Mount of Jupiter or the Aggressive Mars or the centre of the palm. It also ends on the Mount of Venus or the Mount of the

Moon. It takes on the characteristics of the mounts from which it starts or those at which it ends.

Line of Head *(See Fig. 3/3)*

Fig. 3/3

According to *Samudrika Shastra,* it has been called the *Matri Rekha* or the *Dhana Rekha*. Western palmists, however, call it the Line of Head. It is indicative of the mental level or the intelligence of a person. Whether a person would have money or not is also divined from a study of this line. If one goes a little deeper into things one finds that intelligence or a person's mental level has something to do with whether he would have money or not. If a person loses the capacity to act intelligently, he is sure to lose whatever money he has and, conversely, using one's wits·fully can lead to affluence. This line generally originates from a point between the Aggressive Mars and the Mount of Jupiter and terminates at the Defensive Mars, but in most palms it is seen beginning from the Mount of Jupiter or the Aggressive Mars of the Line of Life and terminates at the Mount of Mercury or the Mount of Luna. The point of origin and the point of termination of the line enter into its effect on the life of the individual.

Line of Heart *(See Fig. 3/4)*

Fig. 3/4

According to the *Samudrika Shastra* it is the Line of Life and questions regarding health and longevity are answered with reference to it. It begins from the Mount of Mercury and ends at the Mount of Saturn or the Mount of Jupiter. Western palmists believe it to be the line of emotions, which include love, anger, friendship etc. All the Western palmists are not agreed on its points of origin and termination. The experience of the present author is that this line indicates the emotional state of the individual, his love life and his health. It originates from the Mount of Jupiter and ends somewhere between the Mount of Mercury and the Defensive Mars. In some palms, it originates from the Mount of Saturn and terminates towards the Mount of Mercury.

Other Facets of These Three Lines

According to the *Samudrika Shastra* the Line of Heart indicates the condition of the spouse, the Line of Head tells about the maternal side of a person's life

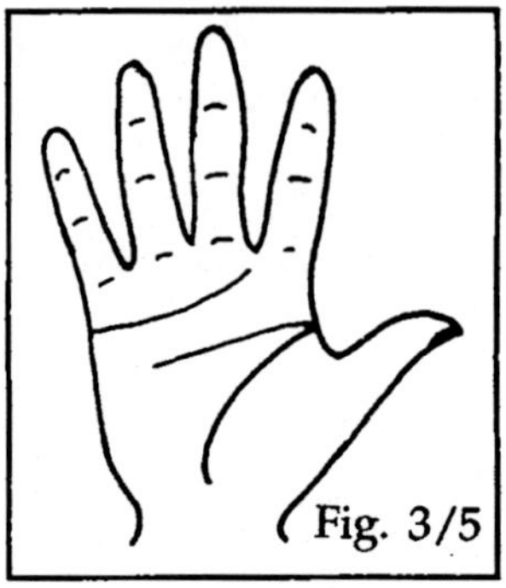
Fig. 3/5

and the Line of Life is consulted to see how the paternal side fares. But a lot of further research in this is indicated and research is a never-ending process. We have on the basis of our experience indicated in this work the points of origin and those where the lines terminate. Fig. 3/5 shows all these three main lines together.

MAIN SECONDARY LINES

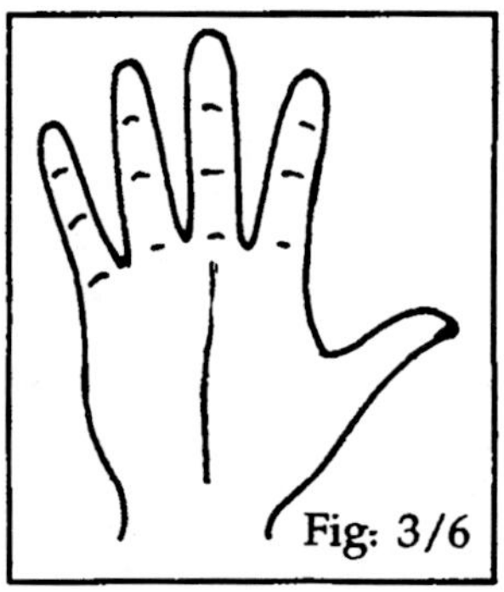
Fig: 3/6

Line of Saturn *(See Fig. 3/6)*

According to *Samudrika Shastra* it is called the *Urdhwa* or *Indira Rekha*. Western palmists, however, consider this as the line of fate or of prosperity. We call it the line of Saturn because it inclines towards the Mount of Saturn. One can answer questions like a person being in possession of worldly goods from a study of this line. It also indicates possibilities of marriage and love for an individual. If this originates from the Line of Life it is considered to be very good. If it originates from the middle of the palm near the wrist, a little away from the Line of Life, it is good. But, if this line originates from a point very near the Line of Life it is not good at all. This line also originates from the Mounts of Moon and Venus, but its effect shows when it straightens and enters the area of the Mount of Saturn.

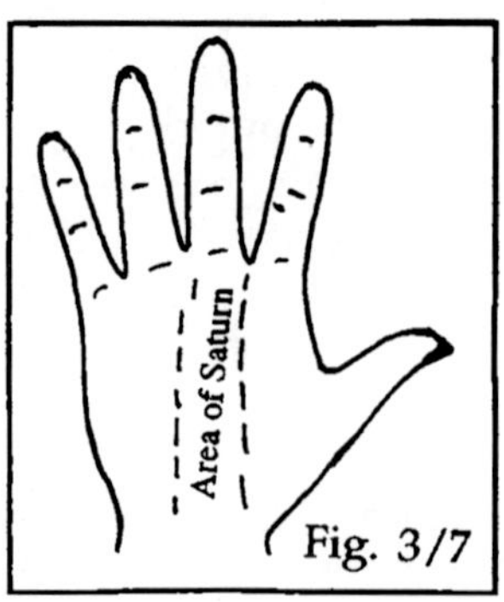

Fig. 3/7

According to *Samudrika Shastra,* the area lying between the base of the middle finger and the wrist is the area controlled by Saturn *(See Fig. 3/7).* The Line of Saturn indicates possibility of wealth. But its effect is seen only when there is another parallel line a little away, or when the Line of the Sun originates. The line which is close to the Line of Saturn is called the *Kuthar Rekha* (axe line) which interferes with the success of efforts to gain the worldly goods.

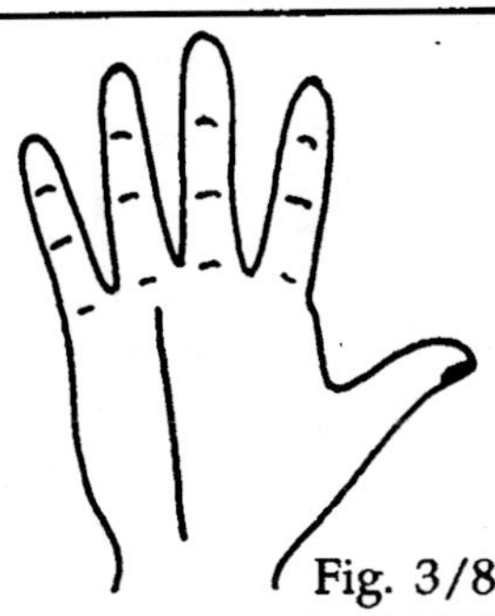

Fig. 3/8

Line of Sun *(See Fig. 3/8)*

This is a subsidiary of the Line of Saturn. According to *Samudrika Shastra* it is called variously as the *Dharma Rekha,* the *Vidya Rekha* and the *Punya Rekha*. It starts from the wrist, the line of life, the line of Saturn or the Mount of the Moon. It inclines towards the Mount of the Sun. This line indicates the success of one's efforts, whether in the acquisition of wealth, politics, a court case, travel or a love affair. A person gets his heart's desire at the time of its coming on the scene. We shall deal with estimating the time when we come to the part of the book where we recap what we have written in this part.

Fig. 3/9

Line of Mercury *(See Fig. 3/9)*

Samudrika Shastra calls it the *Arogya* or *Swasthya Rekha*. Western palmists call it the line of health or the Hepatica (concerned with the health of the liver). Palmists do not agree on its origin or its effect. But the experience of the present author is that this line indicates the sharpness of intelligence or his business sense. It originates from the Mount of Venus, or the Line of Life, the Line of Saturn or the Mount of the Moon and it terminates at the Mount of Mercury. A clear, well-defined line indicates intelligence and good health. A broken-up Line of Mercury is an indication of indifferent health and confused thinking.

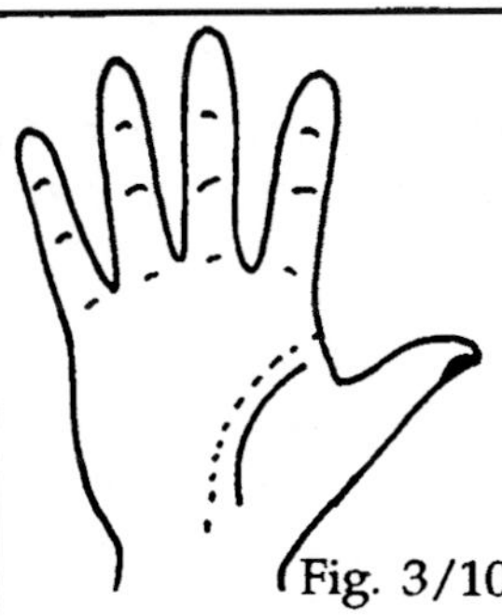

Fig. 3/10

Line of Mars *(See Fig. 3/10)*

Some palmists believe that it is a line of influence of the Mount of Venus. It is a parallel line within the Line of Life. If it is very near the line of life or if it is very deep it indicates the extent to which a person is subject to fits of anger. If it is away from the Line of Life the person is likely to be of an equable temper. It also indicates the state of marital relations. It originates from the Aggressive Mars, runs parallel to the Line of Life towards the Mount of Venus and terminates at the wrist or the Mount of Venus.

Lines of Sexuality or Marriage Lines *(See Fig. 3/11)*

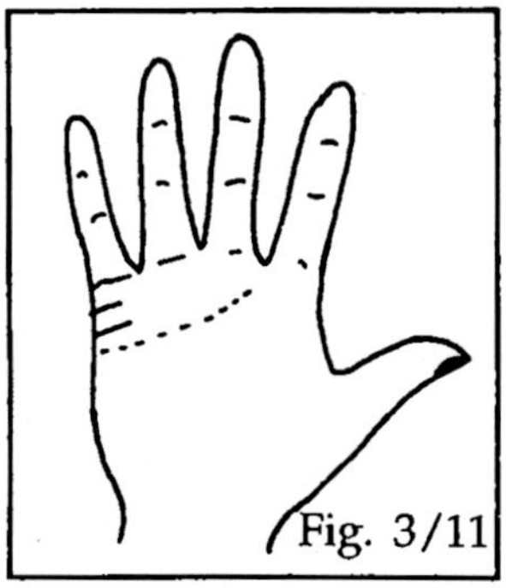

Fig. 3/11

We have called the line popularly known as the Marriage Line as the Line of Sexuality, because it indicates relationships of an individual which are connected with sex. Such a relationship might continue without religious sanction for a long time. This line originates from the percussion (outer part of the palm) near the Mount of Mercury and is inclined towards it.

If the line is straight, it is generally indicative of a good marital relationship or an enduring love affair. If this line inclines towards the Heart Line it indicates an interruption with marital relations or ill health of the spouse. If this line inclines towards the little finger, the spouse is likely to have a long life. This line may not be a single one, but there might be two or even three such lines. But it does not mean that a person would have as many marriages or love affairs. We will deal with this subject of marriage in detail in the second part of the book. It would suffice here to point out that sexual or marital relations or love affairs are not to be inferred from this line alone. One must study the line of Mars, the line of Saturn, the Line of the Sun, the Mount of Venus and the Mount of Jupiter before answering any questions about marriage or its break-up. Many formulae to help you answer such queries are given in the second part of the book.

According to *Samudrika Shastra*, the heart line on the left palm of the man concerns his wife and the same line on the right palm of the woman concerns her husband. But not many proofs are available about the effect of the lines according to this theory.

Line of Children *(See Fig. 3/12)*

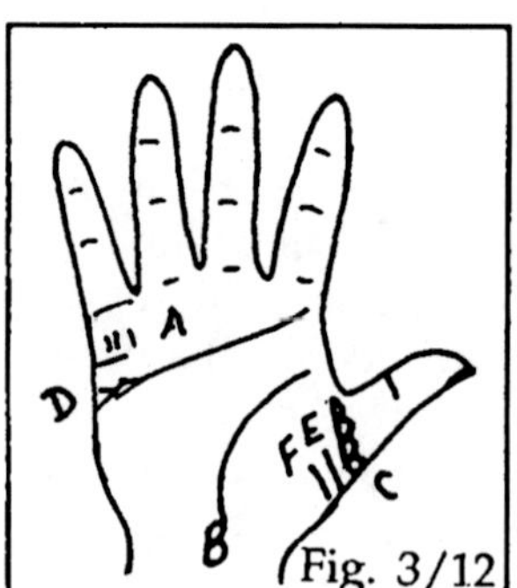

Fig. 3/12

The vertical lines over the line of marriage are, according to Western palmists, the lines of children *(See Fig.3/12A)*.But the experience of the author is that these lines are not true indicators of the children a person is likely to have. According to the *Samudrika Shastra* questions about children can be answered with reference to the circular shape of the Line of Life *(See Fig. 3/12-B)*, the number of islands at the base of the thumb *(See Fig. 3/12-C)*, the branches at the end of the Heart Line *(See Fig. 3/12-D)* and the parallel lines near the base of the thumb *(See Fig.3/12-EF)*. For details see under appropriate heads in Part II.

Bracelets *(See Fig. 3/13)*

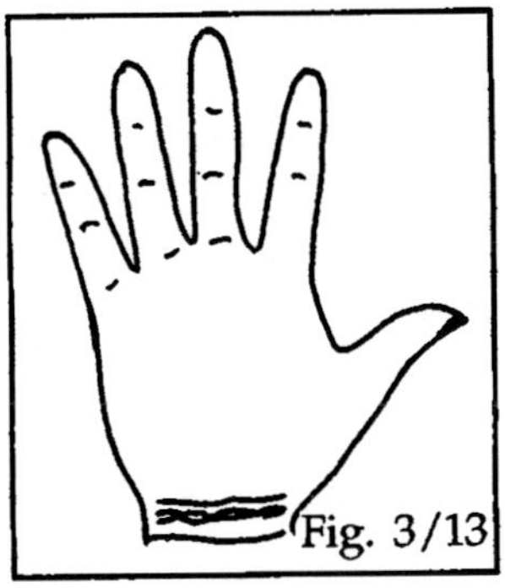

Fig. 3/13

Lines along the breadth of the wrist are known as bracelets, because they resemble the ornament of that name. According to *Samudrika Shastra* questions regarding longevity and health are answered with reference to the bracelets, but Western palmists do not attach much importance to them. We shall, at a later stage, indicate the effect that the bracelets have.

SECONDARY LINES

These lines are not found on most palms and that is why they are known as Secondary Lines.

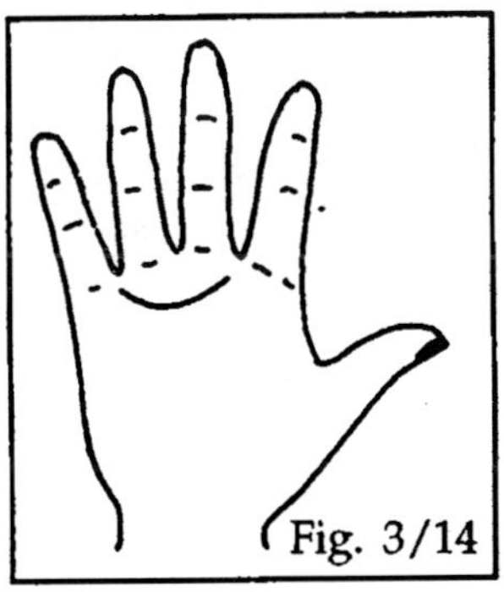

Fig. 3/14

The Girdle of Venus is the semi-circular line enveloping the mounts of Saturn and the Sun *(See Fig. 3/14)*. If Venus, Moon and the Aggressive Mars on a palm are well-developed and the number of lines on the palm is small, it indicates a surfeit of sexuality. If this girdle is found on a thin palm with a large number of lines, it is indicative of worries which beset the owner of such a hand. If the girdle is incomplete, its effect is minimal.

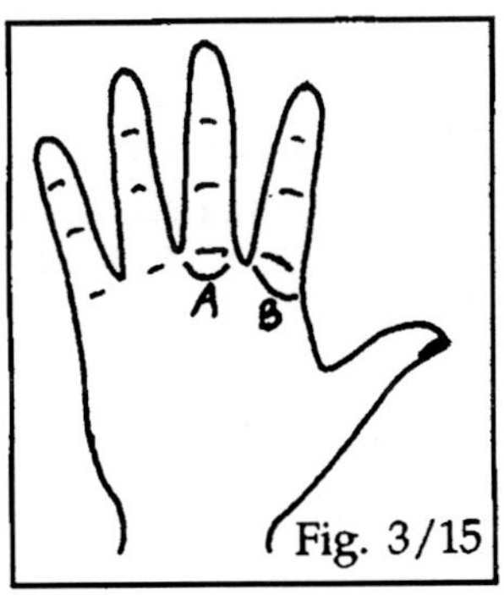

Fig. 3/15

The Ring of Saturn *(See Fig. 3/15-A)* is a semicircular line. If it bisects the line of Saturn, it indicates hurdles in a person becoming wealthy at the point of time in the life. In the alternative, it shows deep interest in subjects of the occult.

The Ring of Solomon indicates the amount of sagacity in a person and his desire for esteem in the eyes of others *(See Fig. 3/15-B)*. There are other lines too on the Mount of Jupiter in addition to the Ring of Solomon. They are called the lines of Jupiter and help a person to get his heart's desire. If lines coming from different directions bisect each other they form a cross. This cross also is a sign of success.

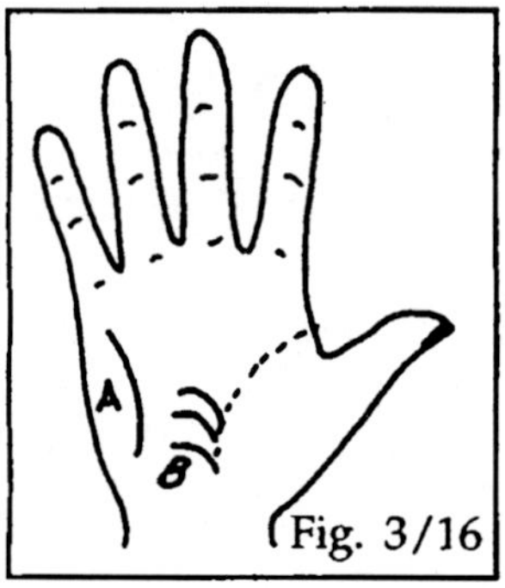

Fig. 3/16

Line of Intuition if found on a palm, indicates great amounts of intuition in a person. This semi-circular line goes from the Mount of the Moon towards the Mount of Mercury *(See Fig.3/16A).* If the Mount of the Moon is well-developed, the effect of this line is heightened, but, if it is incomplete and the Mount of the Moon is not developed, its effect is reduced greatly. The semi-circular lines of influence going from the Line of Life to the Mount of the Moon are also called Lines of intuition *(See Fig.3/16B)* but their effect is minimal.

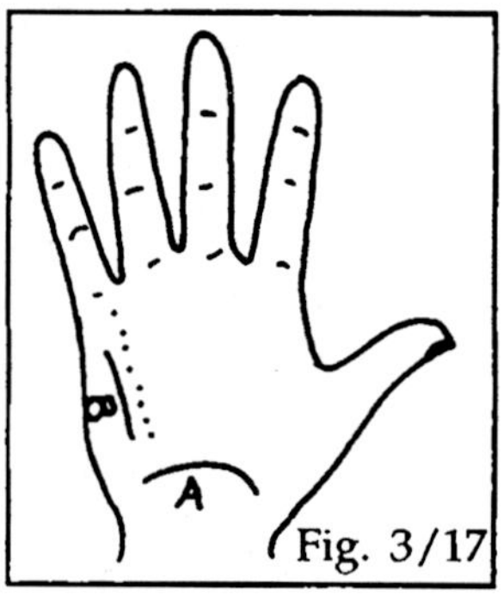

Fig. 3/17

Via Lasciva is a circular line between the Mount of the Moon and the Mount of Venus *(See Fig. 3/17-A)* and is parallel to the Line of Mercury *(See Fig. 3/17-B).* If either of these two lines is found on a heavy hand, it is indicative of excessive sexuality. Occurring on a thin or flabby hand, it is a sign of weakness for drugs. Study Figures 3/16 and 3/17 carefully so that you can distinguish between the Line of Intuition and the Via Lasciva.

Travel Lines

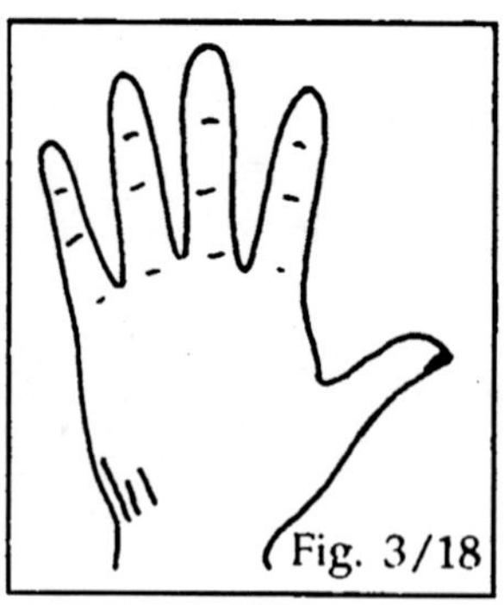

Fig. 3/18

The mounts of the Moon and Mercury have a special affinity for travel. Lines which emanate from the wrist and go towards the Mount of the Moon are generally called Travel Lines *(See Fig. 3/18),* but travel does not depend on these lines alone. We shall come to the signs on the palm later which indicate travel.

Axe Line (*Kuthar Rekha*) and the Parallel Line

A line very near a main line is called an axe line. It tends to reduce the beneficial effect of that main line. If such a line runs parallel a distorted line, it reduces the ill effects of that line. But a line which is a little distance away from the main line it is called a parallel line. A parallel line has the effect of accentuating the influence of that line. For example, if the Line of Mars is very near the line of life, it would be an axe line of that line. But, if it is a little distance away, it is a parallel line. If the Line of Saturn is very near the Line of Life, that period of life represented by that line is the period of the axe line. When the distance between these two lines increases, the effect of the Line of Saturn is heightened. *The Line of the Sun is a parallel line of the Line of Saturn, but lines very near the latter on the right or the left are axe lines for it (the Line of Saturn).*

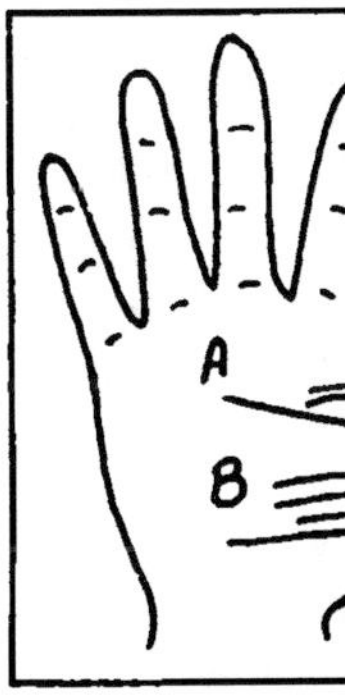

Fig. 3/19

Worry Lines (*Rahu Rekhas*): If the influence line emerges from the Aggressive Mars and intersects the Line of Life, the Line of Saturn or the Head Line, it indicates worries of a serious nature *(See Fig. 3/19-A)*. If it stops short of touching the main line, worries are of a minor nature. Some palmists call them the Rahu Lines. If a worry line reaches the Mount of Jupiter, the Mount of Saturn, the Mount of Apollo or the Sun, or the Mount of Mercury, it strengthens the effect of that mount. For example, the worry line which reaches the Mount of Jupiter gives a person esteem in the eyes of his peers, the one touching the Mount of Saturn gives wealth and prosperity, the one going to the Mount of the Sun gives fame and the one which touches the Mount of Mercury gives success in business and science.

If the worry line coming from the Mount of Venus goes upto the Line of Saturn or the Line of life, it is indicative of anxieties for which the family of a person is responsible *(See Fig. 3/19-B)*. Worry lines which intersect the main lines are indicative of serious worries. The time when such worries would beset the person concerned can be calculated according to at what point of time the worry line intersects the Line of Saturn or the Line of Life. If there is no line on the Aggessive Mars or the Mount of Venus, the person does not have much attachment with his family. He is alone in the struggle for life.

An Auspicious Parallel Line

If a line emerges from the Line of Life and follows the path of the Line of Mars, it is called a line of Extra Fortune *(See Fig. 3/20-A)*. The line emanating from the Mount of Jupiter and running parallel to the Heart Line is also known as the Extra Fortune Line *(See Fig. 3/20-B)*. But I call them the auspicious parallel lines. Let it be repeated here that a line a short distance away from the main

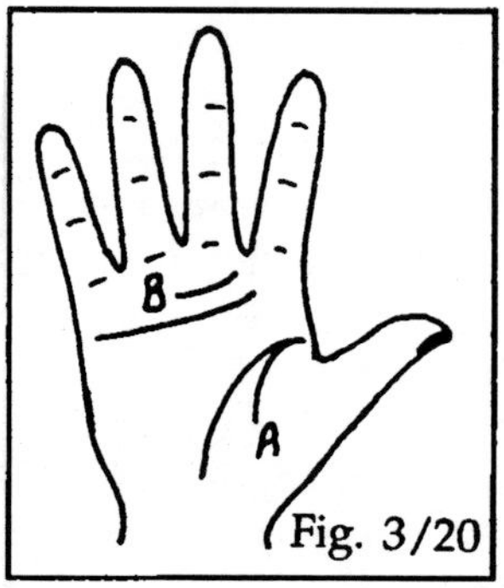

Fig. 3/20

line tends to increase the effect of the latter.

Quality of the Lines

Thin and deep lines are auspicious. A line not very deep, but broad is inauspicious. The strength of a shallow line is meagre. If you want to find out the difference between a shallow and a deep line, stretch it. If a line vanishes on stretching, it is shallow line, but that which remains visible under this condition is a deep line. It is good if a line of influence is shallow. If the main lines on a palm are broad and very deep, their effect is ordinary. If a line is thick at one place and thin at another, fortune smiles on the person at the time of life when the line becomes thin. The stopping of the thick line is also an indication of good fortune.

When you are studying a palm and find that a line has stopped short of its destination, do not think that it is a sign of misfortune. First see whether the line is thin and deep at the place it has stopped or thick and deep. In the latter case all obstacles to a person's fortune disappear at the time the line has stopped. If the thin and deep line has stopped it is an indication of no new sources of income appearing, but greater income from the existing ones. Broken down lines and those intersected by the lines of influence are a sign of fluctuations in a man's fortunes, of what he is likely to gain or to lose.

It must be remembered that the only intersection of a main line by a line of influence is considered intersection. The main or secondary lines follow their paths and any intersection on the way cannot be considered to be a cross.

Other Facts About the Lines

If there are only the three main lines, namely, the Line of Life, the Line of the Head and the Heart Line on a palm, it is a sign of an ordinary life for the individual. If a person is born in a rich or a poor family, his fortunes would follow the fortunes of his family in the ordinary course. There are not many fluctuations in his life. Such persons do not have high ambitions, nor have they any interest in the arts.

If the main lines are thin and deep, a person is usually successful. If there are secondary main lines on the palm too, the person is ambitious. The life of an ambitious person is full of struggle. He tries to do better than what his family has been able to achieve in the way of wordly success.

If there are many lines of influences on a palm in addition to main lines and secondary lines, it mean that the person's mind is active in various directions. If the lines on the active hand are inauspicious as compared to those on the inactive hand, a person might spoil his chances of success because of a wrong decision.

Further on, we are going to use terms like "defective" line, "auspicious" line, "descending" line and "ascending" line. Let us define them and understand their true significance.

A DEFECTIVE line includes any of the following : an incomplete line, a wavy line, a line composed of many segments, cross made on a line by a line of influence, thick line, indistinct line.

An AUSPICIOUS line is a thin, deep line or one which is ascending or has branches.

An ASCENDING LINE means a line going from the wrist to the fingers, like the Line of Saturn.

A DESCENDING line is one which goes from the fingers to the wrist like the Line of Life.

A HORIZONTAL line is one which lies in the middle of the palm in its width, like the Line of Head.

A CIRCULAR line is one which is slightly circular like the Life line, the Line of Mars, the Line of Intuition, the Via Lasciva.

If a part of the line is depressed or there is a well-marked depression on it, that part of the line should be considered as defective. If there is a depression on a mount, the mount is inauspicious to the extent of the depression.

●

THE RIGHT HAND OR THE LEFT

When a client tells you that he is ambidextrous -- that is he is equally proficient in the use of both his hands, take his left hand to be the active hand. To know the reason why it should be so, look at the social milieu in which you live.

Our society looks down upon a person who uses his left hand and he is told repeatedly to use his right hand. Because of these importunings, the person who is used to the use of his left hand starts using his right too. But, he finds it easy to use the left, even if he works with both the hands. According to the principles of palmistry his left hand should be taken to be the active hand. The reason is that his basic instinct is to use his left hand.

A typist used both the hands while he is at his machine, but that is because the use of both the hands is vital to operate a typewriter. Decide whether the right or the left hand is active with reference to the hand with which a person finds it comfortable to write.

- AUTHOR

CHAPTER IV

SIGNS ON THE PALM

We have talked about the lines of influence in the last chapter. When these lines meet on the palm they form many figures to which students must be initiated so that they can recognise them and understand their significance.

Cross

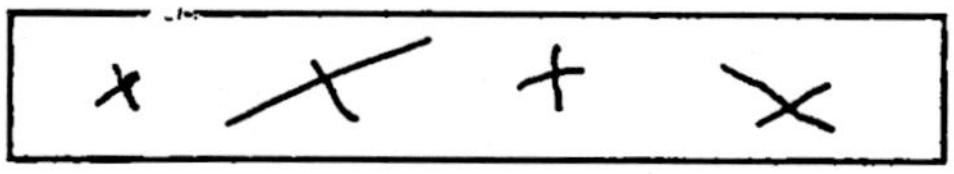

A cross on the Mount of Jupiter is auspicious, but inauspicious on other mounts and lines. Remember that if two lines of influence form a cross it is inauspicious; less inauspicious is the one which is formed when a line of influence intersects a main line.

Star

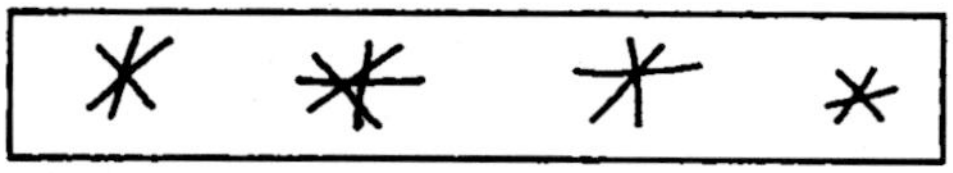

The effect of a star, like that of a cross, can be either good or bad.

Square

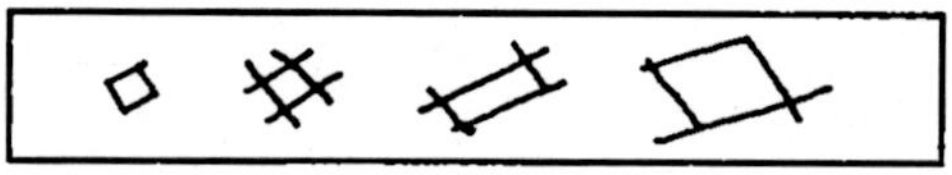

It provides protection against inauspiciousness or obstacles associated with the mount or the line on which it is found.

Island

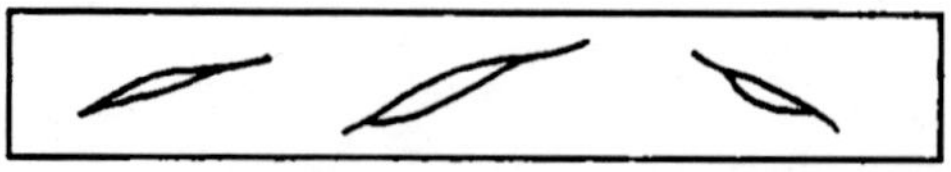

According to the Indian *Samudrika Shastra*, an island is a *Yava*. It is a sign of good if it is found on the phalange of the thumb adjacent to the palm, as it is on the joint between the two phalanges. At other locations it is inauspicious. The widest part of the island is the most harmful at the time of life indicated by its position on the palm. If an island is torn or cut up in two, it is more harmful.

Triangle

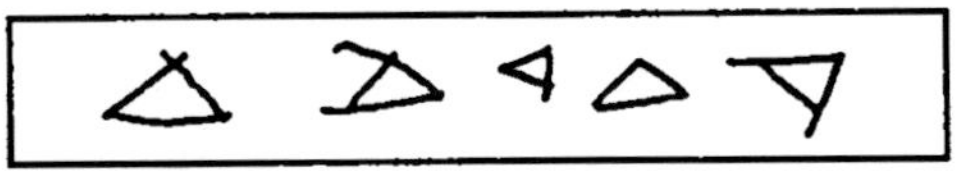

A triangle, wherever it is found on the palm, is auspicious and beneficial.

Grill

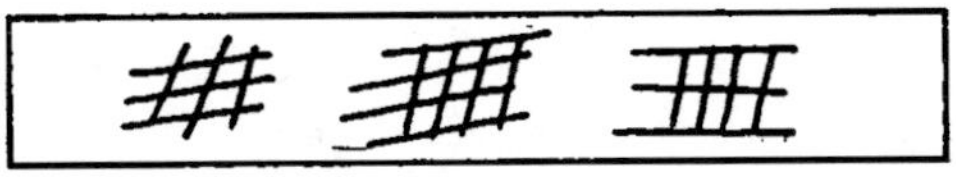

On whatever mount it is found it accentuates its effect; but, as the adage goes, too much of everything is bad.

Trident

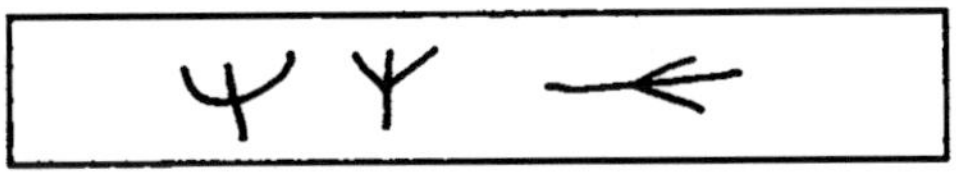

A trident is usually found at the end of the vertical lines towards the fingers. Its effect is beneficial. If it is found at the end of a line towards the wrist, it tends to reduce the power and effect of that line.

Tassle

A tassle is usually found at the end of a line. It tends to reduce the effect of that line. But, if it is at the end of the Heart Line, it is beneficial.

Forked Line

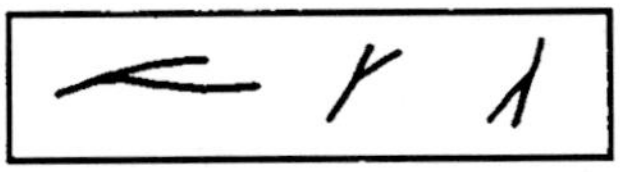

A forked line is indicative of the increased benefit of that line.

Depression

A small depression is sometimes found on a line or on the palm. It is not auspicious. The strength of the mount or the line is reduced at the age at which a depression is found on it. Study the handprint No. 3 'A' (Heart Line) and No. 3 'B' (Line of Saturn), in part IV where there is a depression.

Chain Like Line

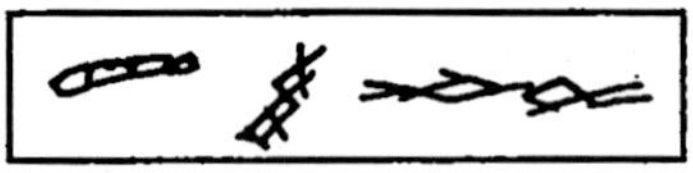

A line twisted like a rope which resembles a chain is defective.

Broken or Wavy Line

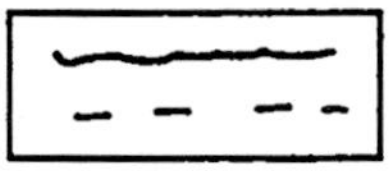

Broken or wavy lines are also defective.

Parallel Line

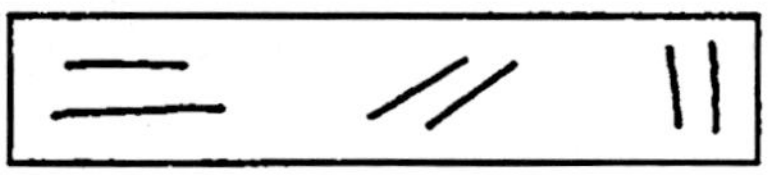

If a thin, clear line runs parallel to a broken or defective line, it tends to remove the fault or the defect of the broken line. If the parallel line runs a little away from a main line, it tends to accentuate the influence of that main line.

Axe Line or *Kuthar Rekha*

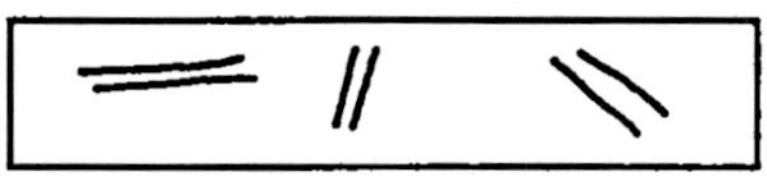

A thin line very near a clear, deep line gives rise to problems. If it is a little distance away it is called a subsidiary or parallel line. The effect of the subsidiary line is beneficial.

Fish Sign

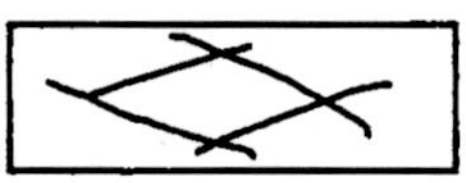

If a square resembles a rectangle, it is called a Fish Sign *(Matsya Chinha)* by the practitioners of the *Samudrika Shastra.* It is auspicious because it endows wealth and knowledge.

Other Features of the Lines

If the number of lines on a palm is limited, they are more effective. Print of a hand with only a few lines is given in Part IV (*Handprint No. 20-B*). Some palms have a network of lines; the effect of these lines is reduced because of their multiplicity. Handprints in part IV, Nos 3-A,B and 15-AB should be studied as examples of multiplicity of lines on a palm. The number of squares, crosses, stars and triangles is so much that they lose all their effect. The only conclusion you can draw from such a handprint is that such persons' brain centres are hyperactive.

For studying how the signs mentioned above appear in handprints consult Part IV (Handprints).

CHAPTER V

LINES AS INDICATORS OF LIFE EXPECTANCY AND IMPORTANT EVENTS IN LIFE

Almost all the eminent palmists are agreed that one can only indicate the approximate time when some events or mishaps would occur in a person's life and that the lines cannot indicate any definite time when such things would happen.

Palmists do not agree about the best method of calculating the time of events from a study of the lines on the palm. The present author, however, believes that Cheiro's System of Seven is accurate to a large degree. Cheiro's formula in its essence is as follows:

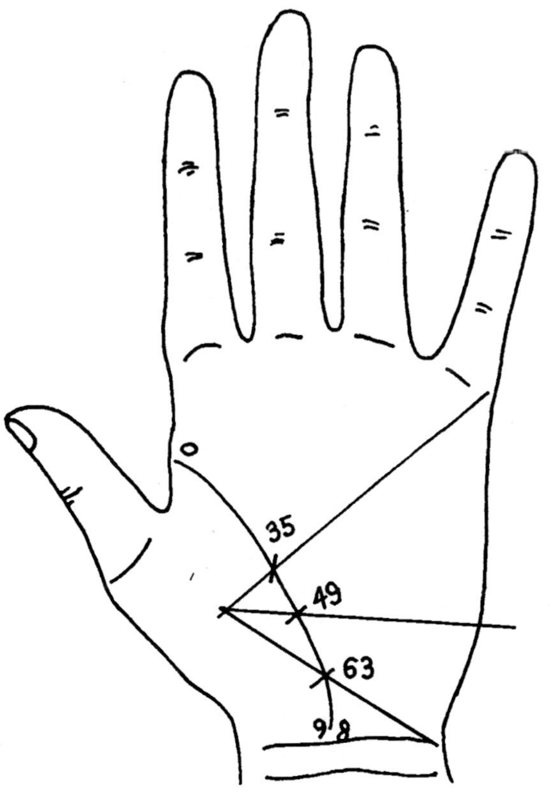

Fig. 5/1- Age on the Line of Life

Cheiro divides the Line of Life and the Line of Saturn according to his System of Seven into segments each representing a span of seven years. He does not divide the Head Line and the Heart Line under this system, but believes that if the Head Line is short it indicates an under-developed mind. As to the Heart Line, Cheiro believes that if it is short, it indicates lack of sentimentality in a person. He applies his System of Seven on the Line of Mercury and the Line of the Sun, as he does on the Line of Saturn. The Line of Mars runs parallel to the Line of Life and he brings it under his system.

To Take the Line of Life First

It begins from a point between the Mounts of Jupiter and the Aggressive Mars *(see Fig. 5/1)*. If you want to find about the childhood of a person consult the origin of this line. The middle of the line represents youth and the part near the wrist old age.

A simple method of marking the age on the Line of Life is to draw a line from the middle of the Mount of Venus to the outer edge of the base of the little finger. The point where this line intresects the Line of Life is the age of 35 years.

Another horizontal line is drawn from the centre of the Mount of Venus to the percussion (the other edge of the palm) and the point at which it intersects the Line of Life is age 49. Draw a third line from the centre of the Mount of Venus to the bracelet. The point at which this line intersects the Line of Life is the age of 63 years.

Fig. 5/1 shows age 98 years at the end of the Line of Life, whereas the beginning of the line represents age 0 years. After you have understood where the three ages in life (35, 49 and 63) are situated between 0 and 98 years lie, it would be easier for you to mark the other points showing the various ages. You can then predict the influence of the Line of Life according to its state and direction.

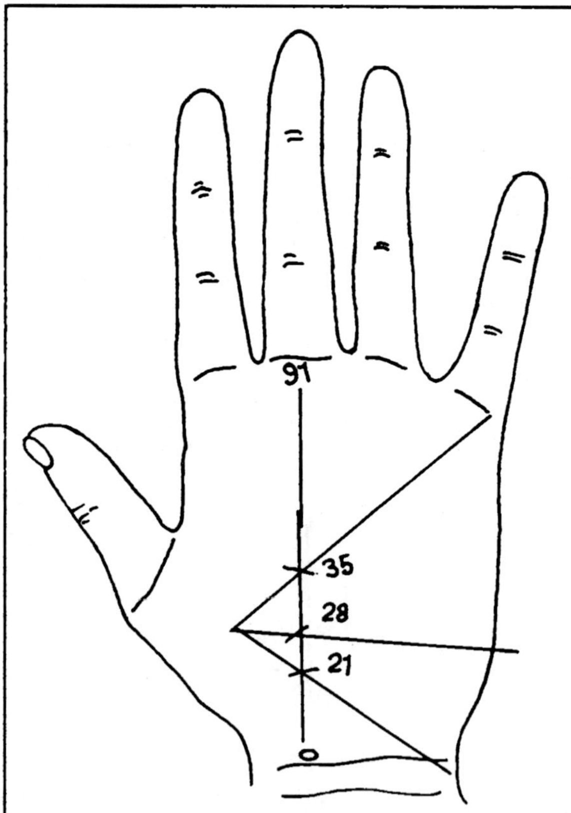

Fig. 5/2 Age on the Line of Saturn

Other Rules Governing the Forecast of Progress, Profit and Career Prospects

If you look at Fig. 5/2, you would find a vertical line. It is the line of Saturn. A person's age can be calculated from this line according to the following method : this line originates from the wrist (*See Fig. 5/2 Zero*) and ends at the base of the middle finger (*Fig. 5/2*). Events during childhood can be seen from the beginning of this line, those of youth from the middle and old age from the end of the line.

Fig. 5/2 shows a line drawn from the centre of the Mount of Venus towards the bracelet. The junction of this line with the Line of Saturn has been marked "21 years". Another line has been drawn from the same point to join the base of the little finger. The point where it intersects the Line of Saturn has been marked "35 years". Another line has been drawn from the centre of the Mount of Venus to the percussion (other end of the palm). Its junction with the Line of Saturn has been marked "28 years"

Between the points 0, 21, 28, 35 and 91 you can mark the ages according to your own understanding of the subject. Keeping them in view and also the Line of Saturn you can know whether at that particular time a person is likely to gain money or lose it.

Some palmists mark the Head Line at 35 years and the Heart Line at 50 years. These lines are not similarly placed in all palms and that is why this rule might give an approximation of the true reading, but the proper course is the one outlined in this chapter.

AN IMPORTANT QUERY AND ITS ANSWER

My students often ask me: why is it that the same Line of Life tells you about the family, the wealth of the individual and also his vital force? Similarly, the Line of Saturn gives an indication of marriage, wealth and many other aspects of human life. The lines of Heart, Head and Mars, in the same manner can be interpreted to mean different things. What bothers the students is how to interpret a line in what manner at what time.

I repeat the answer which I give to my students:

The digits 0 to 9 are used to write figures which may be hundreds or billions. The seven notes in music can be employed to compose myriads of *ragas* and the dictionaries of the world use only 26 letters from A to Z. Similarly the limited number of lines on the palm are interpreted in various ways to read the destiny of human beings.

In so far as the question as to which line mean what in each hand is concerned, it can be answered only in relation to the query of your client and the context in which that is made. Words in any language mean different things according to context. "Right" means the one opposed to left, "correct" and "a legally and morally just claim". "Get" means to obtain, but in conjunction with other words its meaning might change, i.e. in get away, get back, get down, get in, get off, get on, get out, get over, get through, get together and get up etc. Such examples can be multiplied. If, then, each line on the palm has a different meaning according to the context in which it is interpreted, one should not wonder. The lines of the palm have a language of their own and like every other language it has its own grammar and its own rules.

– AUTHOR

PART II

Reading the Signs on the Palm in Response to Specific Queries

INTRODUCTION

When a person goes to consult a palmist he has certain specific questions in his mind which he wants to be answered. But, he wants that the palmist should be the one to guess the questions he has in mind.

When a patient goes to a doctor, he describes his physical symptoms and then asks him for medication to correct the disorder he is suffering from. But the difficulty in being a palmist is that he is expected to guess what his client is bothered with and then suggest remedies. The reason for this is that most palmists spread the word about that they are blessed with mysterious powers which enable them to *know* what their client is worried about. That is why people approach the palmists with great expectations. When those expectations are not fulfilled they blame the palmist for being deficient in his knowledge of palmistry.

Another curious fact is that a common man is unable to distinguish between an astrologer and a palmist and between a palmist and a tantrik. An astrologer consults a horoscope to give his reading of his client's future; a palmist does the same through a reading of the signs on the palm, but the field of a *tantrik* is entirely different. Because of the confusion in the mind of the common man about the roles of these three, the palmist finds it difficult to work in a scientific manner. We would, however, try to get round this difficulty and would indicate the method of interpreting the lines of the palm to answer questions which bother a palmist's client.

Let us take an example from medicine. If a person suffers from diabetes, his eyes and his heart are likely to be affected by that condition. If the liver is malfunctioning, a patient's appetite, thirst and his weight are likely to be affected. This is because the various systems of the body are inter-related; each affects the other. Similar is the case with the lines of the palm. If one of the lines is defective, it is likely to affect the others too adversely. That is why *all* the lines of the palm have to be studied to give a proper reading. The difficulty arises in finding the chief cause of the defect.

If a person is obstinate, for example, it is likely to affect not only his family life, but also his means of livelihood and his love life. Other signs of the palm are also defective in such a case.

Let us take an example. A lady of 30 to 35 years of age came to consult me.

From her way of talking and her dress she appeared to belong to a respectable family. I found that there was a depression in her finger nail which indicated that she had suffered a trauma during the past two and two and a half months. Now a trauma could be of any kind and I looked at her line of marriage/sexuality. It was defective which gave a clue to her marital troubles. I studied the signs carefully and told her that she had suffered a shock at the hands of her husband. She admitted that her husband had fallen in love with his secretary. Even though he showed the same love towards his wife as he did earlier, but the fact he had fallen in love with another woman troubled the lady no end. Her Line of Saturn at that particular point in life was defective, but there were indications of its improving two years hence. That was a hopeful sign, but mental agony, even for a brief period, is something a person cannot face with equanimity and I suggested remedies to lessen her troubles.

Another client, a young man of 25 to 30 years of age came to me for consultations. His Line of Saturn and the Line of Life were both defective, the palm was hard all of which indicated financial troubles. I looked at his nails to find the reason. They were small, the points of origin of the Head Line and the Line of Life were far apart which indicated the obstinacy in his mental make-up. I told him that he was in the habit of sticking to his point in spite of persuasion which led to troubles with family members and the trading community with whom he came in contact in the conduct of his business. He admitted that I was right. It became easier to look into his inner mind and I suggested the spiritual and psychological remedies to correct the fault.

Sometimes when a client is told of certain events in his past he refuses to admit that they ever happened. What I do in such cases is to close his fist and tell him that I have been unable to understand the sign on his palm. In nine out of ten cases, the client spreads his palm and admits that he was only pretending that my reading was wrong and importunes me to give him a reading.

Keep in Mind the Age of the Client While Reading His Palm

The questions of a client between the ages of 18 and 25 years are generally with regard to his love life, marriage, monetary gain etc. The problems which bother a person between the ages of 25 and 40 years pertain to his family, the worldly goods, trade, employment and children. Questions which persons above 40 ask pertain to their children, wealth and health. Keep these priorities in mind and give the reading of those signs first which are positive and the answers to which are in the affirmative.

Scores of signs are being mentioned here so that the readers can answer questions from their clients. But all the signs cannot be found in every palm. *If only four or five signs are to be found you can answer questions with confidence, but if the number is less than that you can indicate possibilities.*

Having said this by way of introduction, we indicate here many signs which concern almost all the questions which a client is likely to ask. No palmist can hope to remember all of them all the time. If you can remember even one fourth of them, you could be a competent palmist. If you study them regularly and go on seeing palms of people constantly, you would manage to remember them and recall them when you need them.

CHAPTER VI

QUESTIONS RELATING TO WEALTH, PROPERTY, BUSINESS, PROFESSION AND EMPLOYMENT

If you want to answer questions with regard to acquisition of wealth and property, indebtedness, business and employment or sudden prosperity through bequests, consult the Line of Saturn first. Afterwards study the Sun Line, the Head Line, the Line of Life, the Line of Mercury and the line which divides the two phalanges of the thumb. If no clear indications are to be found go to the other signs on the palm, the Mounts and the signs on the fingers.

Let us repeat what we said earlier: do not make a prediction on the basis of a single sign. One sign indicates only the possibility of something happening. Only when it is confirmed by the other three or four signs you can go ahead with forestalling the future or saying what happened in the past. If the number of signs is insufficient merely indicate the possibilities.

I tell my students again and again that they should avoid telling of evil things in store for the person whose palm they are reading. If it becomes inevitable that you tell your client of impending tragedies, tell him the remedies too which might reduce the evil influence of the lines. If that is not done, the client would go back with a heavy heart. Remedies which suit every disposition and religious belief are given in Part III of the book.

Auspicious Signs for Acquisition of Wealth, Employment Etc.

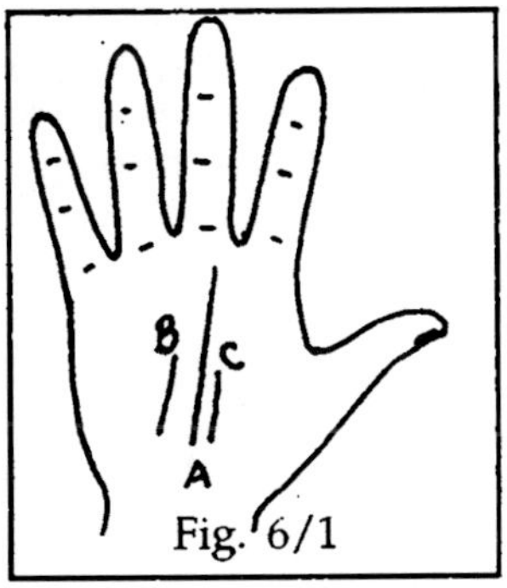

Fig. 6/1

A line parallel to the Line of Saturn a little distance away indicates two sources of income (*See Fig. 6/1-A,B*). The line very close is known as the *kuthar rekha* or the axe line (*See Fig. 6/1-A,C*) which indicates a period of struggle.

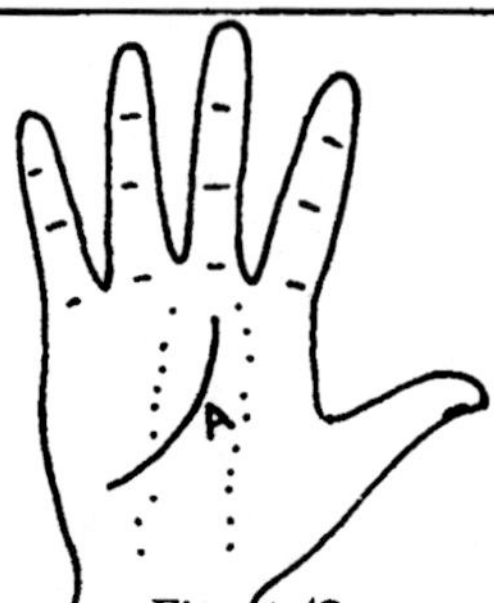

Fig. 6/2

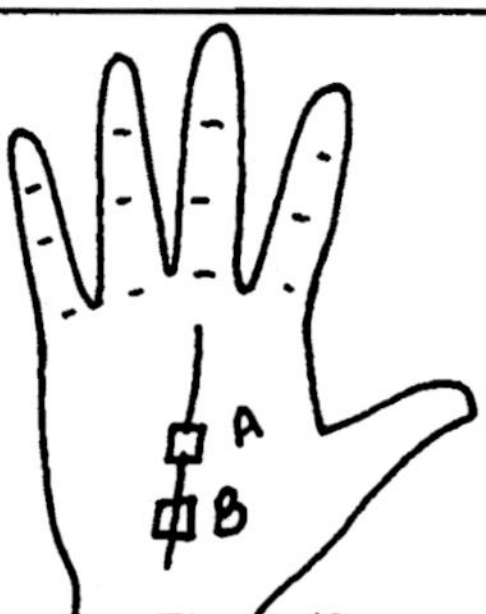

Fig. 6/3

If the Line of Saturn emanating from the Mount of the Moon goes towards the Mount of Saturn, the sources of wealth are moral and legal (*See Fig. 6/2*), but the line shows its beneficial effect at the time it enters the area of Saturn (*See Fig. 6/2-A*) which, as we have already said, lies from the thickness of the middle finger to the wrist. If the Line of the Sun is a little distance away from the Line of Saturn and is parallel to it, there is a certainty of wealth during that period.

More than one Line of Saturn indicate more than one source of income. If the hand is heavy and the Line of Life round and without any fault, monetary benefit is a certainty.

If a broken Line of Saturn is covered with a square, the evil effect of the break is offset (*See Fig. 6/3-A*); in other words, loss is averted. The part of the flawless Line of Saturn which is covered by a square indicates acquisition of wealth in that period of life. (*See Fig. 6/3-B*)

A person with a thin line of Saturn is simple-minded who understands his responsibilities. His word is his bond. But, if the little finger is longer than normal, it indicates more selfishness than a person should be cursed with.

If the Line of Saturn is thick in the beginning and becomes thin later, the period when it gets thin is a lucky period when ill luck leaves a person. If the line is thin from the beginning to the end, the amount of luck increases steadily. If there is a parallel line, it has a decidedly beneficial effect.

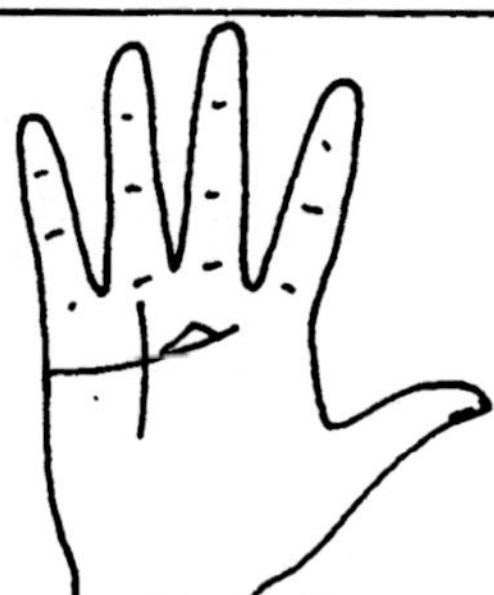

Fig. 6/4

If there is a sun line on the palm and there is a triangle on the Line of Heart, a person acquires property during the period when the sun line begins (*See Fig. 6/4*).

If the sun line emerges from the middle of the palm and the Line of Saturn is in the beginning, wealth is acquired at the time the sun line originates. If there is no Line of Saturn, the sun line indicates results of efforts a man makes to gain fame and to succeed in examinations and tests.

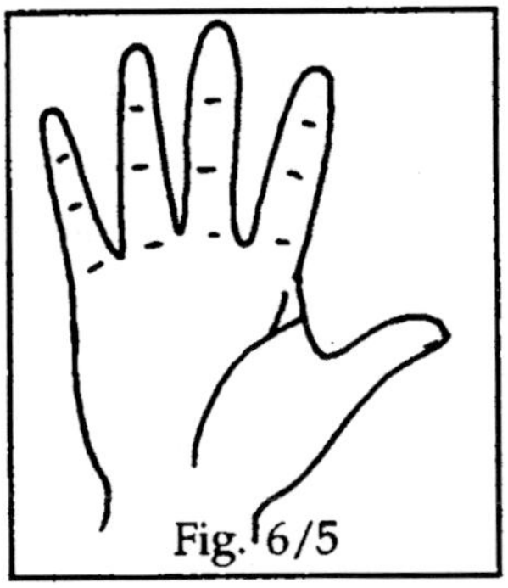
Fig. 6/5

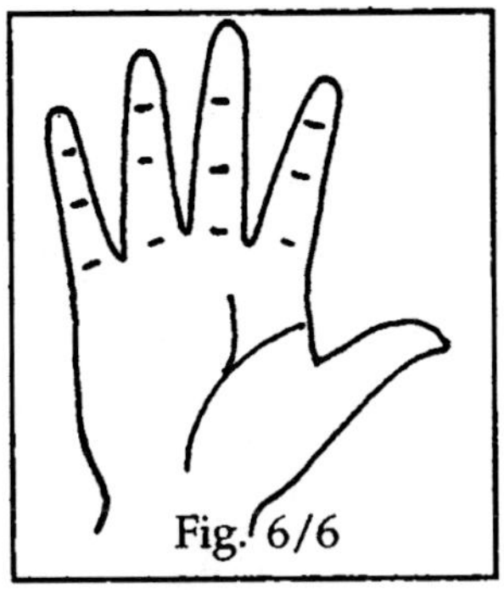
Fig. 6/6

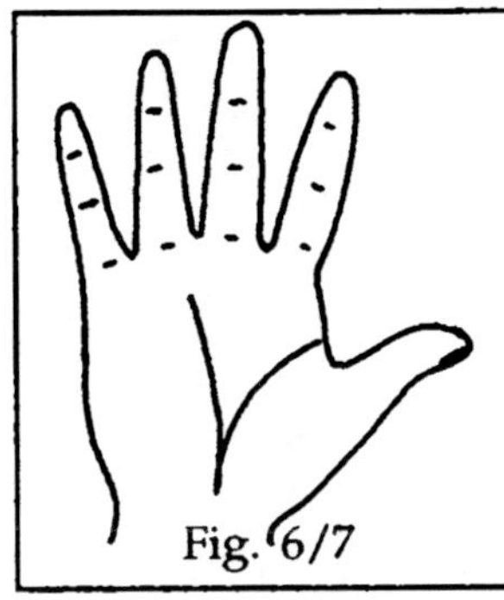
Fig. 6/7

If a branch/branches of the Line of Life proceed towards the Mount of Jupiter (*See Fig. 6/5*) they are indicative of luck. The time when Dame Luck would favour a person can be known from the study of the sun line.

If a branch/branches of the Line of Life proceed towards the Mount of Saturn (*See Fig. 6/6*) there is increase in worldly possessions and better employment prospects during that period.

If a branch/branches of the Line of Life go towards the Mount of the Sun (*See Fig. 6/7*) it gives fame to a person. If they go towards both the Mount of the Sun and the Mount of Saturn, there is increase both in fame and wealth. The period in life when this is likely to happen can be known from the line going towards the Mount of Saturn.

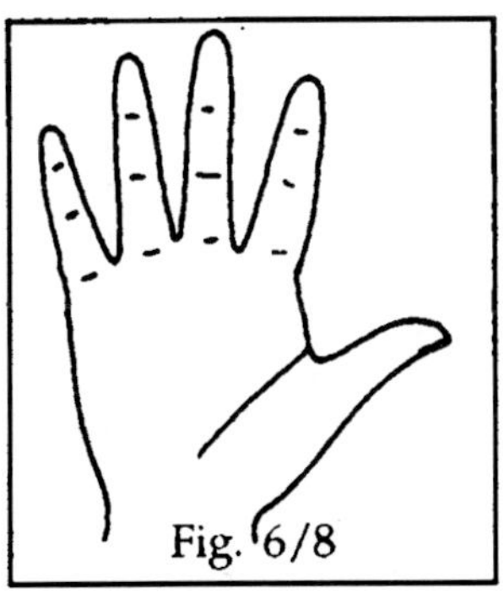
Fig. 6/8

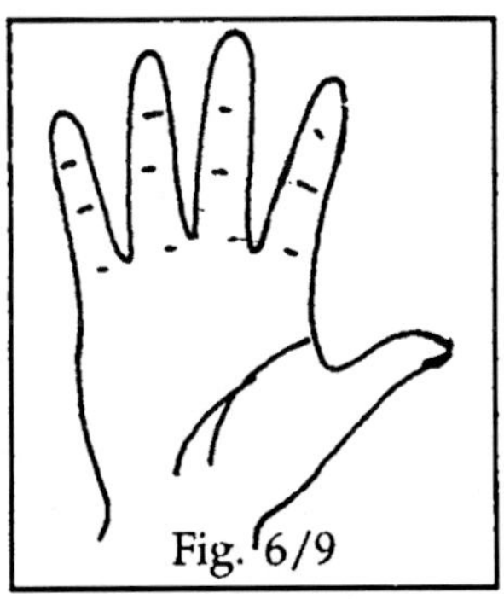
Fig. 6/9

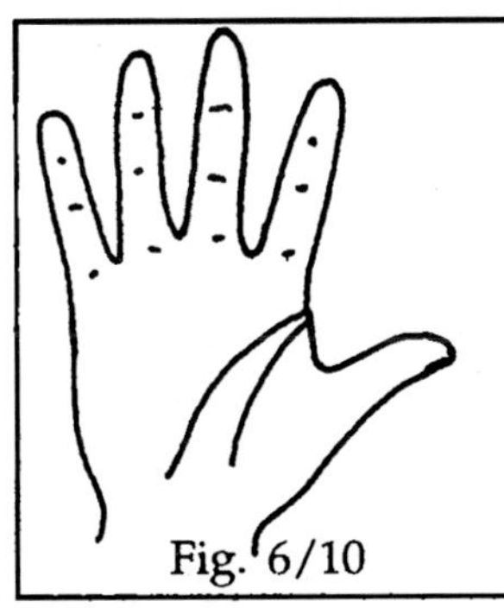
Fig. 6/10

A circular Line of Life (*See again Fig. 6/5, 6/7*) is better than a straight one (*See Fig. 6/8*) from the point of view of gaining wealth.

A thick Line of Life indicates a period of distress; the time when it starts thinning is the time when beneficial changes occur.

If a branch of the Line of Life (*See Fig. 6/9*) goes towards the Mount of Moon there is possibility of foreign travel. The time when it is likely to come about can be estimated from a study of the Line of the Sun or the Line of Saturn.

If the Line of Life bifurcates itself in the beginning (*See Fig. 6/10*) the earlier years of life are full of troubles and luck smiles on the person later in life.

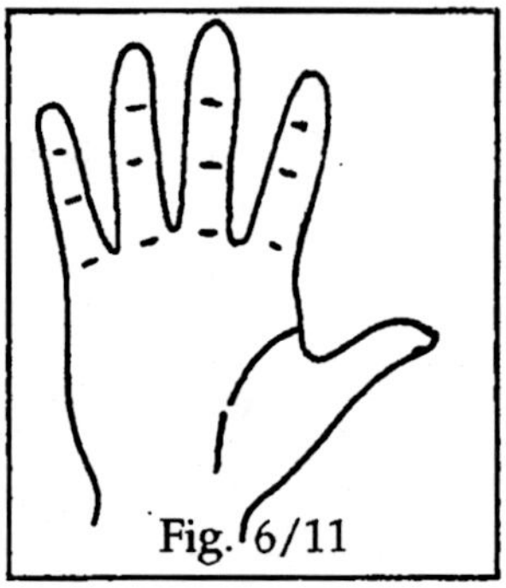

Fig. 6/11

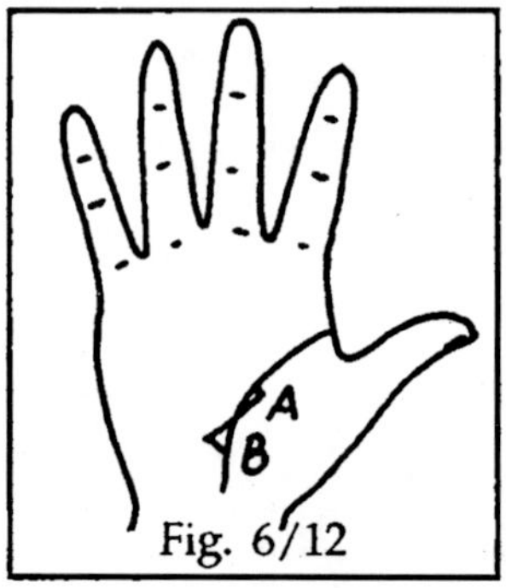

Fig. 6/12

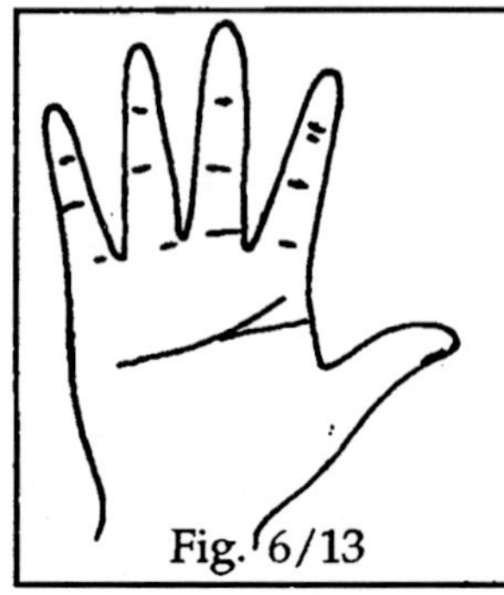

Fig. 6/13

The period in life in which the Line of Life breaks is the time of changes in employment or residence (*See Fig. 6/11*).

When a triangle emerges on the line (*See Fig. 6/12*) it is time for building of property.

If the Head Line is branched in the beginning, one of the branches going towards the Mount of Jupiter (*See Fig. 6/13*), a person is lucky right from childhood.

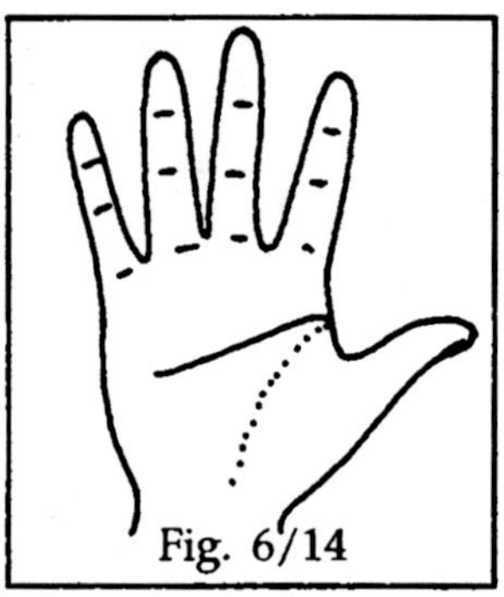

Fig. 6/14

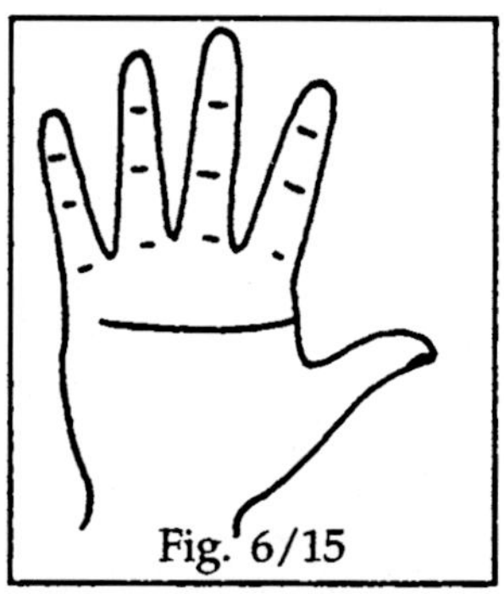

Fig. 6/15

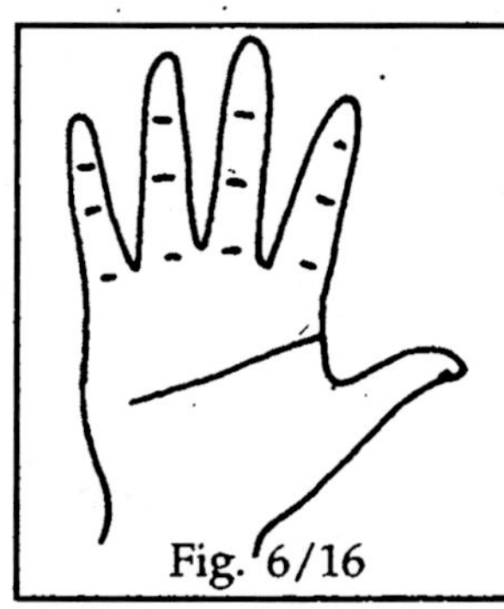

Fig. 6/16

If the Head Line touches the Line of Life at the point of its origin and goes straight to the end of the palm to reach the Defensive Mars (*See Fig. 6/14*) it augurs well for wealth, trade and employment and general affluence.

If the Head Line goes towards Mercury instead of the Defensive Mars (*See Fig. 6/15*), a person gets a lot of wealth, but he is the one who does not bother about any moral codes in the acquisition of that wealth.

If the Head Line is inclined downwards a little and reaches the point between the Defensive Mars and the Mount of the Moon (*See Fig. 6/16*), a person uses only moral means for earning wealth.

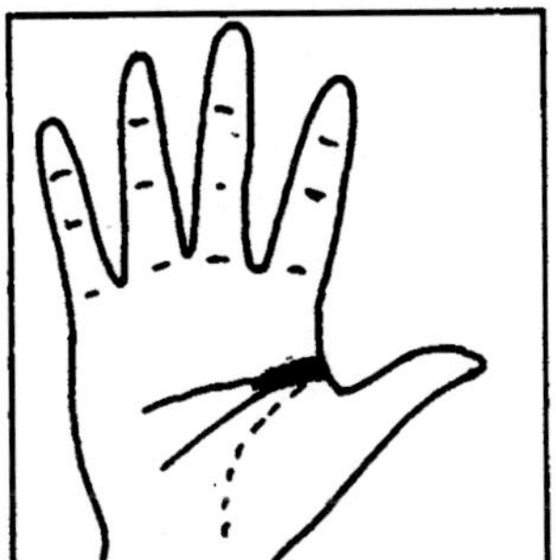

Fig. 6/17

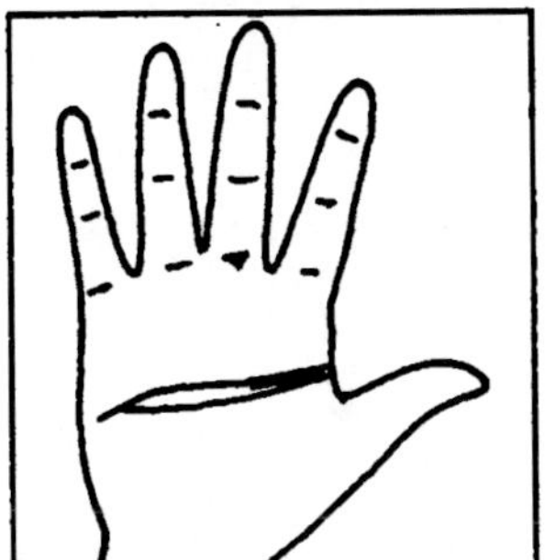

Fig. 6/18

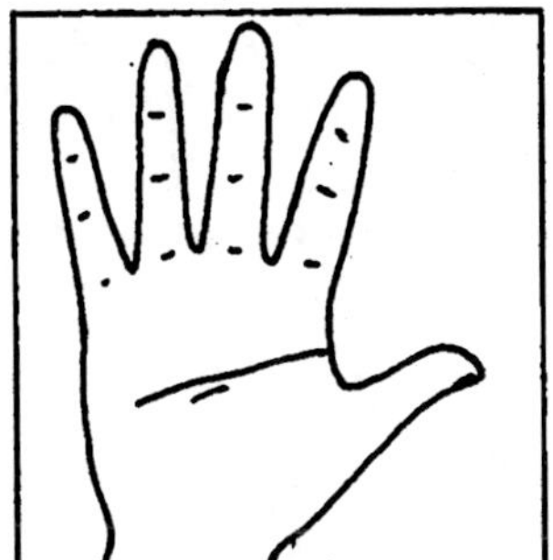

Fig. 6/19

If the Head Line is double, it is good from the point of view of worldly possessions (*See Fig. 6/17*),

But if the ends of the two lines join to form an island (*See Fig. 6/18*) a person gains wealth after a lot of struggle.

If a parallel line runs along a part of the Head Line (*See Fig. 6/19*) a person is engaged in two sources of employment and later on he gives up one kind of work to devote himself wholetime to only one work/employment. The time when it is likely to happen can be known from the Line of Saturn.

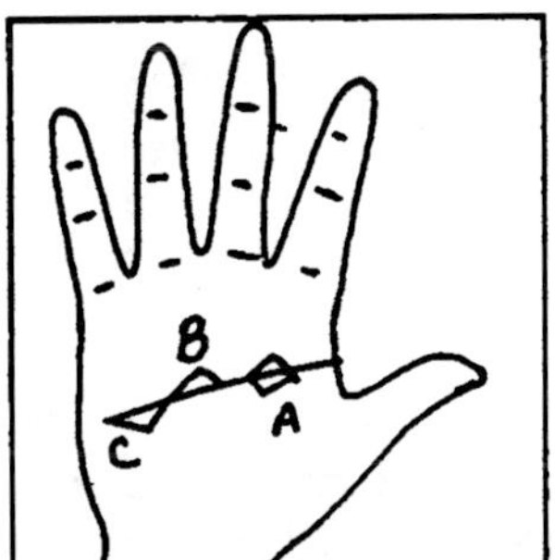

Fig. 6/20

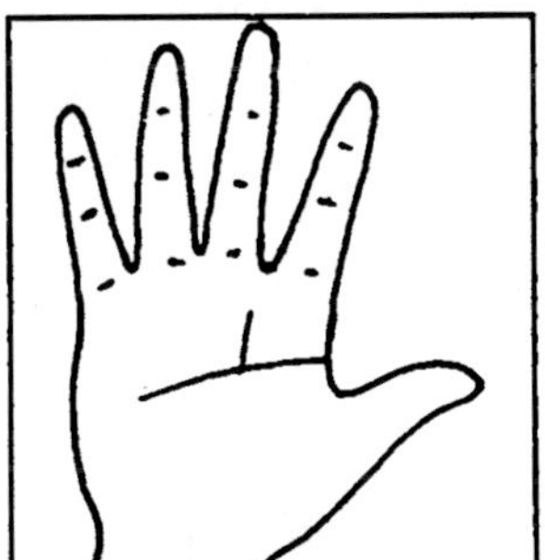

Fig. 6/21

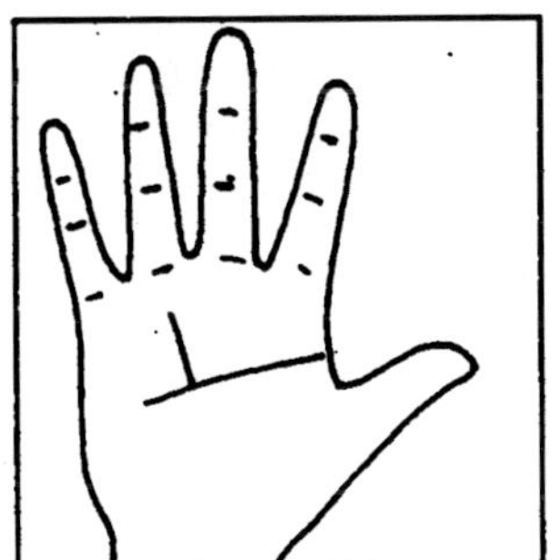

Fig. 6/22

If there are two triangles, above and below the Head Line, they act as a square. In other words, they ward off losses (*See Fig. 6/20-A*). If there are two triangles above and below the Head Line at two different locations, (*See Fig. 6/ 20-B,C*) they are indicative of the time of progress or material gain or building of property. The time when it would be done can be gauged from the Line of Saturn.

If the Line of Saturn emerges from the Head Line (*See Fig. 6/21*) a person gains wealth because of his own efforts.

If the Sun Line originates from the Head Line (*See Fig. 6/22*), it bestows honour at that point of time. If both the Sun and the Saturn lines emerge from that point, a person gets both fame and wordly goods.

If a long thumb accompanies a long Head Line, it indicates that the person would get not only wealth, but also a high office. The time when it would occur can be estimated from the Line of Saturn.

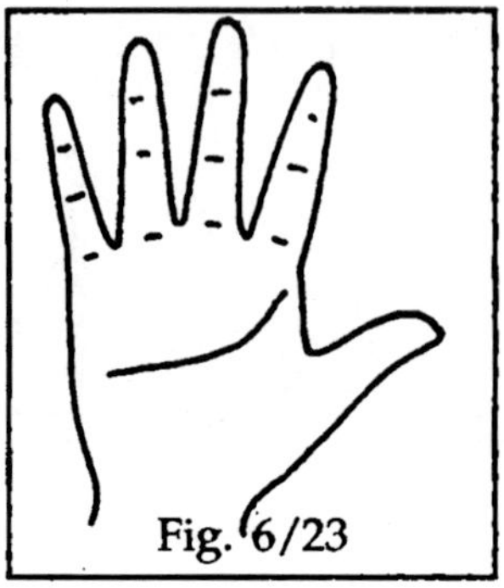
Fig. 6/23

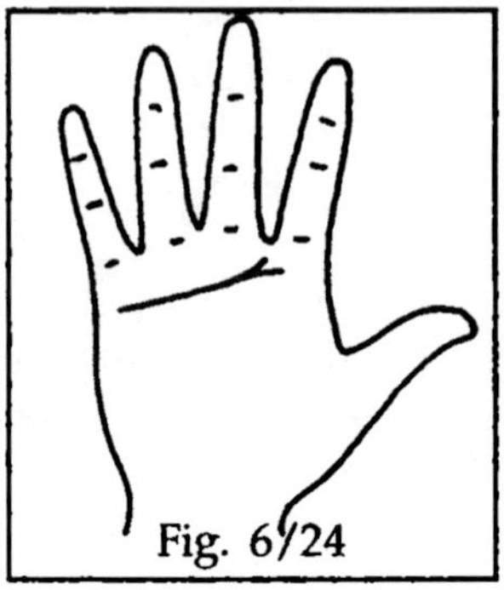
Fig. 6/24

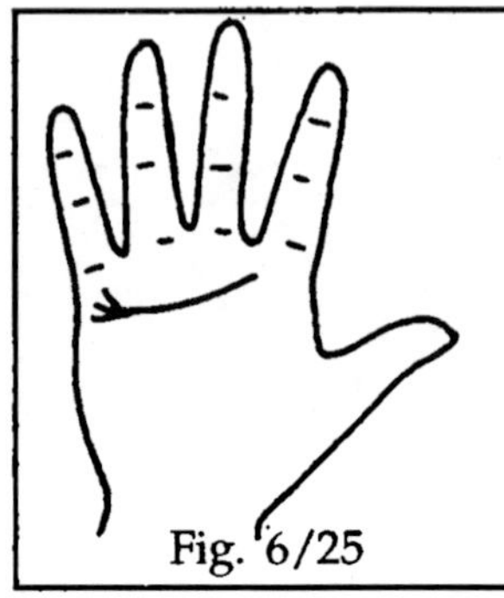
Fig. 6/25

If the Head Line originates from the Mount of Jupiter (*See Fig. 6/23*) there is delay in acquisition of wealth, but a person's prestige endures throughout his life.

If the Heart Line has two forks in the beginning, a person gets opportunities for progress from the beginning of his life (*See Fig. 6/24*). If the number of forks or branches is three, it indicates that alongwith wealth and progress in life a person attains a position where he gets prestige. The origin of the Head Line is from the Mount of Jupiter and it ends at a point between the Mount of Mercury and the Defensive Mars.

If small branches of the Heart Line go towards the Mount of Mercury (*See Fig. 6/25*), a man is likely to add to his wealth because of his business sense.

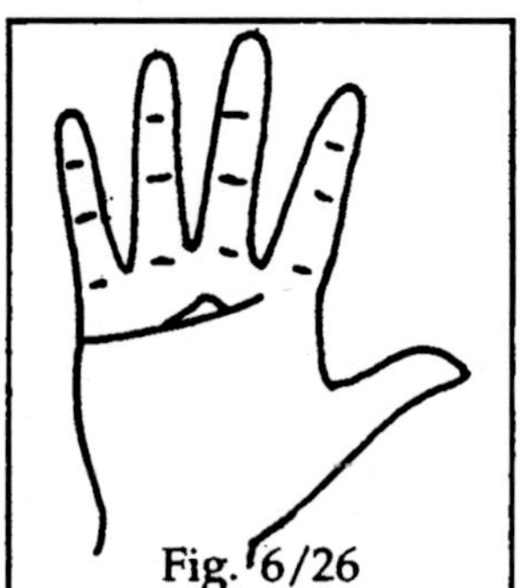
Fig. 6/26

A triangle on the Heart Line makes a person economically independent. Many small triangles indicate that the person has got money. The triangles over the Heart Line (*See Fig.6/26*) are more beneficial, while those on the lower side, towards the Head Line are not that fruitful. The time when a person with these triangles would have money can be estimated from the study of the Line of Saturn. If the Line of Saturn and the Line of Life are both defective, the benefit of those triangles is possible after a period of struggle during a person's advanced years.

A branch of the Heart Line going towards the fingers helps in achieving one's desires.

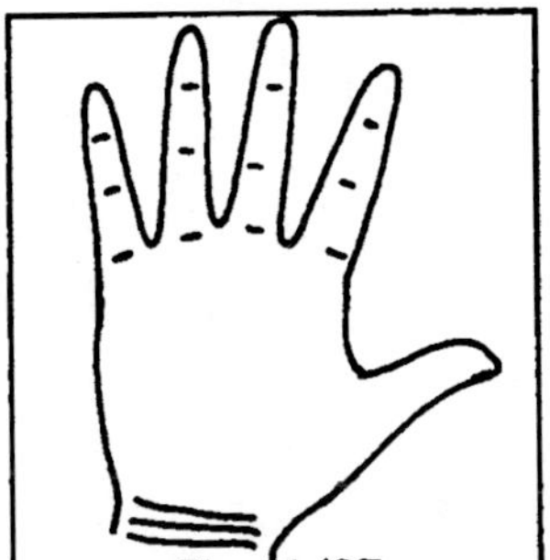

Fig. 6/27

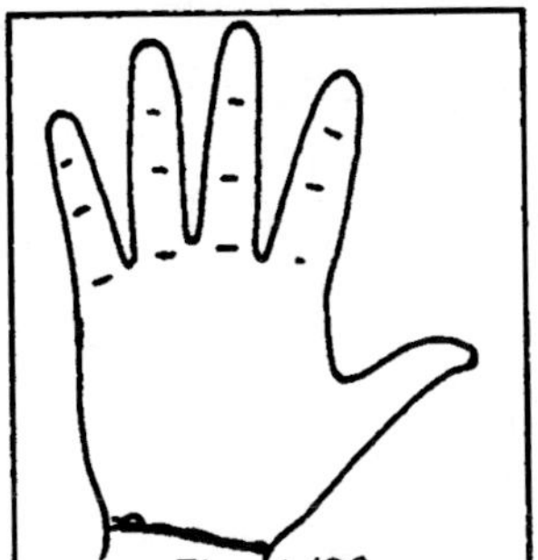

Fig. 6/28

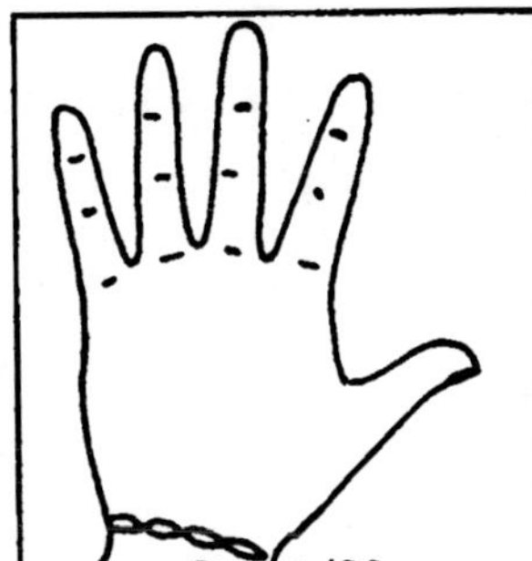

Fig. 6/29

Three well-defined bracelets (*See Fig. 6/27*) are a sure indication of acquisition of wealth.

If the first bracelet is twisted like a rope (*See Fig. 6/28*) one gets the benefits of struggles he waged during youth in his old age.

If the first bracelet is composed of large islands (*See Fig. 6/29*) the owner of such a hand is likely to get huge wealth. If more than one bracelet are composed of islands, one gets not only huge wealth, but also honour and prestige and high position.

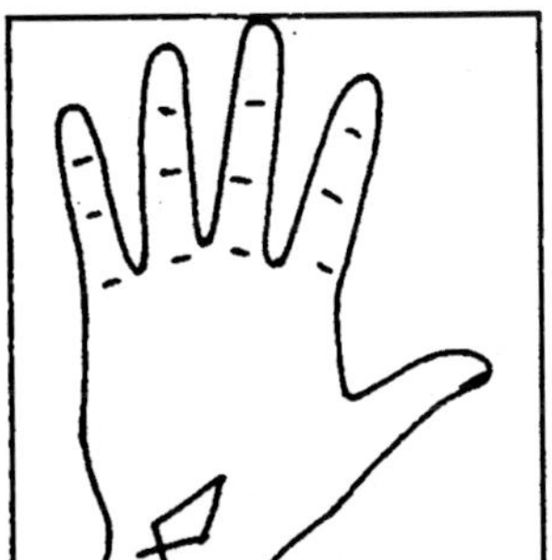

Fig. 6/30

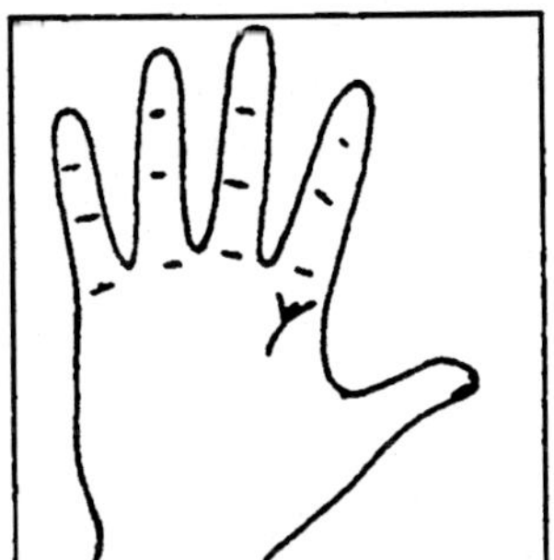

Fig. 6/31

If there is a sign of the fish on a palm a person is never short of money. If the tail of the fish faces the bracelet and the mouth is towards the fingers (*See Fig. 6/30*), a person is likely to be highly educated.

Some palms have very few lines or the lines fail to reveal any thing with clarity; other signs which indicate success should be studied in that case.

Lines on a heavy hand show their beneficial effect more easily than they do on a thin hand. If the hand is flabby, mental work rather than physical labour produces better results.

If there is a trident on the Mount of Jupiter (*See Fig. 6/31*) it is indicative of money as well as a vehicle.

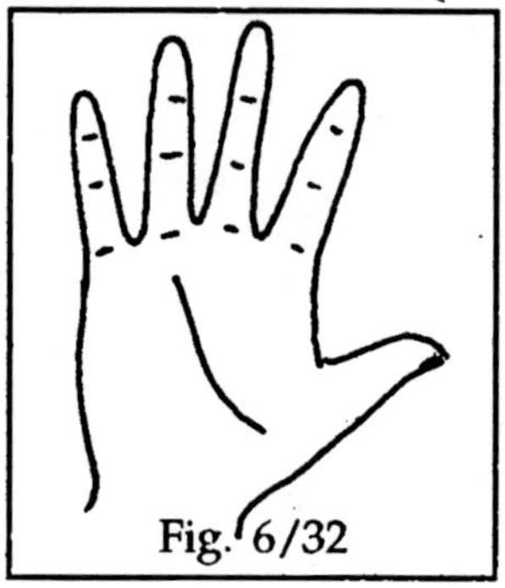

Fig. 6/32

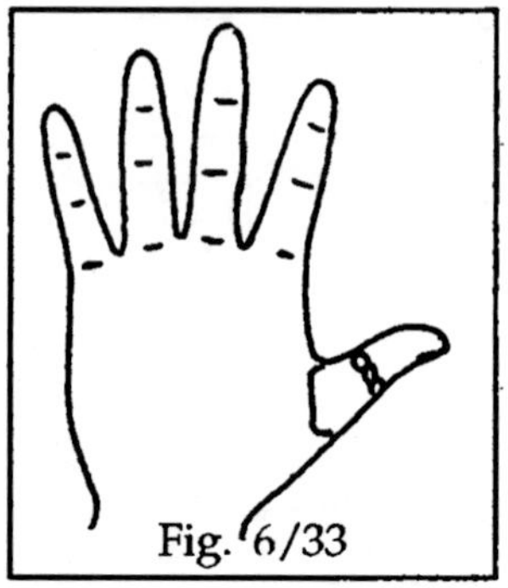

Fig. 6/33

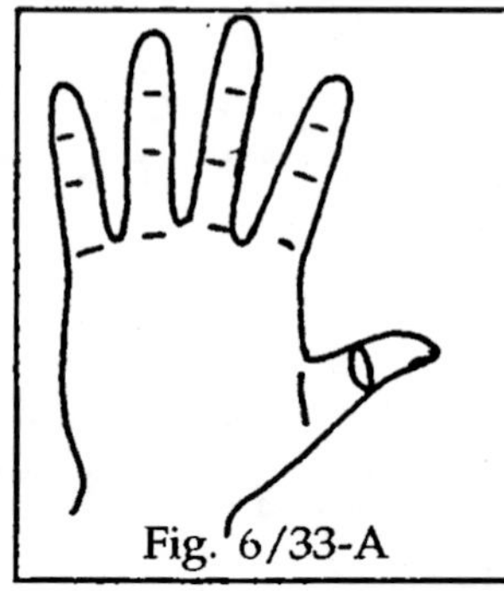

Fig. 6/33-A

The line of influence going from the Mount of Venus to the Mount of Apollo or the sun (*See Fig. 6/32*) indicates wealth, property and fame.

If the Heart Line starts from the Mount of Jupiter and has three forks or branches, it means that the owner of such a hand would have wealth and also vehicle.

If there is a rectangle on the Mount of Saturn, it indicates that monetary troubles would soon vanish and a man would get wealth.

If at the middle joint of the thumb there are chain like islands (*See Fig. 6/33*) wealth endures with such a person.

If there is one large island instead of many smaller ones, it indicates more wealth (*See Fig. 6/33-A*), and if the island is cut up a person gets wealth after the age of 50 and if there is a clear, well-defined line instead of these island, there is happiness and contentment.

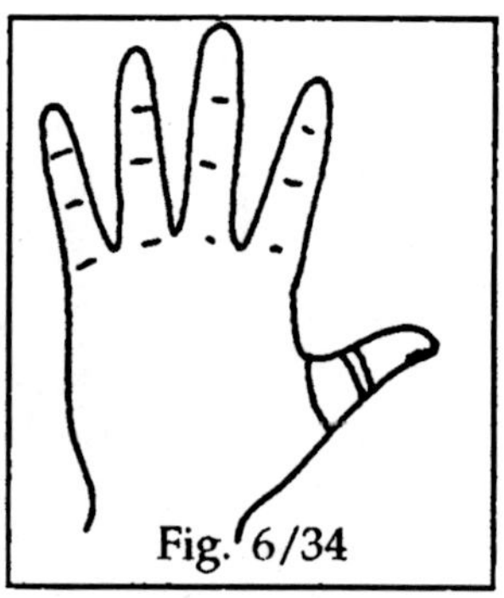

Fig. 6/34

If there are two instead of one line (*See Fig. 6/34*) a person is never short of money.

If the little finger is long, its second phalange being longer, it indicates success in business. A person with a long little finger does not let ideals came in the way of acquisition of money; he always hankers after wealth.

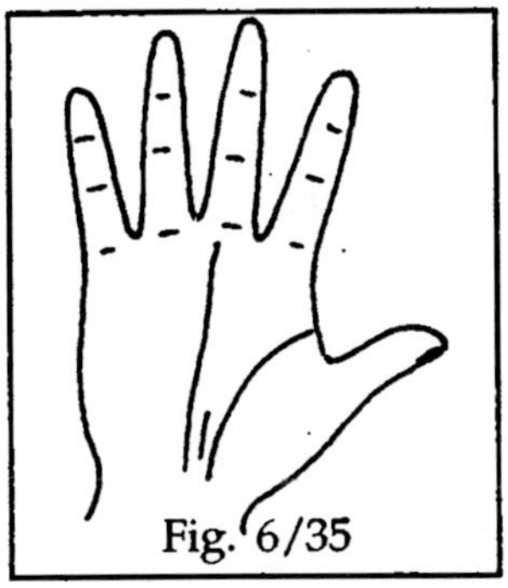
Fig. 6/35

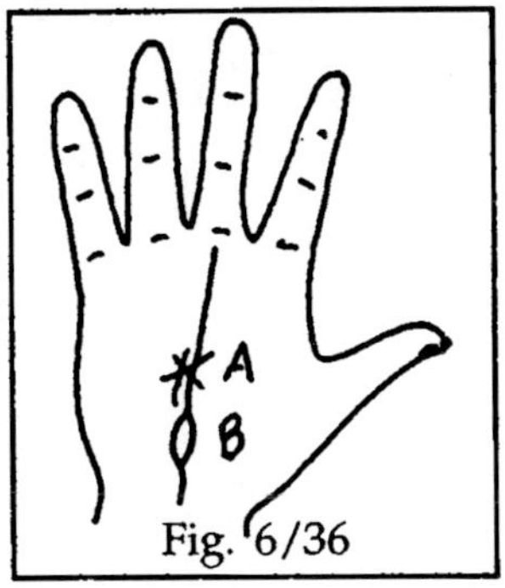

Fig. 6/36

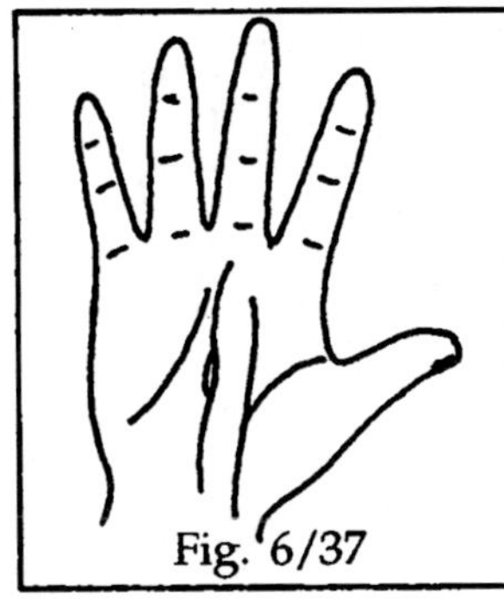
Fig. 6/37

Signs Indicating Success after Struggle and Many Obstacles

If there is an axe line between the line of Saturn and the Line of Life (*See Fig. 6/35*) success greets a person at the time the axe line ends.

If there is a star on the Line of Saturn (*See Fig. 6/36-A*) it indicates obstacles during the period represented by the star.

If there are islands on this line (*See Fig.6/36-B*) it indicates many obstacles to success including litigation.

If there are many Lines of Saturn and on one of them you find an island (*See Fig. 6/37*), there is ultimate gain in spite of initial losses.

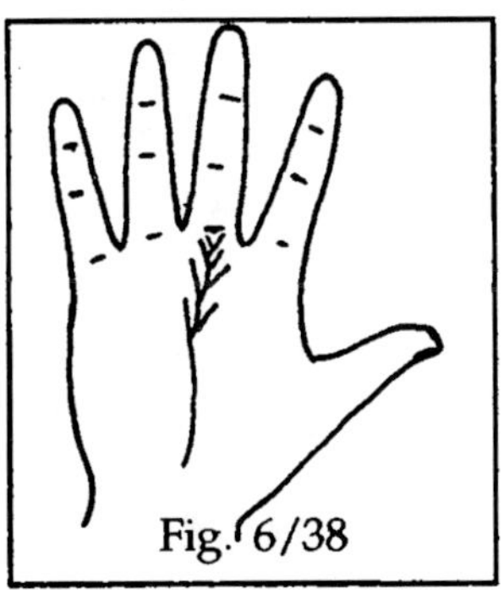
Fig. 6/38

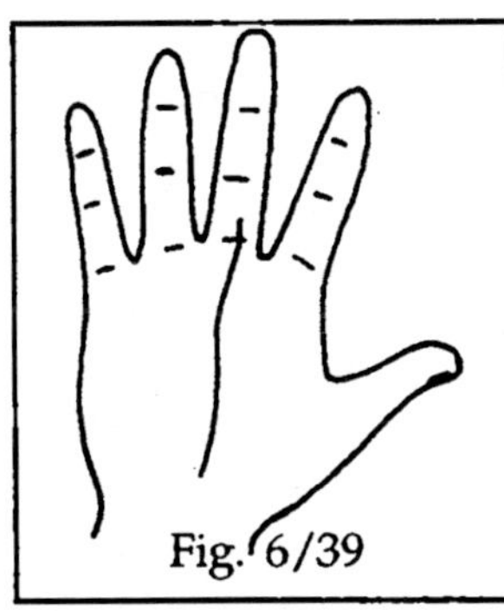
Fig. 6/39

If there is a tassel at the end of the Line of Saturn (*See Fig. 6/38*) a person faces financial difficulties after the age of 50.

If the Line of Saturn enters the third phalange of the middle finger (*See Fig. 6/39*) it indicates financial difficulties in old age.

If there is a single Line of Saturn without any parallel line to it, a person gets wealth after a lot of struggle.

Let us try to understand the significance of the end of the Line of Saturn. The

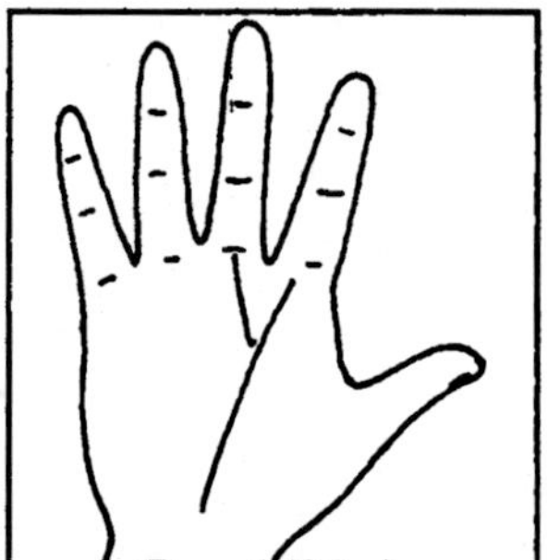
Fig. 6/39-A

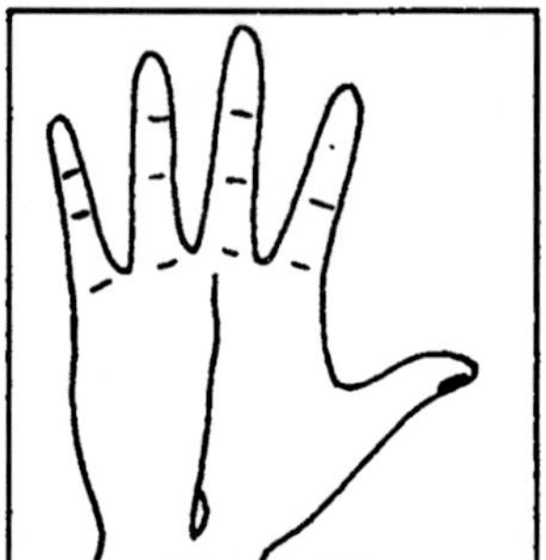
Fig. 6/40

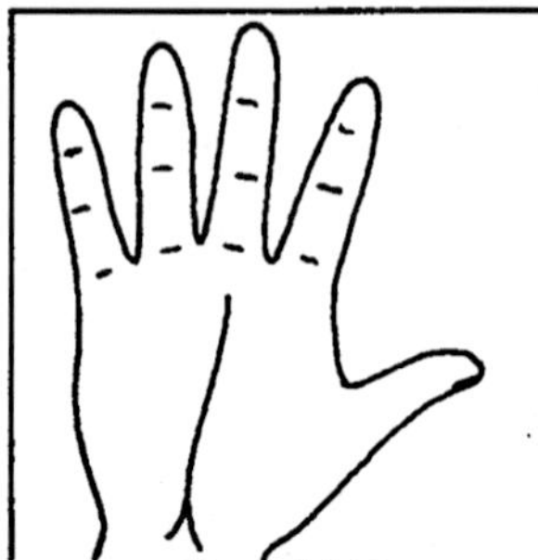
Fig. 6/41

period in life indicated by the end of a thick Line of Saturn signifies end to all misfortunes. It is better to have no line of Saturn then a thick one. If the thick Line of Saturn gets thinner and thinner, it indicates good days.

After the thin Line of Saturn ends it signifies a period when new sources of income are not created, but income continues from the old sources.

If the number of Lines of Saturn is more and all of them are defective, it means that a person faces a lot of struggle in his life. Persons with a thick hand are able to withstand the stress that comes with struggle, while those with thin hands give up the ghost.

If the Line of Saturn ends in two forks or branches, one of them going to the Mount of Jupiter and the other to the Mount of Saturn (*See Fig. 6/39-A*) it is indicative of acquisition of wealth and honour after the age of 50.

If there is an island at the beginning of the Line of Saturn (*See Fig. 6/40*) a person faces struggle in earlier years or his parents are likely to leave him.

If it is forked at the beginning, it has the same effect as an island (*See Fig. 6/41*).

There is no likelihood of a person having any property at the age where the line of Saturn is broken, but if there is a flawless circular Line of Life, such possibilities arise later in life.

Persons with broken Lines of Saturn go on changing their jobs. If along with a broken Line of Saturn, the Line of Sexuality and the Line of Mars are also defective, there are obstacles to a happy family life.

A person with an indistinct Line of Saturn is dependent on others for financial sustenance.

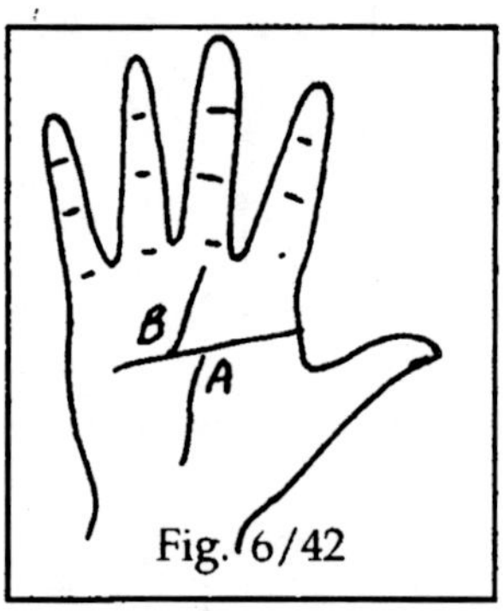

Fig. 6/42

If a thin Line of Saturn stops at the Head Line (*See Fig. 6/42-A*) it indicates harm flowing out of a wrong decision. If in addition to this another thin Line of Saturn originates from another point on the Head Line it indicates that the individual would gain from some decision of his (*See Fig. 6/42-B*). If the new line is thick, benefit comes after some struggle.

If there is no Line of Saturn a person does not have any ambitions for money or wealth. He goes on expanding his business/work slowly and gradually and gains success. If born in a family of millionaires he can become a billionnaire through persistent efforts.

The effect of the Line of Saturn on a thick hand is more than it is on a thin hand.

If the Line of Saturn stops at the Head Line or the Heart Line, a person faces struggles at that period in his life.

If the Line of Saturn is good, but the Head Line defective, a person gets money but cannot accumulate it.

A person with a thick Line of Saturn, a thick Head Line or a straight Line of Life should be advised not to borrow beyond his capacity to pay for investment in any large business, but should proceed with his limited means and work persistently to gain success.

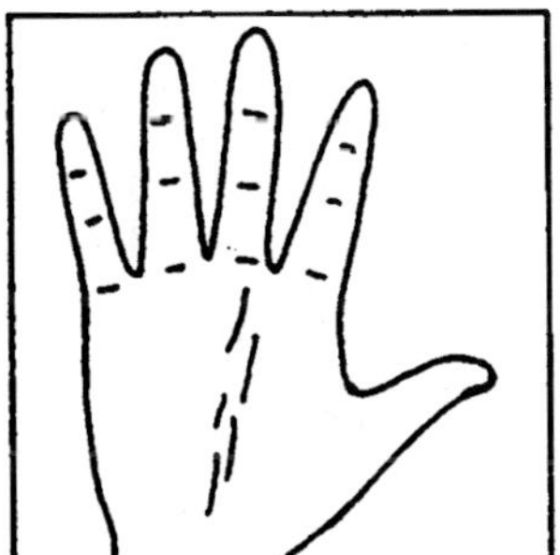
Fig. 6/43

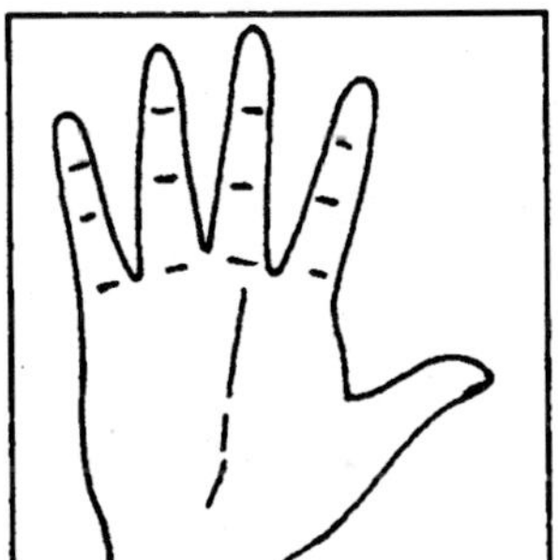
Fig. 6/44

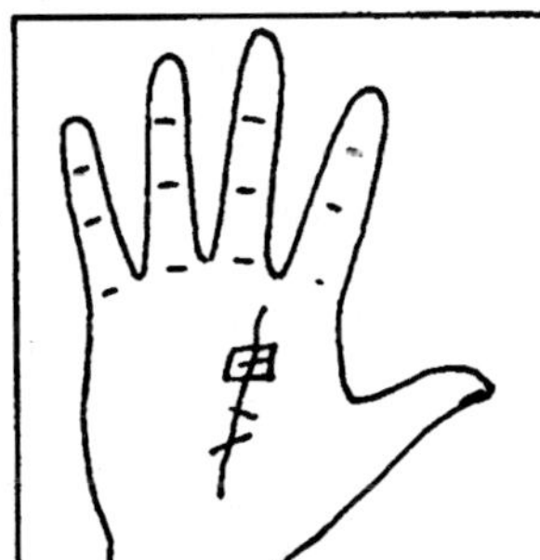
Fig. 6/45

If the Line of Saturn is broken, but its ends overlap (*See Fig. 6/43*) a business succeeds in spite of troubles. If there is a space between the two ends (*See Fig. 6/44)* the obstacles are more and severer.

If oblique lines of influence bisect the Line of Saturn a person faces monetary difficulties or problems connected with his family. If there is a square on the point of bisection, one can escape damage or loss. (*See Fig. 6/45*)

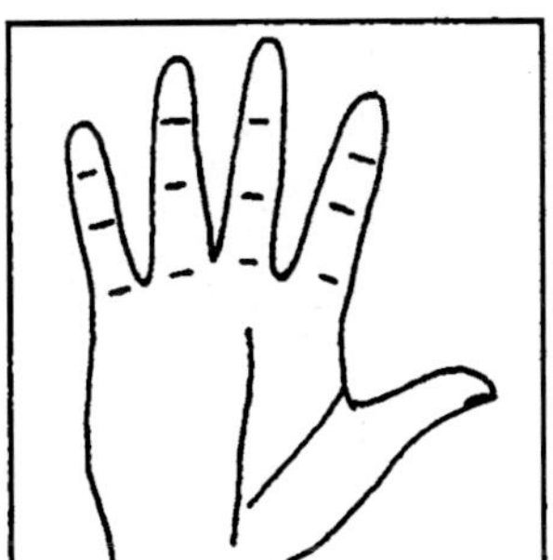
Fig. 6/46

The pace of success till the period signified by a straight Line of Life is reached is slow. If such a Line of Life is supported by the Line of Saturn (*See Fig. 6/46*), the defect of the Line of life is removed at the time calculated under the rules pertaining to the Line of Saturn.

If the Line of Life is thicker than the other lines, one gets the benefit after some struggle.

During the period signified by the thick and wide portion of the Line of Life, one is likely to face economic difficulties. Difficulties evaporate when the Line becomes thin.

If the Line of Life is broken, there are problems with regard to health or there is a change of residence not to the liking or according to the choice of the person. A study of the Mount of Luna or the Moon can help you decide the time when there would be a change of residence. A supportive diagnosis of the health Problems is possible with reference to the Heart Line or the Line of Mercury. Problems with regard to employment can be known from the study of the Line of Saturn.

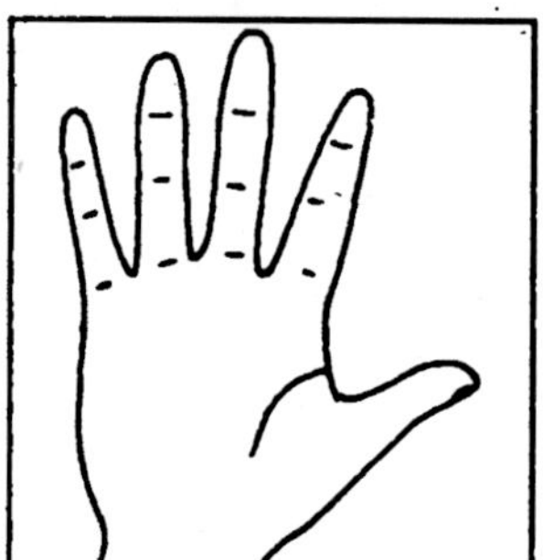

Fig. 6/47

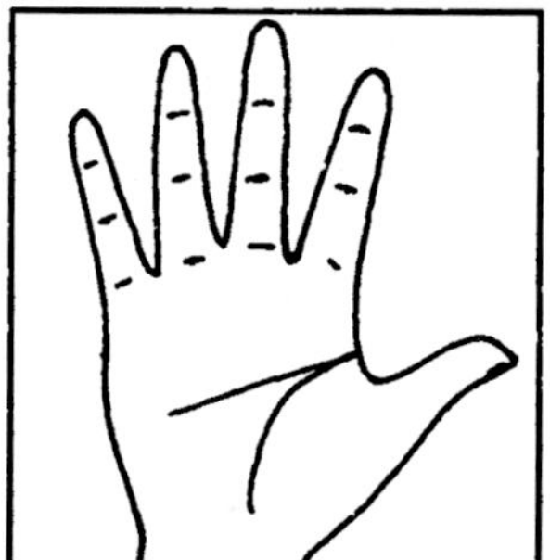

Fig. 6/48

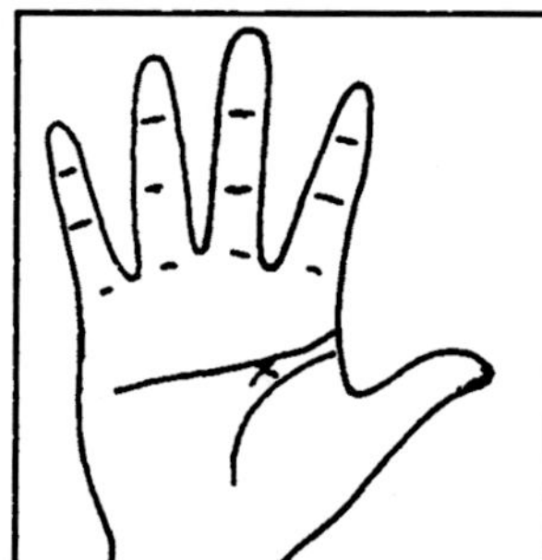

Fig. 6/49

If the Line of Life is incomplete (*See Fig. 6/47*) see whether the thick lines has stopped or the thin one. If the thin one has stopped it indicates economic difficulties and troubles in the family. Troubles continue so long as the thick line continues to run. If a thick line stops before it makes a loop, all troubles vanish.

If the Head Line and the Line of Life originate from the same point and proceed together for quite a long time (*See Fig. 6/48*) the lucky period starts when the lines separate from each other. The point of time when it does can be calculated according to the rules governing the Line of Life.

If there is a cross between the Head Line and the Line of Life (*See Fig. 6/49*) there are obstructions in the way of a person getting wealth.

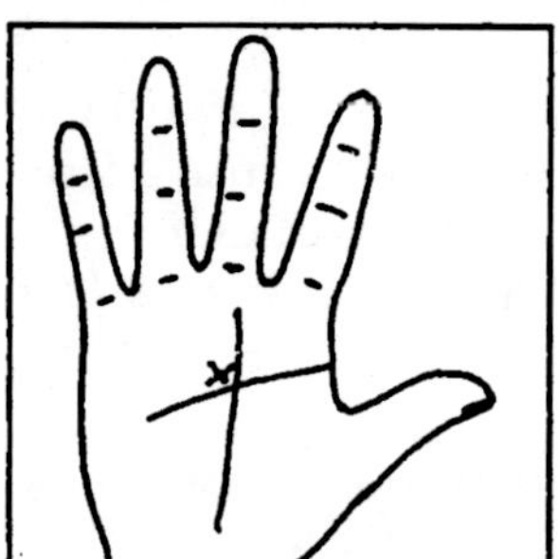

Fig. 6/50

Similar is the effect when there is a cross near the Head Line and the Line of Saturn (*See Fig. 6/50*). Financial difficulties persist in that case too. The period of such difficulties can be calculated from the Line of Saturn following the rules which apply to it.

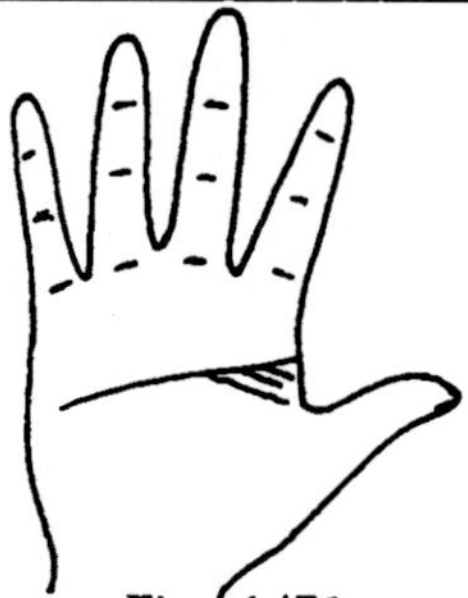

Fig. 6/51

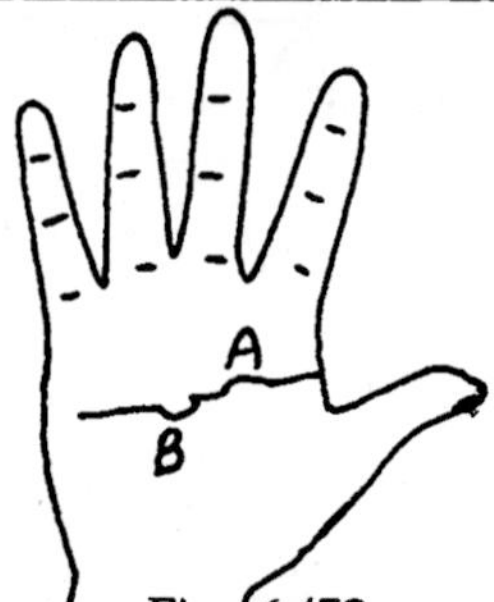

Fig. 6/52

Fig. 6/53

If branches of the Head Line go towards the Aggressive Mars (*See Fig. 6/51*) there are obstructions in matters of money.

If there are small, point like depressions on the Head Line it is an indication of loss or change of profession.

If the Head Line is twisted like a rope, it indicates that the financial position of a person would improve after his fluctuating fortunes.

A thick Head Line indicates lack of mental peace or loss. If it is thick at places, gains would equal losses. The period when this is likely to happen can be calculated from the state of the Line of Saturn.

A broken Head Line indicates obstructions in the running of a business due to worries; the time here again can be calculated from the Line of Saturn.

If there is a hump upwards (*See Fig. 6/52-A*) or downwards (*See Fig. 6/52-B*) in the Head Line it means that the line is defective. The period during which loss would occur can be calculated from the Line of Saturn.

If the Heart Line originates from the Mount of Apollo (*See Fig. 6/53*) it indicates financial stringency. If you want to answer any question with regard to the love life of a person with such a Heart Line, you can tell him that there would be obstacles in the fulfilment of his desires.

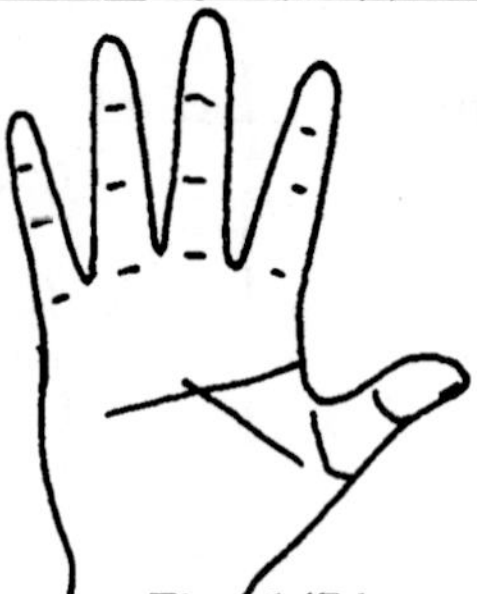

Fig. 6/54

If a line of influence on the Mount of Venus bisects the Head Line (*See Fig. 6/54*) financial troubles are in store for a person. If there is an island on the Head Line on the point of intersection of this life of influence emanating from the Mount of Venus, financial stringency is a certainty.

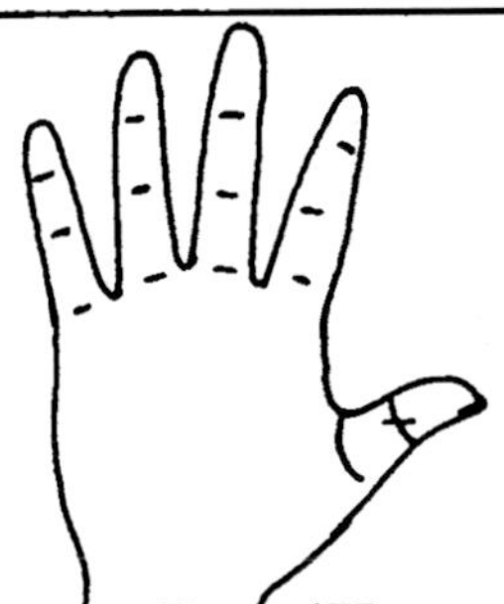
Fig. 6/55

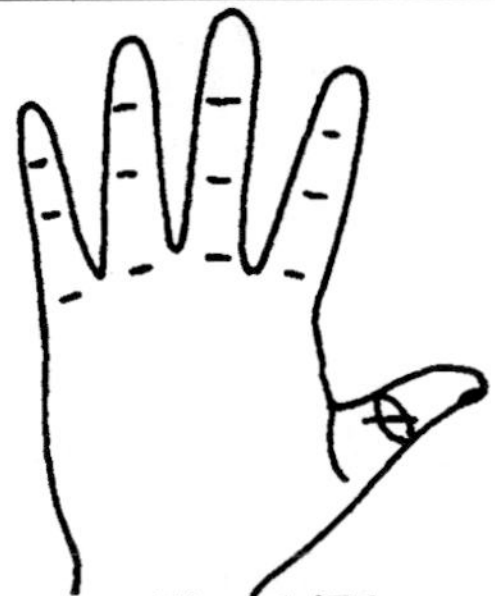
Fig. 6/56

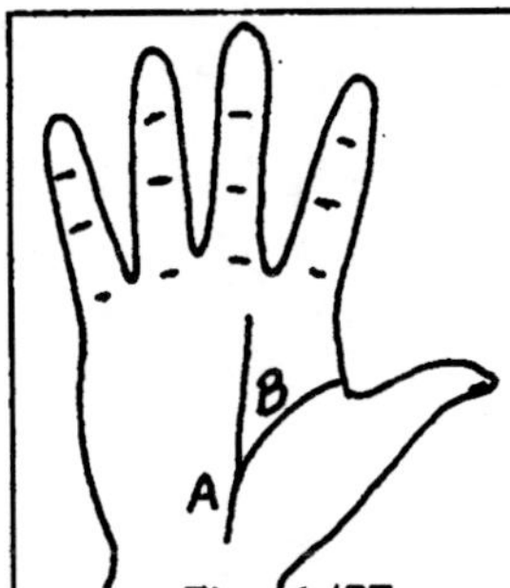

Fig. 6/57

If the line at the junction of the two phalanges of the thumb is broken or crossed (*See Fig. 6/55*) there are fluctuations in the finances of the person.

If an island on the junction of the phalanges of the thumb is broken or crossed (*See Fig. 6/56*) monetary troubles vanish after some time. If the island is not broken up, even with a defective Line of Saturn a person retains wealth and lives comfortably.

If the little finger is short, the progress is slow.

Very small fingers indicate monetary troubles. The reason for this is that the man is likely to be hasty in his decisions.

Very long fingers presage delay in success. The reason for this is that the person is likely to lose an opportunity because he takes too long to take a decision.

Matters Relating to Partnerships and Choice of Employment/Business

If the first part of the Line of Saturn merged the Line of Life (*See Fig. 6/57-A*) a person gains from the help extended to him by members of his family. When the Line of Saturn separates from the Line of Life (*See Fig. 6/57-B*) it signifies the beginning of a period when a person stands on his own feet. The time when it will happen can be calculated according to the rules pertaining to the Line of Saturn.

If the Line of Saturn starts from the wrist and is away from the Line of Life a person tends to give up the family business and strikes out in a different direction. His efforts bear fruit when the Line of the Sun starts to emerge. The Line of Saturn in the palm of a housewife indicates the financial position of her husband/family.

If the Line of Saturn emerges from the Head Line (*See again Fig. 6/42-B*) it indicates gain from intellectual pursuits. If the Line of Saturn ends at another part of the Head Line (*See again Fig. 6/42-A*) it indicates that intellectual efforts would help in gain when a person changes direction.

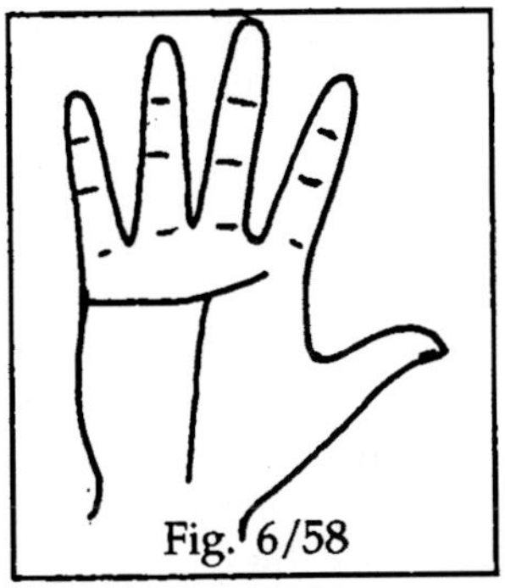
Fig. 6/58

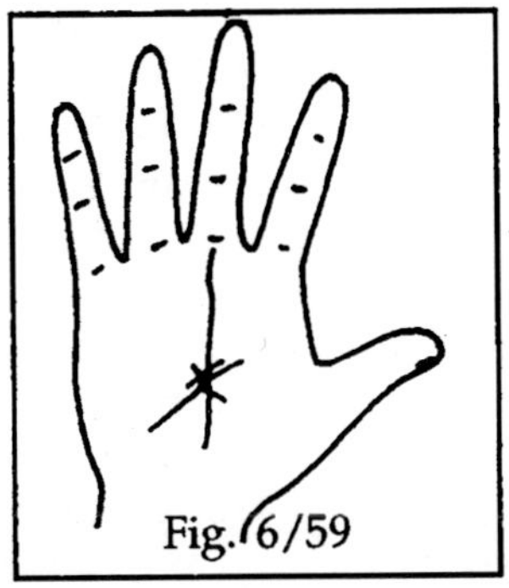
Fig. 6/59

If a deep Line of Saturn stops at the Heart Line (*See Fig. 6/58*), a partnership would end in a loss. If, later on, the Line improves, it might help in gain. If it does not, loss is a certainty.

If a thick line of influence from the Mount of Luna or the Moon joins the Line of Saturn, it indicates a partnership or a marriage, but the ties would be troublesome.

If a line of influence from the Mount of the Moon meets the Line of Saturn and there is a star on the junction of the lines, (*See Fig. 6/59*), there would be troubles or crises in a partnership or marriage.

If the Line of Life is incomplete, that is the time when there are troubles in a partnership.

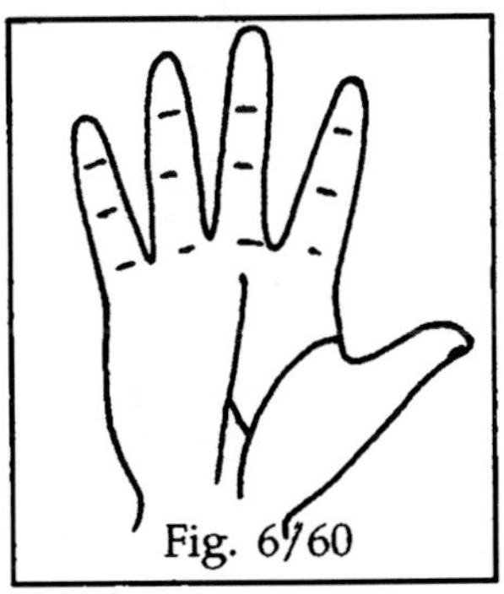
Fig. 6/60

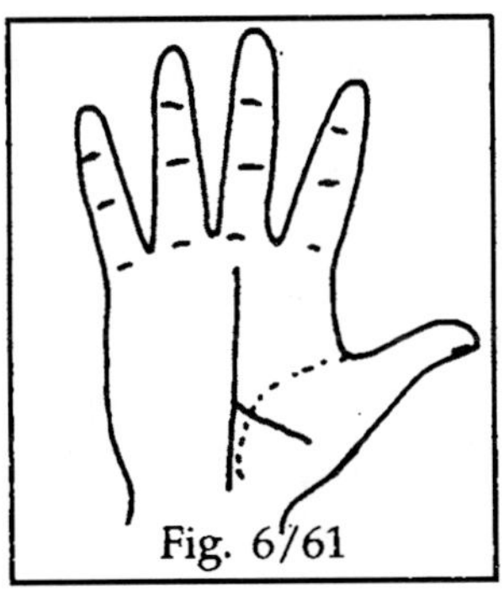
Fig. 6/61

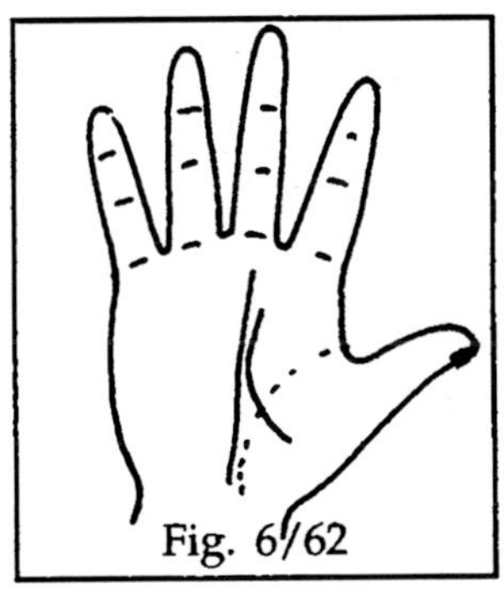
Fig. 6/62

If there is a line resembling a bridge between the Line of Life and the Line of Saturn (*See Fig. 6/60*), it indicates ties of partnership or between families. If a line of influence from the Mount of Venus touches the Line of Saturn (*See Fig. 6/61*), a family partnership is a possibility. For a person desirous of marriage these ties might be that of love or marriage. If a line of influence runs parallel to the Line of Saturn instead of touching it (*See Fig. 6/62*), the ties are long-lasting. If the line of influence or the Line of Saturn are defective, these ties result in lack of mental peace.

While going in for a partnership look at the little finger of your intended partner. If that finger is very longer or has a high setting or is twisted, your capital is at risk from him/her.

Persons with small, thick fingers, small hand and a rough skin gain from physical labour.

Persons with long fingers, an elongated palm and a soft, pliable skin are more suited than others to planning and things in which mental effort is needed more than physical labour.

Persons with soft, flabby hands are gifted with imagination. The knots of their fingers are not prominent. They are not suited to physical labour, but more for the artistic fields. They gain from their endeavours if their Saturn and Sun lines are good.

If the Head Line is similarly positioned in both the palms, gain comes from continuing the family business. If the Head Lines in both the hands are dissimilar, there are chances of the line of business/service/profession changing. If the Line of Mercury and the little finger are without any fault, it indicates profit from trade.

If there is a triangle on the Mount of Saturn, a person is likely to succeed in the sciences of the occult, like astrology, palmistry, psychiatry, *mantras*, yoga and spiritualism.

A rectangle or a triangle on the Mount of Mercury indicates skill in oratory. Such a person should go into politics. The time when success comes can be calculated with reference to the Lines of Sun and Saturn.

If a line of influence emerges from the Defensive Mars and goes towards the Mount of Apollo, it is indicative of success in politics.

A long index finger, along with a triangle on the Mount of Jupiter indicates that the person would practise clean politics, make a name for himself, but would lose money.

A triangle on the Mount of the Moon indicates spirituality in a person. If his middle finger is long and the Line of Saturn is without any defects, he is likely to spend his life in solitude. But if instead of the middle finger the little finger is long, the person would make spirituality into a money-making vocation.

A Look at the Fingers

If the fingers are knotty, a person is more inclined towards research.

If the fingers are soft, i.e., the knots of the fingers are not prominent, a person is more inclined towards the arts and things best done with imaginativeness. If there is a Sun Line it leads to gain and fame.

Signs on the Hand Which Indicate Indebtedness and Involvement in Litigation

If the Line of Saturn is thick in parts and thin in others, the period represented by the thick part is the time when a person incurs debts. The period represented by the thin part is the time when he pays back the debts. Similar is the prognosis in the case of the Line of Life.

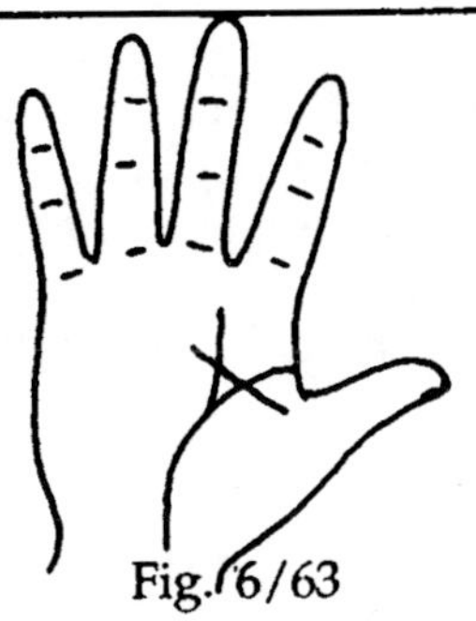

Fig. 6/63

If a line of influence from the Aggressive Mars intersects an ascending branch of the Line of Life (*See Fig. 6/63*) it indicates involvement in litigation. If the hand is heavy it presages success in a suit. Similar is the result if the line of influence reaches a mount at the base of the fingers.

Fig. 6/64

Fig. 6/65

Fig. 6/66

The area between the Heart Line and the Head Line is called by palmists as the Great Rectangle. When a client asks a question about indebtedness, look at this Great Rectangle. If it is wider towards the Mount of Jupiter (*See Fig. 6/64*) it would be difficult to recover the money lent. If it is broader towards the Defensive Mars (*See Fig. 6/65*) even then the recovery would be difficult. But if the Great Rectangle is narrow towards the Defensive Mars (*See Fig. 6/66*) the money lent would never be lost.

If an island lying on the area between the two phalanges of the thumb is cut up (*See again Fig. 6/56*) it indicates worries connected with the money lent.

If an influence line cuts the line between the two phalanges of the thumb (*See Fig. 6/55*) there are troubles in getting one's patrimony.

Gain from Bequests, Lotteries and Windfalls

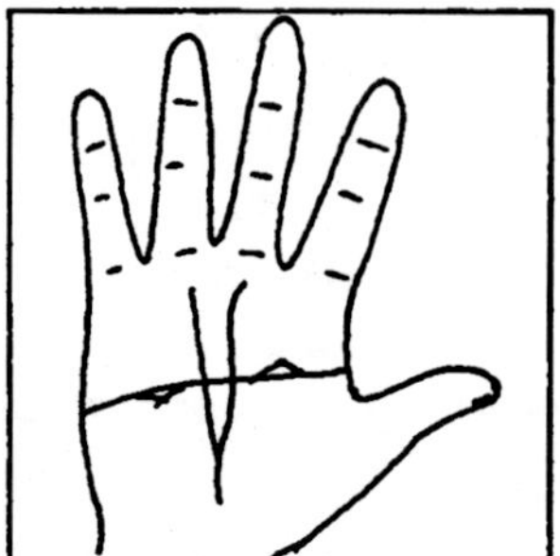
Fig. 6/67

If the Line of Sun emerges from the Line of Saturn and there are many triangles on the Head Line (*See Fig. 6/67*) it indicates the possibility of a windfall, like the winning of a lottery. The time when this is likely to happen can be calculated from the emergence of the Line of the Sun.

Triangles on the Line of Saturn indicate windfalls.

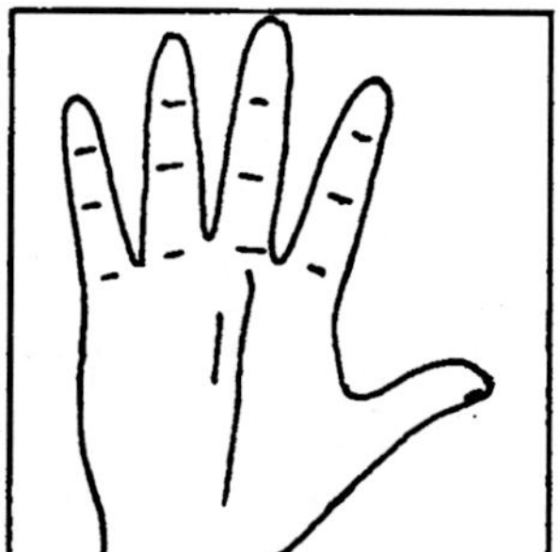
Fig. 6/68

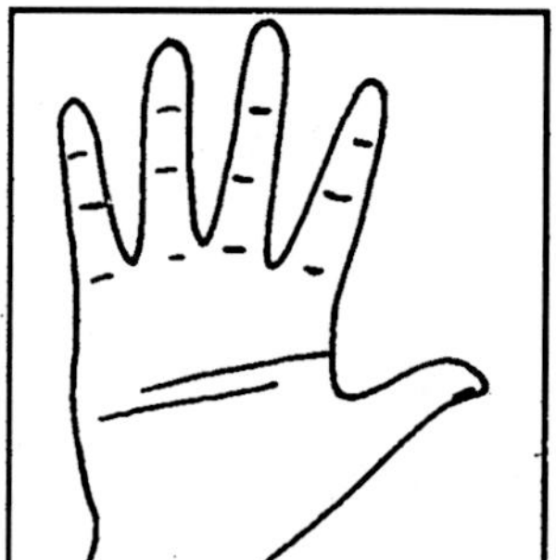
Fig. 6/69

The time when a line parallel to the Line of Saturn starts emerging is the period of sudden, unexpected gain (*See Fig. 6/68*). But please keep in mind the fact that a line parallel to the Line of Saturn, which is very near, is known as an axe line or *kuthar rekha*.

If there is a double Line of the Sun, the time when the second line starts emerging is the time when a windfall is likely.

If the middle and the third finger are equal in length and lines parallel to the Line of Life on the Mount of Venus are without any faults, it indicates gain from lotteries/speculation.

If at the beginning of the Line of the Sun there is a triangle, a person is likely to get sudden wealth or a windfall.

If there are triangles on the Line of Life one is likely to get patrimony or property bequeathed by father/grandfather. A triangle on the Head Line indicates a bequest from the mother or her family.

If there is a subsidiary line running along with the Head Line (*See Fig. 6/69*), it indicates gain from a bequest. The time when it would come about can be calculated from the study of the Line of Saturn.

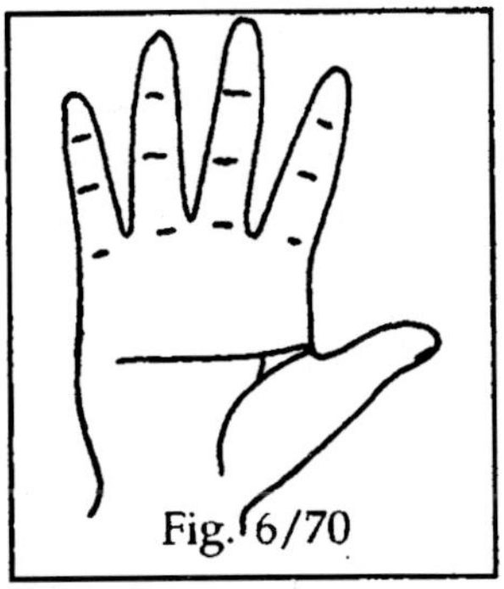

Fig. 6/70

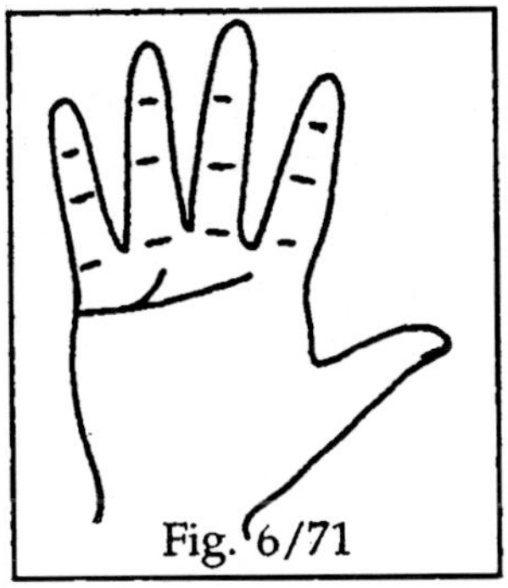

Fig. 6/71

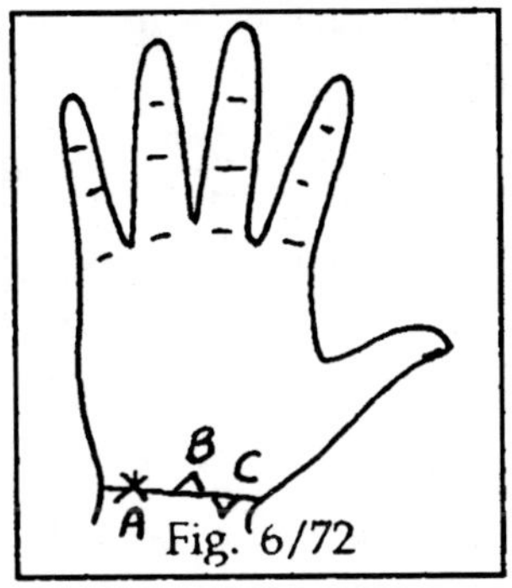

Fig. 6/72

If a small line emerging from the Line of Life meets the Head Line (*See Fig. 6/70*) one inherits property. But, if oblique lines intersect the Head Line, it is an indication of litigation concerned with property.

If there are signs of a bequest, but the Line of Saturn is indistinct, a person would have to struggle to get his patrimony.

A triangle in the middle of the Heart Line is also an indication of gain from inheritance.

If a branch of the Heart Line goes towards the Mount of Sun (*See Fig. 6/71*) one gets a bequest or a windfall.

If there is a star on the bracelet (*See Fig. 6/72-A*) it indicates a bequest. Similar is the result if there is a sign of a triangle (*See Fig. 6/72 B,C*) on the bracelet.

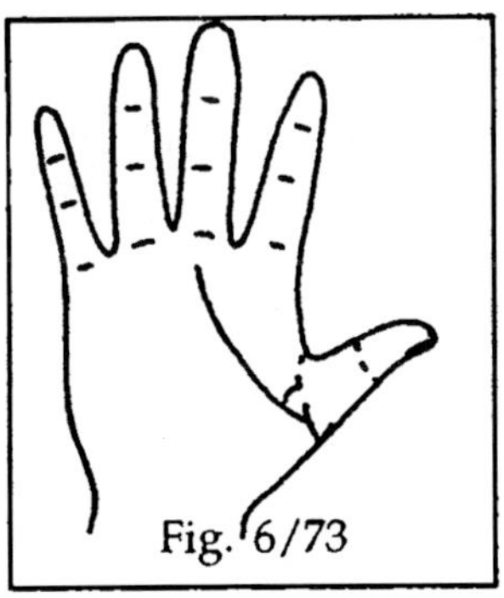

Fig. 6/73

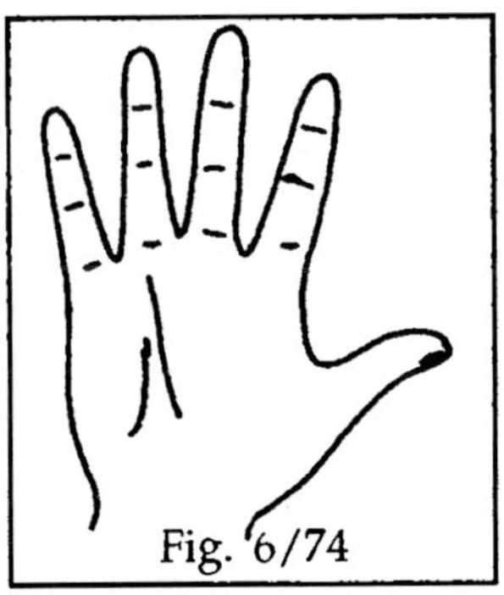

Fig. 6/74

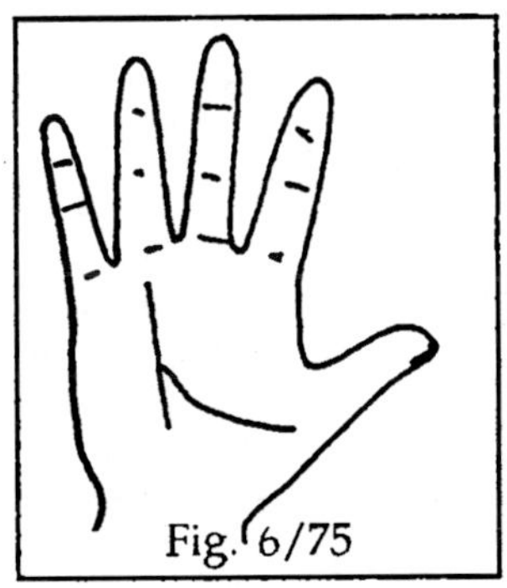

Fig. 6/75

If a line of influence emerges from a triangle from the base of the thumb (*See Fig. 6/73*) and goes towards the Mount of Saturn and the ring finger is equal in length to the middle finger, one benefits by a bequest from his father.

If a line of influence emerging from the Mount of the Moon runs along the Line of the Sun but does not touch it (*See Fig. 6/74*) one gets ancestral property. Similar is the result when a line of influence from the Mount of Venus merges with the Line of the Sun (*See Fig. 6/75*).

Some Lucky Signs

1. A straight, long thumb, straight fingers, equal length of the middle and the third finger. All main lines should be thin and deep; the Head Line should emerge from the point of origin of the Line of Life and should slightly touch it; the Head Line should be without any faults; it should branch out in two forks as it ends; there should be a Line of Saturn and the Line of the Sun; ascending branches of the Line of Life should go towards the Mounts of Jupiter, Saturn and Sun.

2. *Vriksha Shakha Yoga (lines like the branches of a tree)* - It is the three lines going from the wrist towards the fingers. They are: the Line of Saturn, the Line of Sun, the Line of Mercury and a circular Line of Life. When they combine they look like the branches of a tree. If all these lines are there in a palm and are thin and deep, a person is lucky.

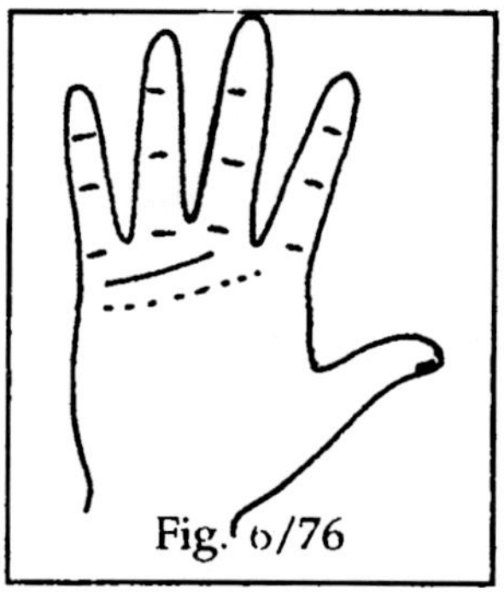

Fig. 6/76

3. *Supplementary Line of Luck* - A line parallel to the Heart Line which originates from the centre of the Mount of Saturn and ends at the centre of the Mount of Mercury (*See Fig. 6/76*) is called the Supplementary Line of Luck. It must be distinguished from the Girdle of Venus, because the two are different and should not be confused with each other. The Girdle is semi-circular whereas the Supplementary Line of Luck is parallel to the Heart Line. The time when this line will start having its effect can be calculated with reference to the Line of Life or the Line of Saturn.

4. The double circular Line of Life can be considered as the Supplementary Line of Luck. The ascending branches of the Heart Line or the Head Line are also indicative of good luck and increased affluence.

5. A well-demarcated island on the skin between the two phalanges of the thumb (*See again Fig. 6/33-A*) leads to acquisition of wealth, education and a name or fame. If the island is complete or a line cuts across it, a person gets wealth after the age of 50.

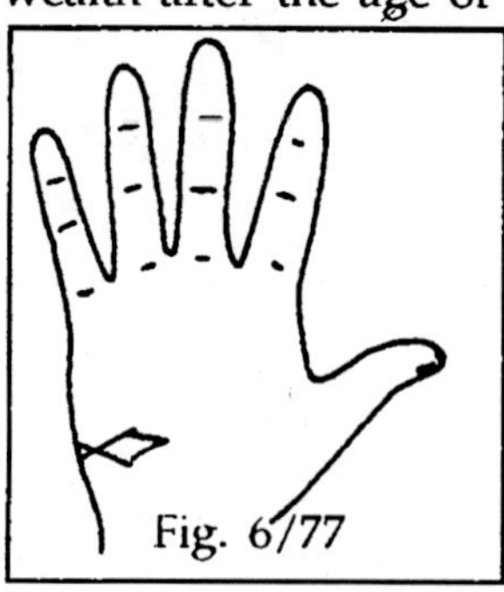

Fig. 6/77

6. If there is the sign of a fish on the Mount of the Moon (*See Fig. 6/77*) it is indicative of luck. If the tail of the fish is towards the wrist (*See Fig. 6/78*) it presages greater amount of luck.

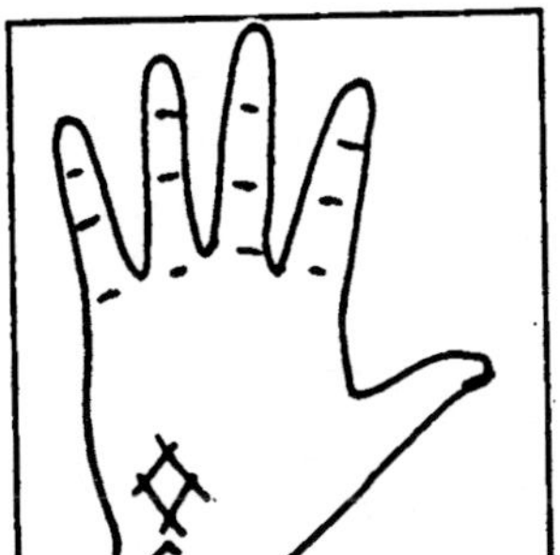

Fig. 6/78

All these signs are not generally found on a palm, but even if five of them are it indicates luck. Greater than this number is indicative of greater luck. If there is a line cutting across any of these signs, it means that Dame Luck smiles on a person after an initial period of difficulties.

●

INFLUENCE OF INDIVIDUAL ON SOCIETY AND VICE VERSA

Individuals are the units which make up a society or community. The mass and its constituents interact with each other and influence each other in a good or bad way. This fact should not be lost sight of while studying the hand signs.

As an Example I would mention Saddam Hussain, the dictator of Iraq. His invasion of Kuwait shook the whole world. It led to increase in the prices of oil and the pollution which his actions caused – the world is paying the price of his sins. The future of hundreds of thousands of Indians settled in Kuwait became dim after the invasion. This is the example of an individual affecting society.

Another example is of how society affects individuals. During the mid-term elections in Uttar Pradesh, a minister in the Mulayam Singh Yadav Government came to consult me professionally. He wanted me to study the lines in his hands and to tell him what his chances of winning the elections were.

I found that the Sun Line was passing through the Defensive Mars and was clearly going towards the Mount of Apollo. The other signs were also good. I told him: "There is a strong possibility of your victory, but the possibilities of the party with which you are associated are dim." I meant the Samajvadi Janata Party.

He asked me: "Hsve you seen the future of that party"

And I told him: "I am seeing the mood of the people. The sentiment in favour of "Ram Ratha" is stronger than it is in favour of the Mandal Commission." But he had an idea fixed in his mind that if a person's Line of Life was long, even a shower of bullets cannot harm him.

He fought the mid-term poll on the ticket of the Samajvadi Janata Party in 1991. His party was swept away in Uttar Pradesh and he also lost the elections.

The purpose in quoting these examples is that in addition to the stars, the lines on the palm one should also see what is happening around one. Ignoring the current events has led many a ruler to defeat in spite of the fact that they had prominent court astrologers to tell them the auspicious moments when elections should be announced.

– Author

CHAPTER VII

ANSWERS TO QUESTIONS RELATING TO LOVE, MARRIAGE, DIVORCE AND OTHER MARITAL PROBLEMS

It cannot be over-emphasised that no predictions should be made on the basis of only one sign, because no definite answer is possible from one sign or the position of a single line. If a question with regard to love or marital relations is to be answered, the first thing to do is to study the line of sexuality. And then, the Line of Saturn and the lines of influence coming to meet it from the Mount of the Moon or the Mount of Venus should be studied. It should be followed by a study of -- in that order -- the Line of Mars, Heart Line, Head Line, the Line of Life and cross on the Mount of Jupiter.

Having said this we come to the signs which should be studied to answer questions with regard to love or marital relations. What follows is based on the author's experience and it can be stated that even if four or five of the signs are found, one can safely predict the future in regard to this subject. If the number of signs is less than four, you should only say that there is a possibility of these things happening. One cannot overemphasize this because one would not like students of palmistry to go out on a limb and say things which are only possible and not probable.

According to *Samudrika Shastra*, the ancient Indian science, the heart line on the right palm of a woman is indicative of the type of husband she would have and the heart line on the left palm of a man tells you about his wife. Enough research has not, however, been undertaken to support this view, but it cannot be rejected out of hand as a mere opinion. But, before one reaches any conclusion on the basis of the study of the heart line of a man or a woman, the marriage lines and the Line of Mars should be studied.

Age at Which Marriage or an Affair of the Heart Would Come About

The line/lines which we have designated as the line/lines of sexuality are generally known as the marriage line/lines (*See Fig. 7/1*). These horizontal lines emanate from the outer edge of the Mount of Mercury and end on the Mount itself. But questions with regard to marriage cannot be answered with reference to these lines alone and it would not be proper to call them marriage lines. Another reason why these lines cannot be truly called marriage lines is the fact that they are found on the palms of confirmed bachelors and spinsters.

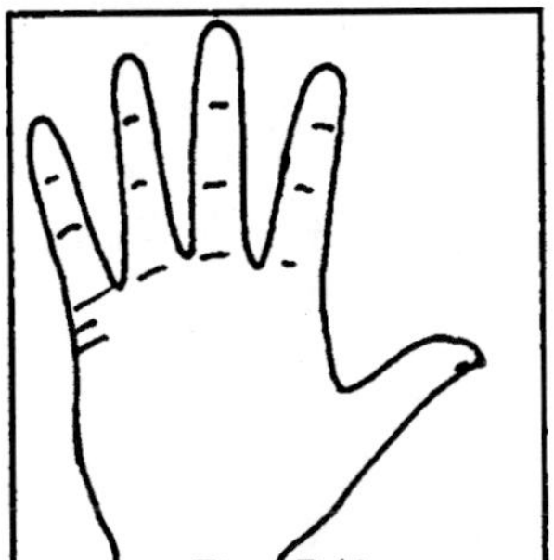

Fig. 7/1

That is why these lines have been called the lines of sexuality.

If there is only one line of sexuality on a palm, the owner of the hand would, normally, be apathetic towards marriage or a love affair. But, if the Mount of Venus is well-developed such a person would surely marry. If there are two lines of sexuality the desire for love or marriage is strong. Three lines indicate hyper sexuality which might also mean extra-marital affairs.

If one of the two marriage lines, the one near the little finger is short, marriage might be delayed. Conversely, if that upper line is long, early marriage is indicated.

"Early" or "late" does not indicate the age at which marriage would take place. The matter needs to be clarified. Time was when a girl of twelve or thirteen was thought old enough to marry and a boy was normally married at 16. Even today marriages take place at these ages at many places, but in the cities, it is unusual for a girl under 18 and boys under 21 to marry. Boys generally wait till they are well-settled in life before they marry and the age at marriage for boys is generally in the range of 25 and 30 years. It is commonly seen that girls attain the age of 25 or 26 years because they wait for a suitable husband. Whether an "early" or a "late" marriage is indicated should be decided in view of the above parameters. If you see the lines of influence emanating from the Mount of the Moon and the Mount of Venus which meet the Line of Saturn, you will be able to calculate the age at which a person would marry. But, in addition, the other lines should also be studied.

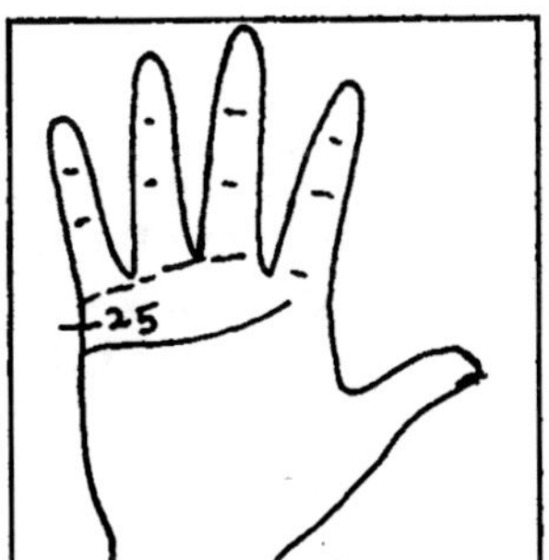

Fig. 7/2

Let us first take the line of sexuality. The portion between the base of the little finger and the Heart Line would indicate an age of 50 years. If the line of sexuality is in the middle of that area (*See Fig. 7/2*), marriage is likely to take place around the year 25. Or, a love affair would develop at that age. If the line is near the little finger marriage is likely to be delayed by the years represented by that distance of the line from the little finger. If the line is near the Heart Line, early marital relations are indicated. If the lines of sexuality are more than one, marriage is indicated according to the line of sexuality near the Heart Line. But the Line of Saturn has to be consulted to indicate the time when the marriage would take place. Keep this in mind while you go to the other signs, which are :

If the line of sexuality is thick, a late marriage is indicated.

If the line of sexuality is thin and short, late marriage is indicated or the sentimental side of marriage or a love affair is weak. If the lines of sexuality are two, the sentimental side is strong and there is possibility that the libido would remain strong till after middle age.

If the lines of sexuality are three in number there might be two marriages or a marriage and a love affair. If along with these signs, the Mount of Venus, the Aggressive Mars and the Mount of Mercury are firm and the little finger is long, extra-marital relations are a certainty. But if these are under-developed, the relationship is only platonic and not physical.

In order to find out the age at marriage, see the Line of Saturn and calculate at what age it has originated, or the age at which the thick Line of Saturn has thinned out or the time when the defect of the Line of Saturn has been removed. Marriage can be expected after the defect in the Line of Saturn has been removed.

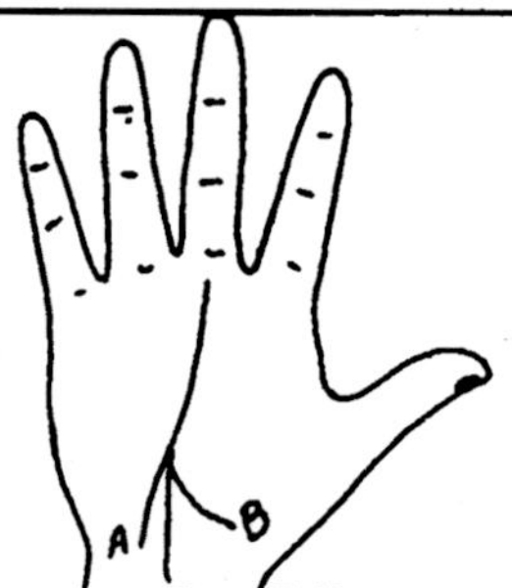

Fig. 7/3

The time when the line of influence from the Mount of the Moon (*See Fig. 7/3-A*) meets the Line of Saturn is the time when marriage would take place. Or, a love affair would develop.

Similar is the result when the line of influence from the Mount of Venus meets the Line of Saturn (*See Fig. 7/3-B*). If your client wants to know about partnership, you can tell him that the time the line of influence meets the Line of Saturn, he would go into partnership with another person. Whether the query is about marriage or about monetary prospects would depend on how the question is phrased by the client and the experience of the palmist. The question can be answered with reference to the time when the line of influence meets the Line of Saturn.

Fig. 7/4

If there is a cross on the Mount of Jupiter (*See Fig. 7/4*) the marriage is likely to be at the customary age. If the cross on the Mount is near the Line of Life, marriage might take place before the customary age. If there is a cross on this mount near the base of the index finger, a late marriage is indicated. The customary age of marriage, let it be repeated, change according to the customs prevalent in a place.

Signs Indicating a Happy Married Life or a Pleasant Love Affair

If the two lines of sexuality are straight emotional attachment to the spouse is indicated.

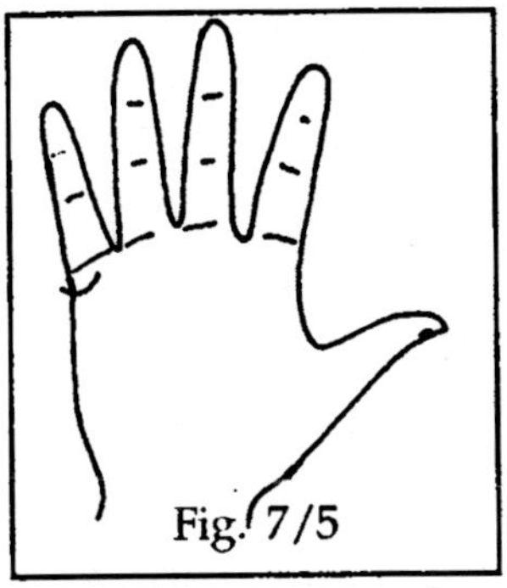

Fig. 7/5

If the line of sexuality is towards the fingers, the spouse is likely to have a long life. (*See Fig. 7/5*)

If the line/lines of sexuality is/are without any fault, the Line of Life is thin and circular, the Line of Saturn is thin and without any fault and is away from the Line of Life, the Head and the Heart Lines are away from each other, but run parallel and their branches do not merge with each other, the thumb and the index finger are long, the fingers are straight, marital relations are very happy.

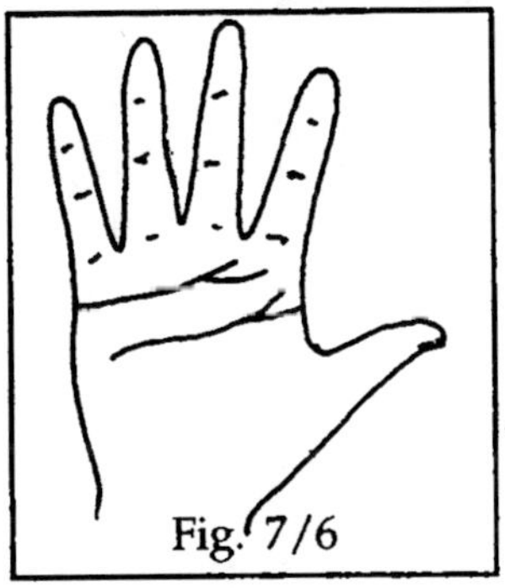

Fig. 7/6

Persons whose Heart Line emanates from the Mount of Jupiter tend to show solicitude for the welfare of their spouses. If the Heart Line or the Head Line has a branch which faces the Mount of Jupiter, a person shows consideration for his spouse. (*See Fig. 7/6*)

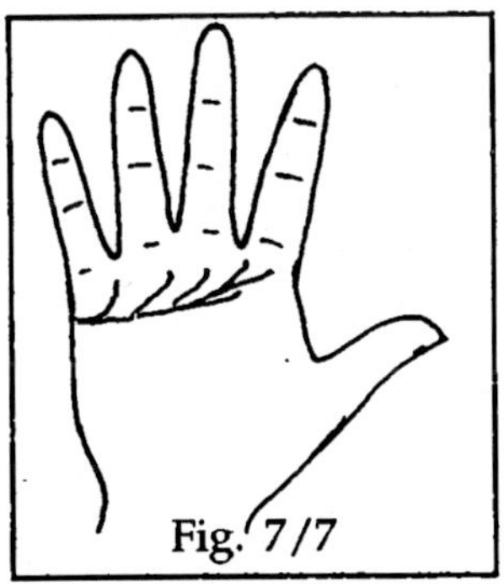

Fig. 7/7

If the Heart Line has three branches in the beginning or its branches go towards the mounts on the bases of the fingers, (*See Fig. 7/7*), a happy married life with financial security is indicated.

If the Line of Saturn is thin and deep, the hand beautiful and plump and there are clear islands at the junction of the phalanges of the thumbs, a long and happy married life is indicated.

If the Heart Line on both the palms of a woman is thin, deep and forked, she is likely to be happy with her husband and her children.

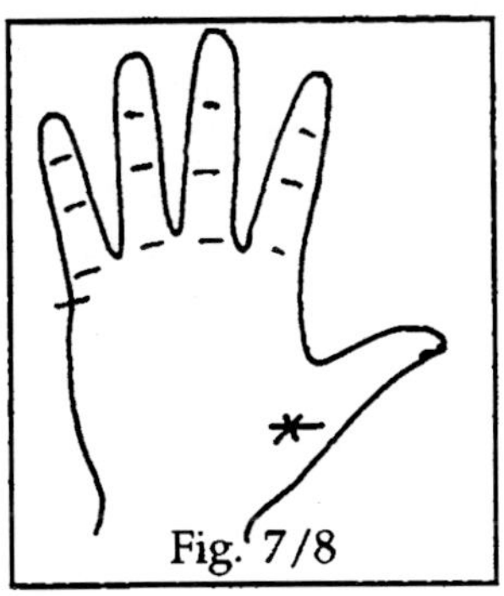

Fig. 7/8

If the marriage line is good and there is a star on the Mount of Venus (*See Fig. 7/8*) marriage follows a love affair or there is marriage in a prosperous family.

Branches of the Heart Line going towards the Mount of Apollo indicate marital relations with a happy family.

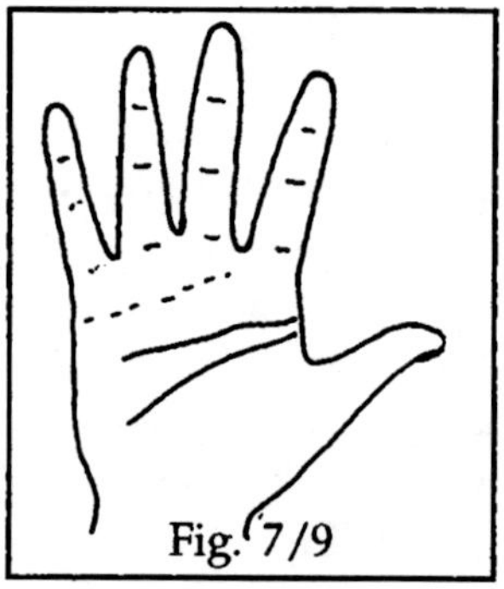

Fig. 7/9

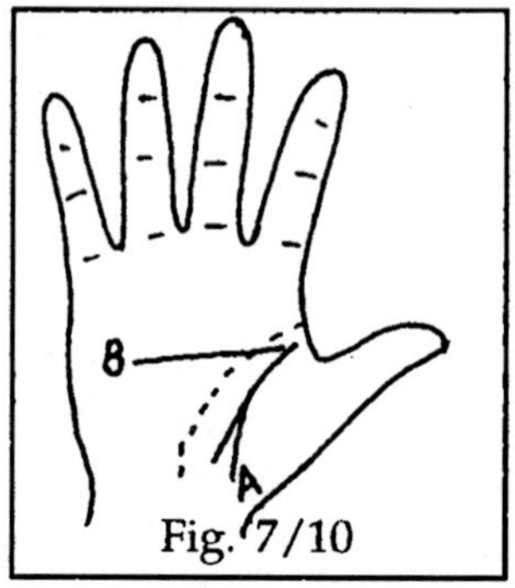

Fig. 7/10

If a woman has two Head Lines and both are distinct and separate she is likely to be married to a man belonging to a rich family. If one of the lines faces the Mount of the Moon (*See Fig. 7/9*) a love affair precedes the marriage.

Signs Indicating Unhappy Marriage/Love Affair

The following signs indicate an unhappy marriage or love affair :

If the Line of Mars has two forks at the end (*See Fig. 7/10-A*), the Line of Life is straight, incomplete or broken, there is a cross on the Line of Saturn or an island or the line is broken, the Head Line emanates from the Aggressive Mars (*See Fig. 7/10-B*) or emanates away from the Line of Life, these are inauspicious signs. Study these signs alongwith a defective line of sexuality and forecast the future.

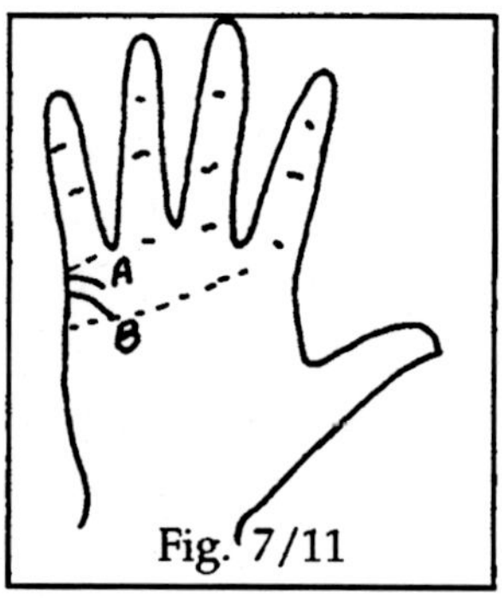

Fig. 7/11

If the Line/Lines of sexuality tilt towards the Heart Line (*See Fig. 7/11-A*) there would be differences of opinion and quarrels with the spouse. If the Line of Marriage or one of its branches touches the Heart Line (*See Fig. 7/11-B*) quarrels with the spouse are indicated. If the Line of Marriage or its branch touches the Heart Line (*See Fig. 7/11-B*) ill-health of the spouse is indicated or there is possibility of a divorce. Whether there would be divorce can be found from the study of the Line of Mars and the Line of Saturn.

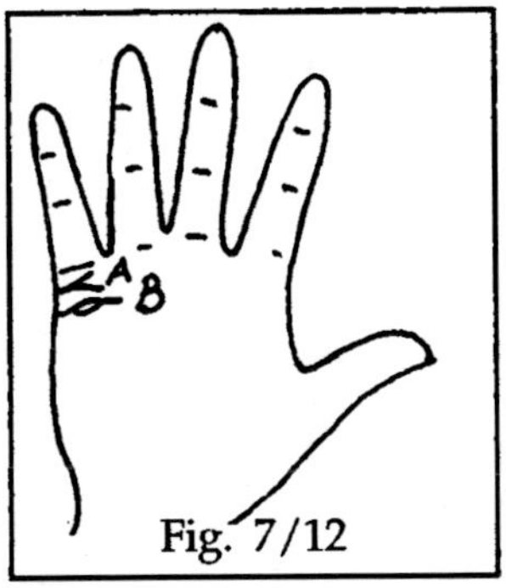

Fig. 7/12

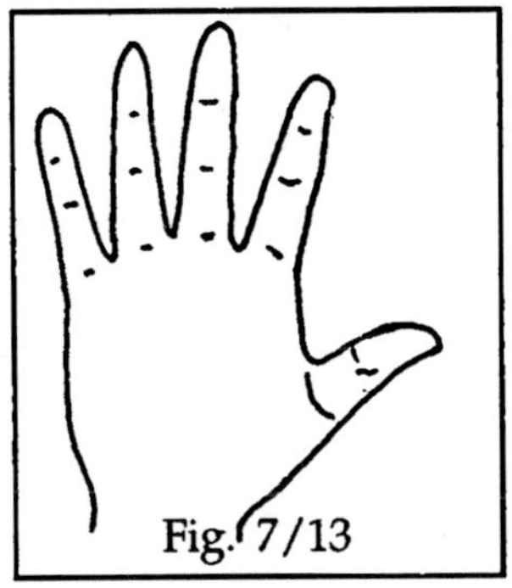
Fig. 7/13

If there is a fork at the end of the Line of Sexuality (*See Fig. 7/12-A*) or there are any islands on it (*See Fig. 7/12-B*) there would be troubles between the partners to a marriage.

One should not be hasty in predicting any matrimonial troubles or problems merely because the Line of Sexuality is defective. One should ask the client whether the health of the spouse is a source of worry. After the question has been answered, one should ask about any quarrels or differences of opinion.

A cross or a star on the line of sexuality indicates either a divorce or trouble for the spouse.

If the end of the thumb is thick like a club or is flat or the thumb is short, it tends to aggravate the ill-effects of a defective line of sexuality.

If the line dividing the two phalanges of the thumb (*See Fig. 7/13*) is broken or disjointed, an unhappy marital state is indicated.

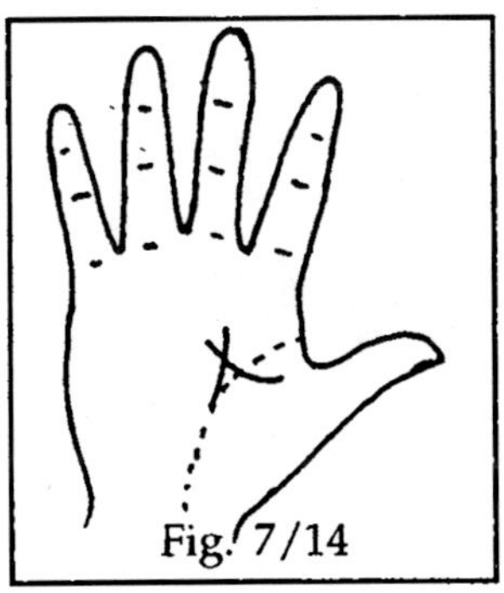
Fig. 7/14

If the line of influence emanating from the Aggressive Mars intersects the ascending branch of the Line of Life (*See Fig. 7/14*) there are marital troubles. If a question of a client relates to an on-going court case this state of affairs can indicate difficulty in realising the dues.

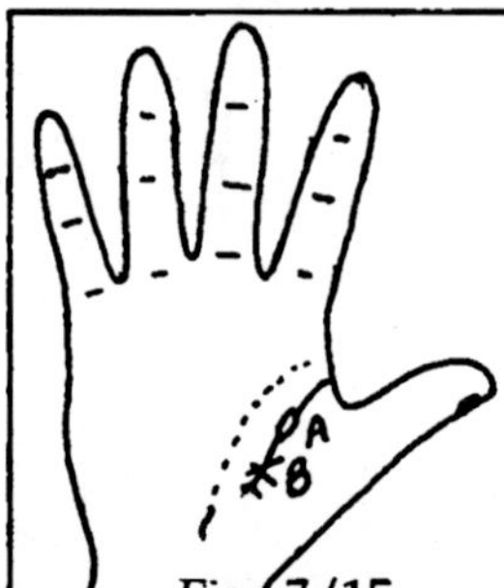

Fig. 7/15

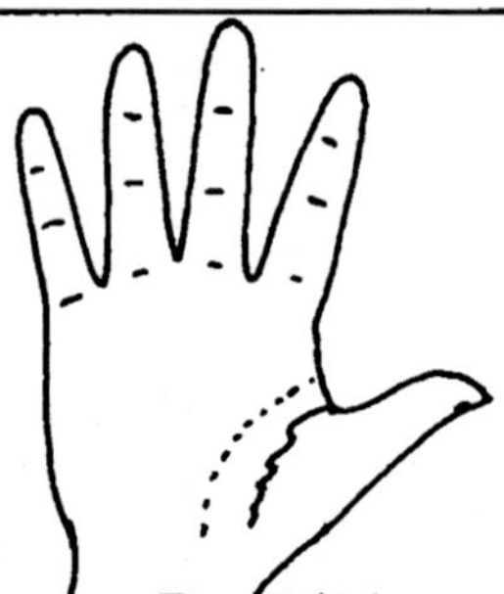

Fig. 7/16

If there is a star or an island on the Line of Mars (*See Fig. 7/15, A, B*) or the Line of Mars is wavy (*See Fig. 7/16*) there is no peace in married life, but if there is a square which mitigates the fault of the line, such a contingency would not arise.

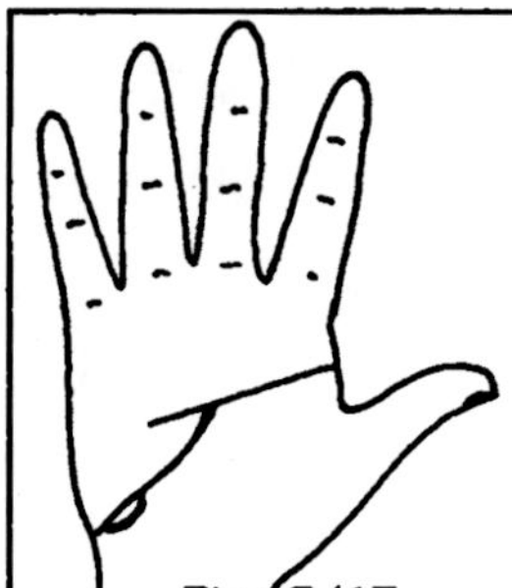

Fig. 7/17

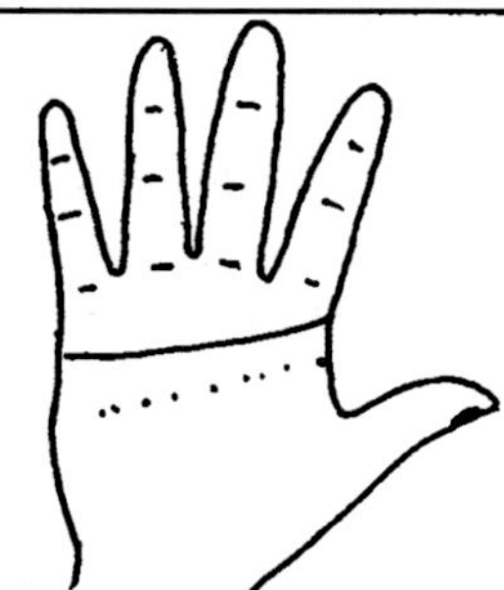

Fig. 7/18

If the Line of Saturn is thick and begins from an island on the Mount of Luna and stops at the Head Line (*See Fig. 7/17*) there are quarrels between the spouses.

If the Heart Line emanates from the Mount of Saturn, it is called a short line. If alongwith a short Line of Heart the index finger is short, a person is mean and petty-minded in his marital relations and his spouse cannot be happy.

If the Heart Line spans the whole width of the palm (*See Fig. 7/18*) a person seeks to dominate the object of his affections, which leads to bitterness with his beloved or his wife.

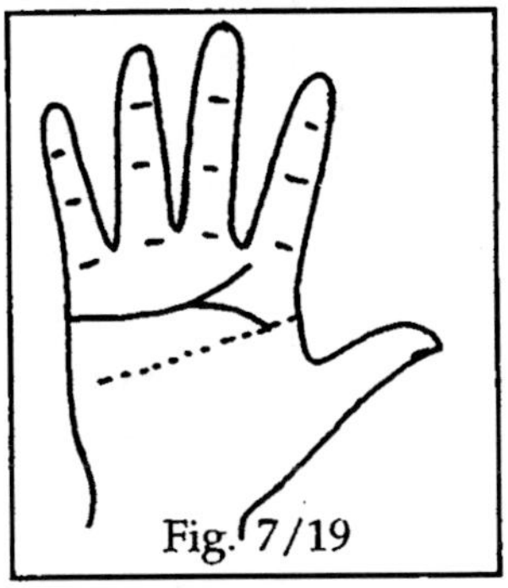

Fig. 7/19

If a deep branch of the Heart Line intersects the defective Head Line under the Mount of Jupiter (*See Fig. 7/19*) there is likely to be failure in love or in marriage. Alternatively, the spouse of the client asking such a question would predecease him/her.

If the Heart Line does not have a branch it means that there is no sentiment involved in the marital relations and married life cannot be happy.

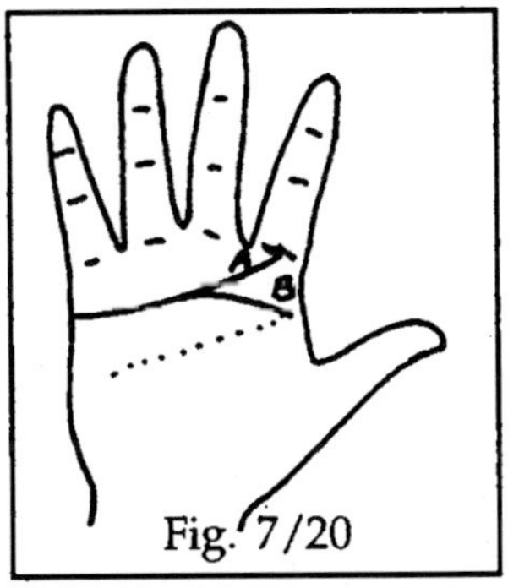

Fig. 7/20

Persons whose Heart Line emanates from the base of the index finger (*See Fig. 7/20-A*) wish to see such qualities in their objects of affection/spouses which are just not found among human beings. That is why they face disappointment in love/marriage. If a branch of such a Heart Line reaches the Head Line (*See Fig. 7/20-B*) there is possibility of a divorce.

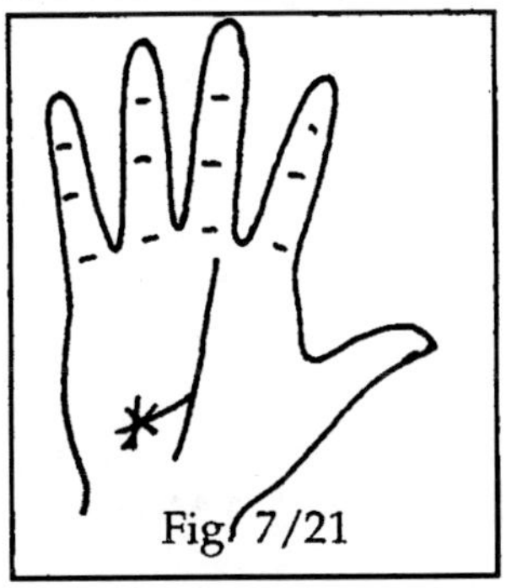

Fig. 7/21

If the line of influence emanating from the Mount of Luna meeting the Line of Saturn has a star (*See Fig. 7/21*) bad luck is indicated for the object of affections/spouse.

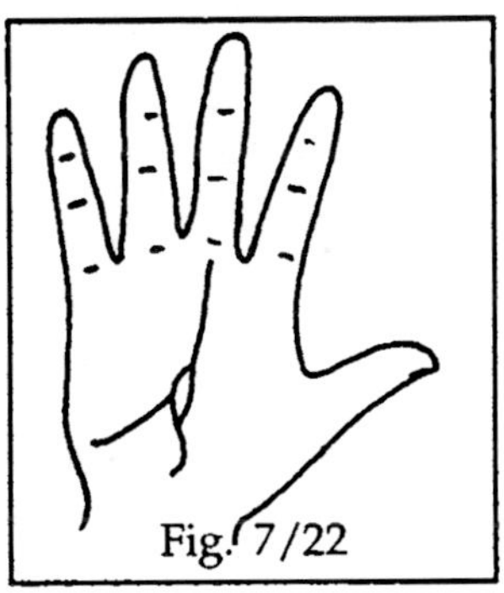

Fig. 7/22

At the time the line of influence emanating from the Mount of Luna touches the Line of Saturn where there are islands (*See Fig. 7/22*) there is bitterness in marital relations. But a firm conclusion can be reached only after studying all the other signs.

If there are islands or stars on the Line of Saturn, one does not get any happiness due to one's spouse and is likely to lose money.

A marriage contracted at the time when there is an island on the Line of Saturn (*See Fig. 7/22*) is never successful. The time where island is the widest is the time of great difficulty.

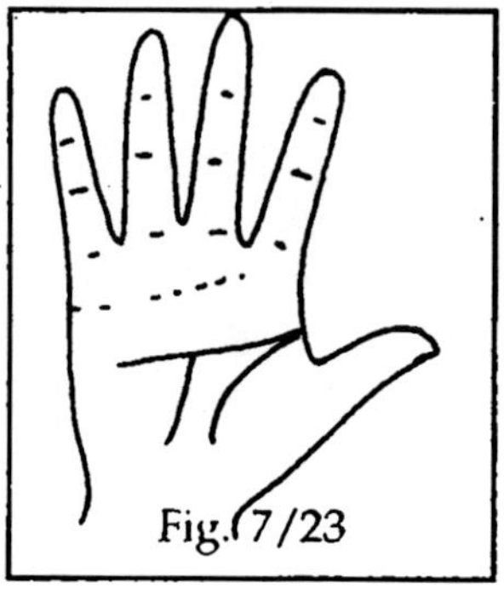

Fig. 7/23

If the Line of Saturn stops at the Head Line (*See Fig. 7/23*), the Line of Life is incomplete or straight and the index finger is short, it indicates troubles for the spouse.

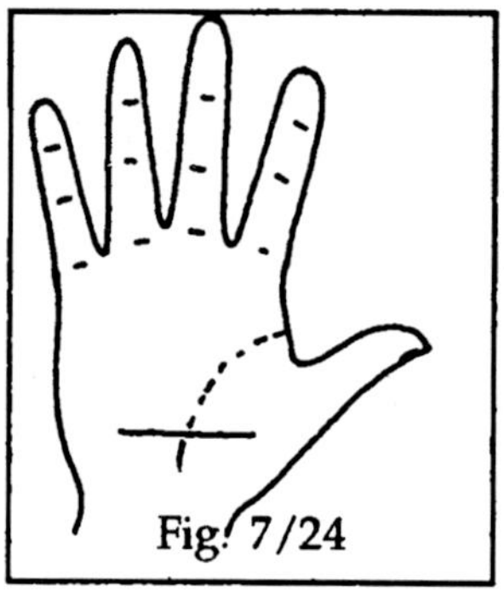

Fig. 7/24

If the line of influence from the Mount of Venus cuts across the Line of Life and goes towards the Mount of Moon (*See Fig. 7/24*) there is apprehension of troubles caused by a person of the opposite sex. Western palmists call it the Via Lasciva which indicates hyper-sexuality on a heavy and rough hand. In a thin and flabby hand it is indicative of a tendency towards addiction to drugs.

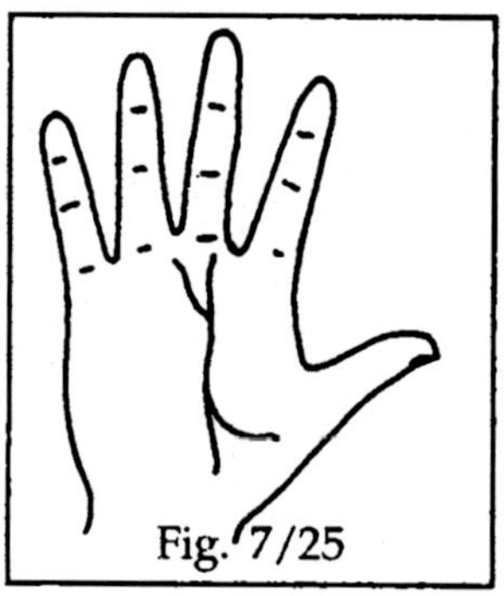

Fig. 7/25

If a line of influence emanating from the Mount of Venus touches the Line of Saturn and divides in two branches (*See Fig. 7/25*) an unhappy marriage is indicated.

Signs Indicating Obstructions to Marriage/Love Affair

There is difficulty in establishing marital/love relations at the time there is an island in the Line of Saturn.

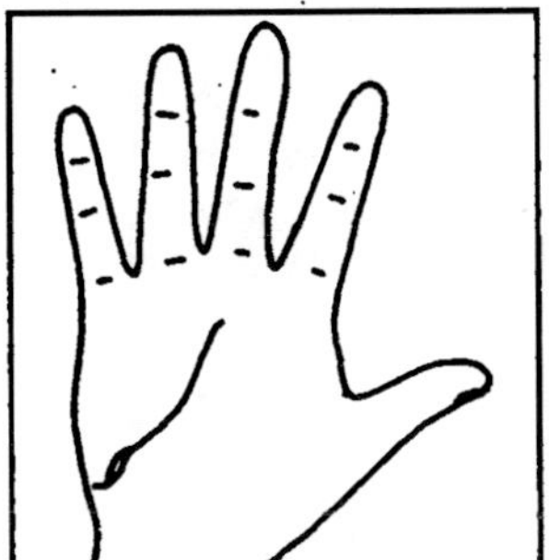

Fig. 7/26

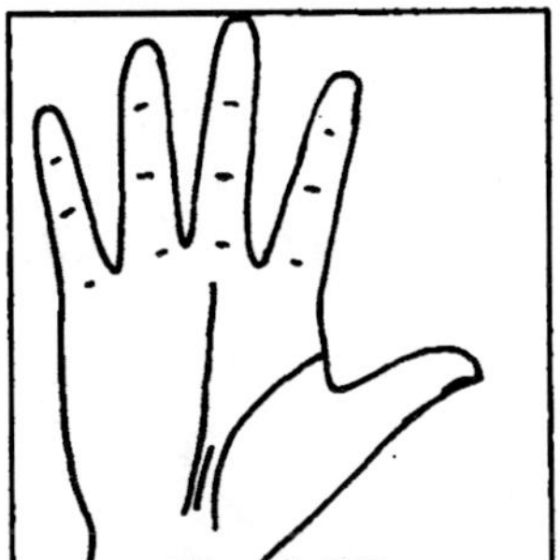

Fig. 7/27

If the Line of Saturn originates from an island in the Mount of Luna (*See Fig. 7/26*) there is disappointment in marital relations/love affair.

So long as the Line of Saturn remains defective, there are obstructions in marital relations.

If there is an axe line (*kuthar rekha*) between the Line of Life and the Line of Saturn (*See Fig. 7/27*) obstructions persist till the time of the *kuthar rekha*. The time of this line can be calculated by reference to the rules pertaining to finding the age from the Line of Saturn.

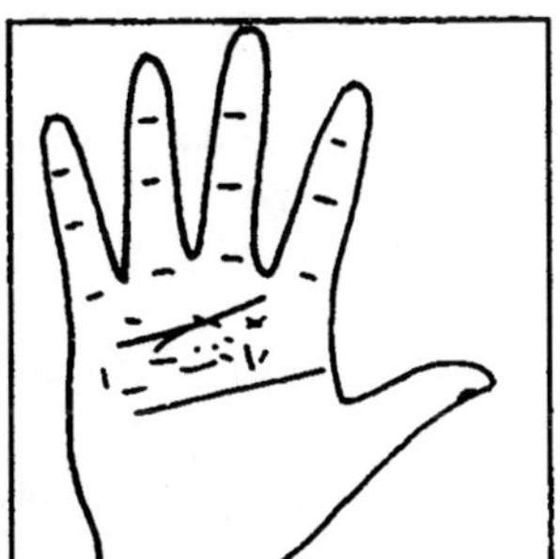

Fig. 7/28

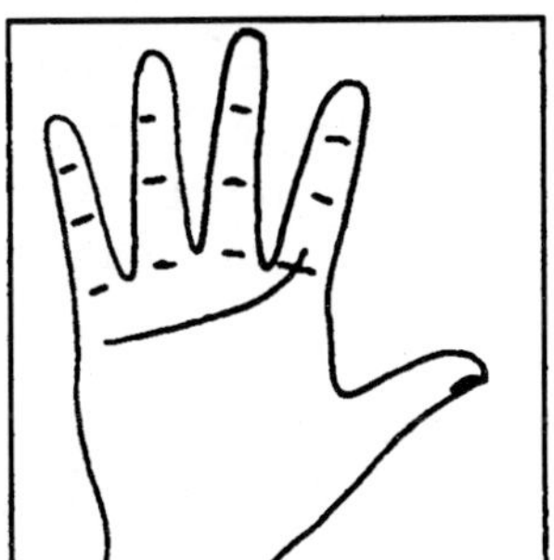

Fig. 7/29

If there are short lines between the Heart Line and the Head Line which intersect the Heart Line (*See Fig. 7/28*) they indicate disappointment in love.

If the Heart Line starts from the third phalange of the index finger (*See Fig. 7/29*) there is disappointment in love. A study of the Line of Saturn can tell you when that disappointment would turn into hope.

If the Heart Line is broken there is disappointment in love.

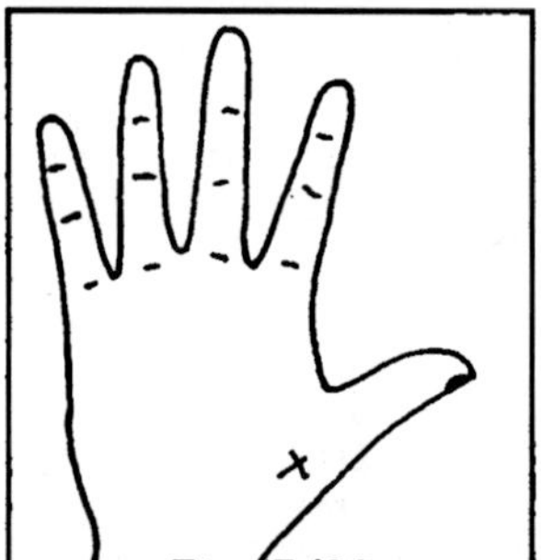

Fig. 7/30

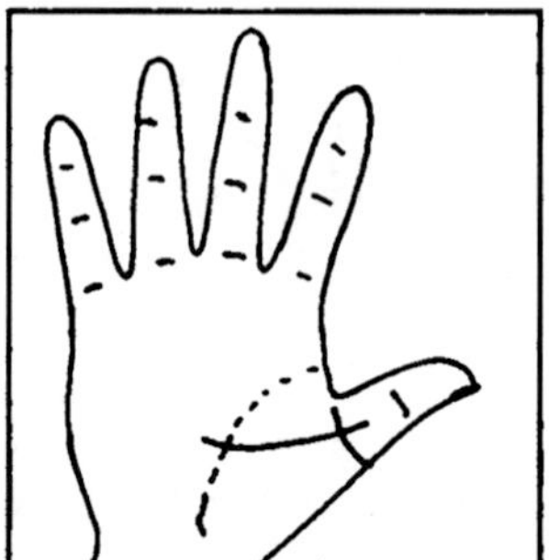

Fig. 7/31

If there is a cross in the middle of the Mount of Venus (*See Fig. 7/30*) it indicates disappointment in love.

An over-developed Aggressive Mars is indicative of obstructions in marriage/love.

If a line of influence emanating from the second phalange of the thumb intersects the Line of Life (*See Fig. 7/31*) a love affair ends in misfortune.

A Love Marriage or an Arranged One?

Persons with a thick Line of Saturn are self-willed and there is greater likelihood in their case of marrying someone they love or like. Persons with a thin line of Saturn are clear-headed and marry after they have taken all the factors into consideration. They might fall in love with someone but when the time for marriage comes they bow before their parents and accept their choice of a spouse.

If the Head Line is long, straight and without any fault, there is greater possibility of an arranged marriage.

If the Heart Line is forked and the third finger is long there is possibility of a love marriage.

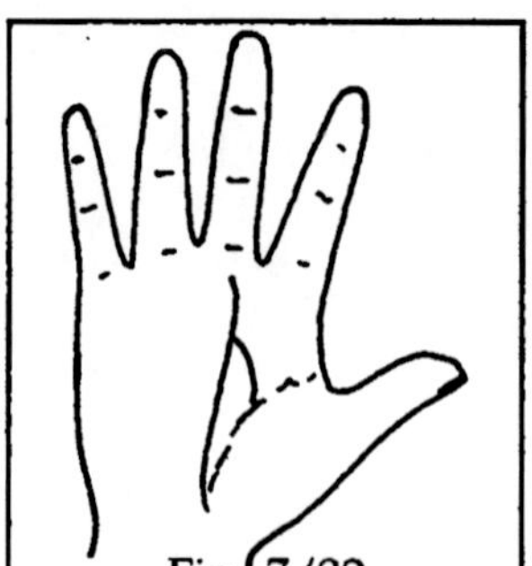

Fig. 7/32

If a branch of the Line of Life makes a loop and describes an island with the Line of Saturn (*See Fig. 7/32*) a love marriage is indicated.

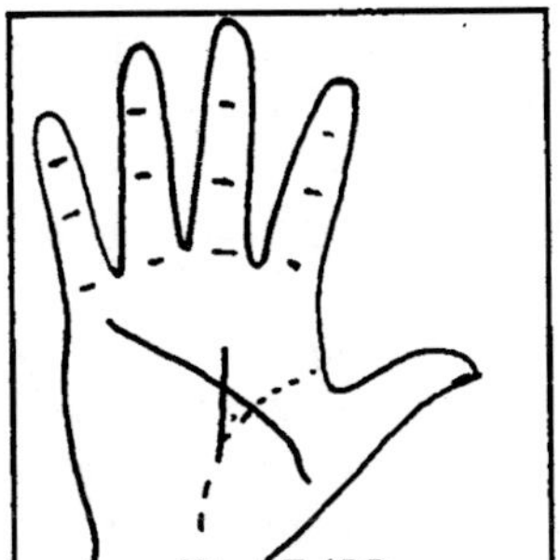

Fig. 7/33

If a line of influence from the Mount of Venus intersects an ascending branch of the Line of Life to proceed towards the Mount of Mercury (*See Fig. 7/33*), a love affair is indicated.

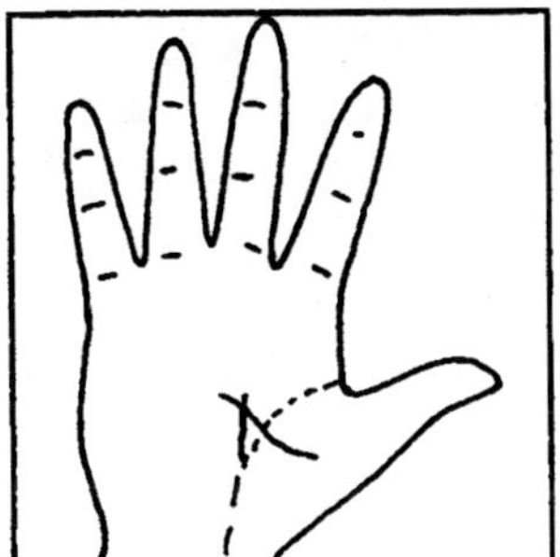

Fig. 7/34

If this line of influence fails to reach the Mount of Mercury after intersecting the ascending branch of the Line of Life (*See Fig. 7/34*) a divorce is possible.

If a line of influence emanating from the Mount of Venus touches the Line of Saturn it is indicative of a love affair. If the question of your client refers to trade, it indicates possibility of a partnership. (*See again Fig. 6/61 in Chapter VI*)

If a line of influence emanating from the Mount of Venus runs parallel to the Line of Saturn the love affair would be long-lasting (*See again Fig 6/62*). In case there is a query with regard to trading, a partnership would subsist for a long time.

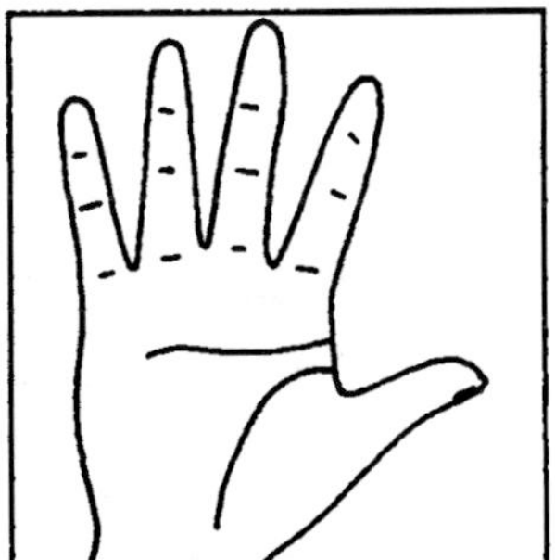

Fig. 7/35

If the distance between the points of origin of the Line of Life and the Head Line (*See Fig. 7/35*) is considerable, there is possibility of a love marriage, but the marriage is not fortunate. Persons whose Head Line and the Line of Life combine and run for a considerable distance, generally go in for arranged marriages.

Signs Indicating Divorce, Reconciliation and Second Marriage

If the line of sexuality meets the Heart Line (*See again Fig. 7/11-B*) or there is an island on the line of sexuality (*See again Fig. 7/12-B*), an island on the Line of Saturn, the Heart Line touches the Head Line, there is an island on the Line of Mars (*See Fig. 7/36*), or the Line of Mars stops at a point and restarts from another (*See Fig. 7/42*) -- if three or more such signs are found in a hand -- there is likelihood of a second marriage after divorce/ death of the spouse.

There are some other signs too, but before you study them see that you have properly studied and made your calculations from the line of sexuality. The other signs would only confirm your analysis.

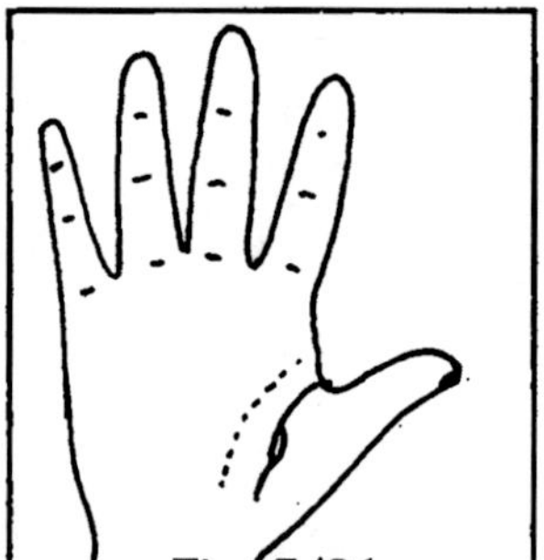

Fig. 7/36

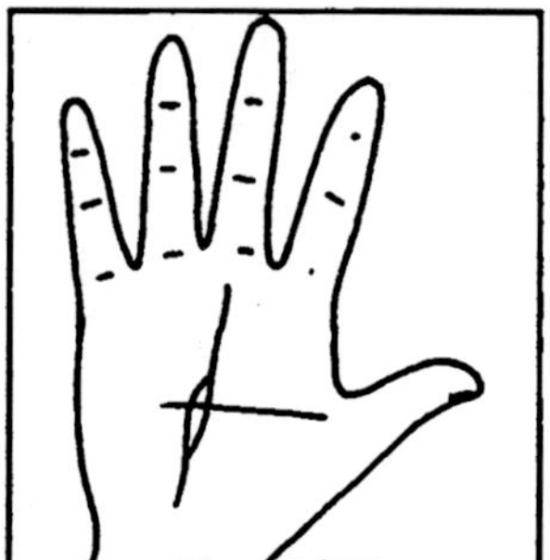

Fig. 7/37

If a line of influence emanating from the Aggressive Mars cuts across an island on the Line of Saturn (*See Fig. 7/37*), there is likelihood of the break-up of a marriage.

If the line of sexuality meets the Heart Line, there are islands on the Line of Saturn on both the palms, there is an island on the Line of Mars, it indicates breaking off of relations with spouse or his/her death and a second marriage thereafter.

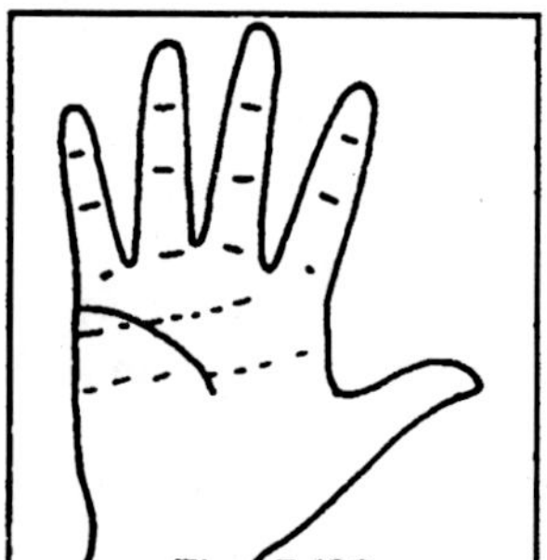

Fig. 7/38

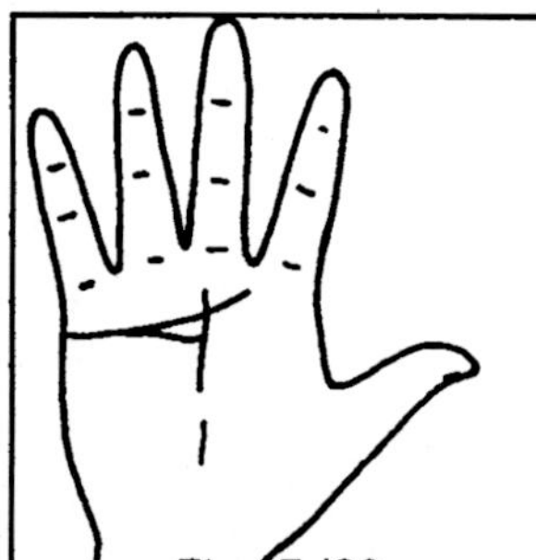

Fig. 7/39

If the line of sexuality intersects the defective Head Line and the Heart Line (*See Fig. 7/38*), a divorce is a certainty.

If a thick branch of the Heart Line touches the Line of Saturn (*See Fig. 7/39*), there is a possibility of divorce.

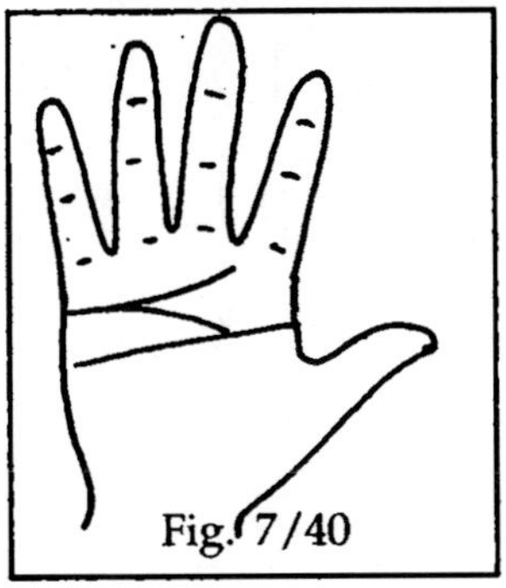

Fig. 7/40

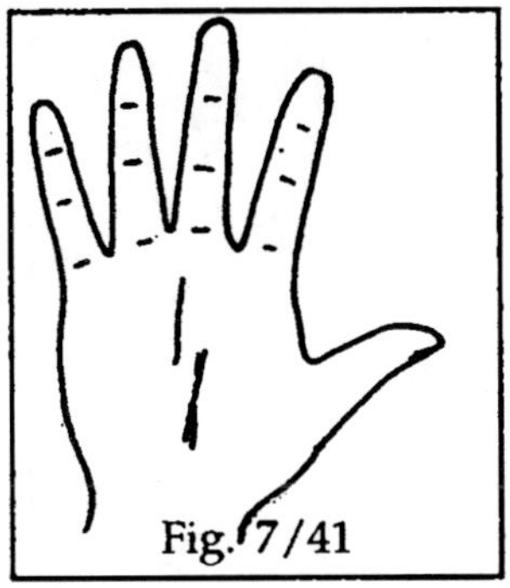

Fig. 7/41

There is possibility of divorce also if the branch of the Heart Line meets the Head Line (*See Fig. 4/40*) and the index finger is small.

There is a possibility of divorce if the Line of Saturn is broken at many places.

If the Line of Saturn stops at a point and then re-starts a little distance away (*See Fig. 7/41*) there is likelihood of a second marriage after divorce.

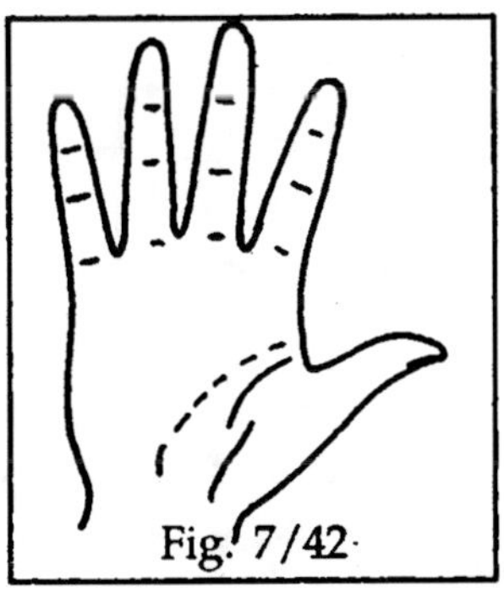

Fig. 7/42

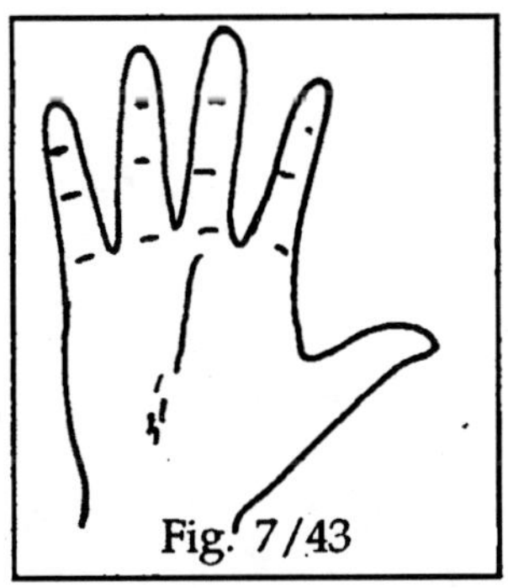

Fig. 7/43

Similar is the result when the Line of Mars stops at a point and a parallel line of Mars starts a little distance away (*See Fig. 7/42*).

If the Line of Saturn is broken and its pieces overlap each other, the spouses would quarrel, separate and then reconcile with each other. If in the age when the Line of Saturn comes to an end and then re-starts (*See Fig. 7/43*) there is likelihood of a new marriage after divorce.

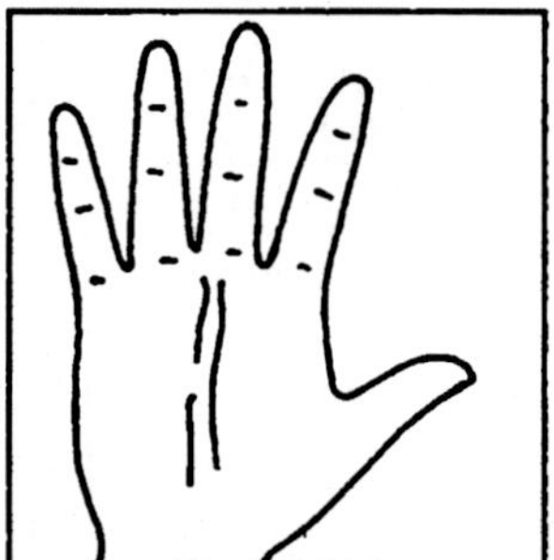

Fig. 7/44

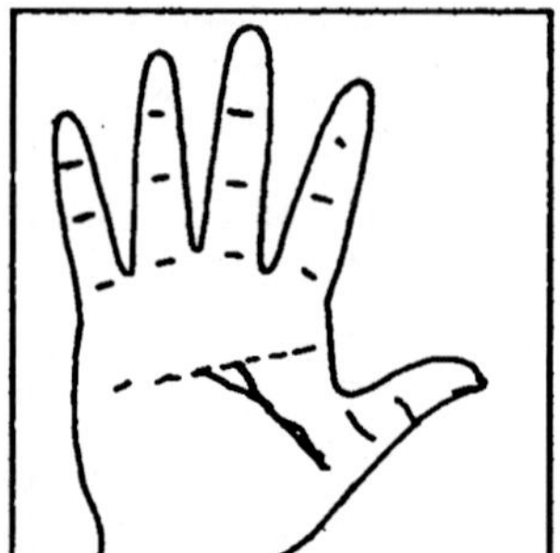

Fig. 7/45

If there are two Lines of Saturn, one of which is broken and the other without any fault (*See Fig. 7/44*) reconciliation is indicated after tensions in marriage/love affair.

If a line of influence emanating from the Mount of Venus reaches the Head line and divides into two branches (*See Fig. 7/45*) there are chances of a divorce or a scandal.

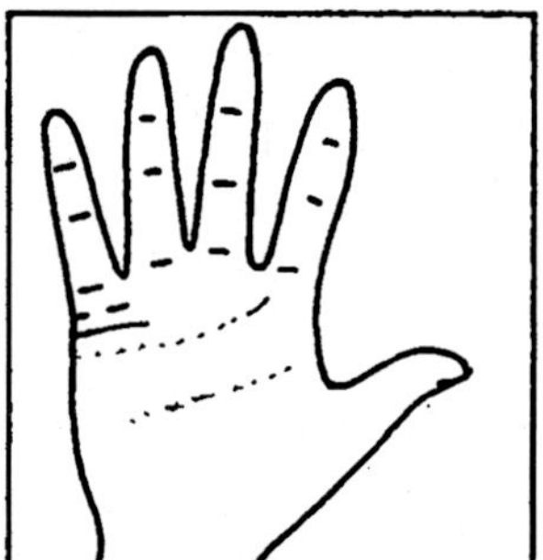

Fig. 7/46

If there are two lines of sexuality, one of which is broken, but the other line overlaps the first (*See Fig. 7/46*) a reconciliation between the spouses is possible after initial stresses and strains.

If the Line of Mars and the Line of Sexuality is without any fault, but the Lines of Saturn and of Life are faulty, it indicates monetary and health problems. We shall deal with these lines in separate chapters.

Signs Indicating Lack of Fidelity in Love/Marriage

If the Line of Mars is deep and is near the Line of Life, the little finger is long and thick, the Aggressive Mars, the Mount of Mercury and the Mount of Venus are developed, it indicates extra-marital relations. Study carefully the third phalange of the little finger. If it is long and thick such relations are a certainty. If the Mount of Apollo is defective or there is a fault on the Line of the Sun one is likely to face disgrace or infamy.

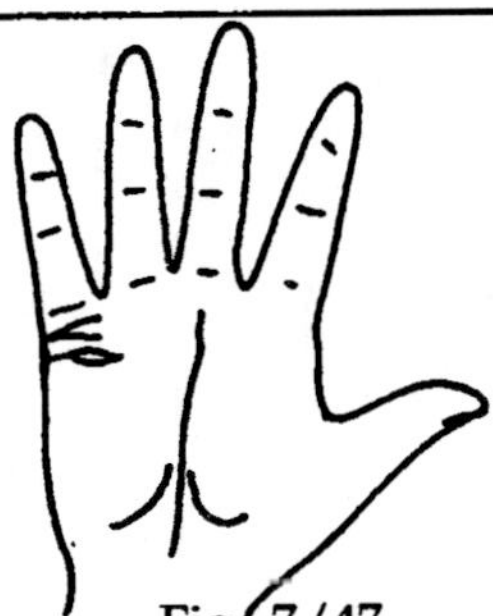

Fig. 7/47

If the Line of Sexuality is forked or there are islands on it, if the Mount of Venus is over-developed and lines of influence emanating from it and the Mount of Luna run parallel to the Line of Saturn (*See Fig. 7/47*) extra-marital relations are indicated. If the marriage line is without any fault, the line of influence emanating from the Mount of Venus indicates partnership in business.

Fig. 7/48

If the line of marriage is defective and the Heart Line is very close to the base of the fingers, (*See Fig. 7/48*) the Mount of Venus is over-developed, extra-marital relations are probable.

Similar is the case when the Heart Line emanates from the Mount of Saturn and the Mount of Venus is over-developed.

Fig. 7/49

If two lines from the Mount of Luna meet the Line of Saturn (*See Fig. 7/49*) there might be two love affairs or marriage with extra-marital relations. Whether such relations would be happy or unhappy can be found from the position of the Line of Saturn.

Fig. 7/50

If alongwith other signs, a line of influence emanating from the Mount of Venus goes upto the Mount of Mercury (*See Fig. 7/50*) it is an indication of extra-marital relations. The other signs include : a developed Mount of Venus or a grill on it, a long thick little finger and a developed Mount of Mercury.

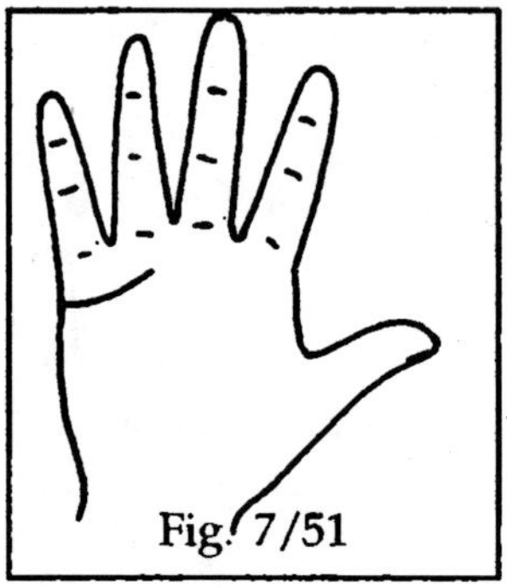

Fig. 7/51

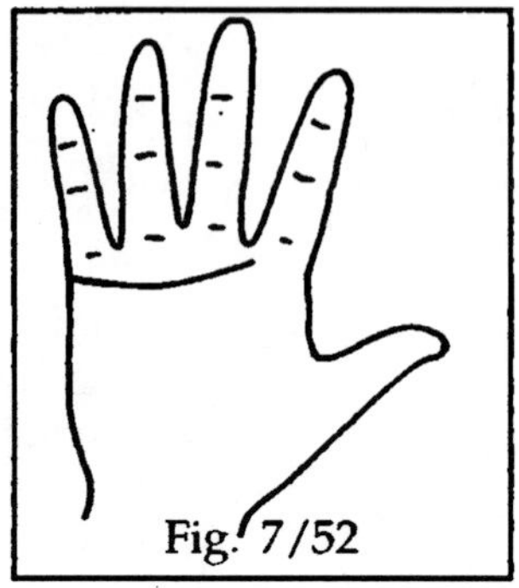

Fig. 7/52

If the Heart Line starts from the Mount of Apollo (*See Fig. 7/51*) and there are other signs mentioned in the preceding paragraph, there is loss of money accompanied by extra-marital relations.

If the Heart Line ends near the base of the little finger (*See Fig. 7/52*) a person loses all moral rectitude in the matter of extra-marital relations.

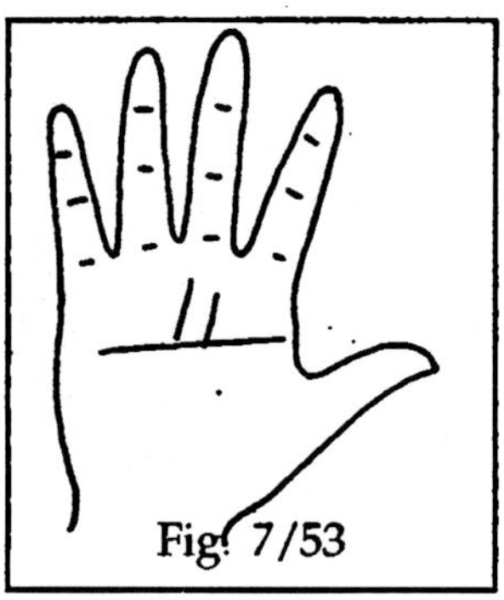

Fig. 7/53

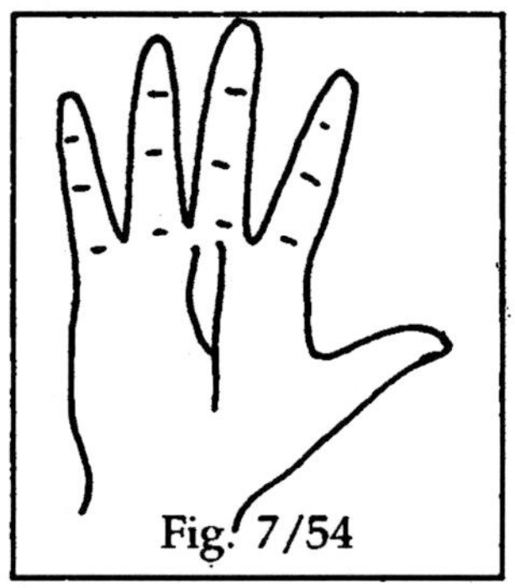

Fig. 7/54

If two Lines of Saturn emanate from the Head Line (*See Fig. 7/53*) and other signs support it, there is likelihood of sexual relations with two persons at the same time. The other signs have been referred to more than once in this chapter.

If another Line of Saturn emanates from the main Line of Saturn (*See Fig. 7/54*) and other signs favour such a conclusion, then there are many sexual relations.

If the Line of Saturn stops at a defective Heart Line and other signs are favourable there is likelihood of multiple sexual relations.

It should be noted that if there is a grill on the Mount of Venus it should be taken to be a developed one and a reading should be given with reference to other signs in conjunction with it.

CHAPTER VIII

ANSWERS TO QUESTIONS REGARDING CHILDREN AND FAMILY

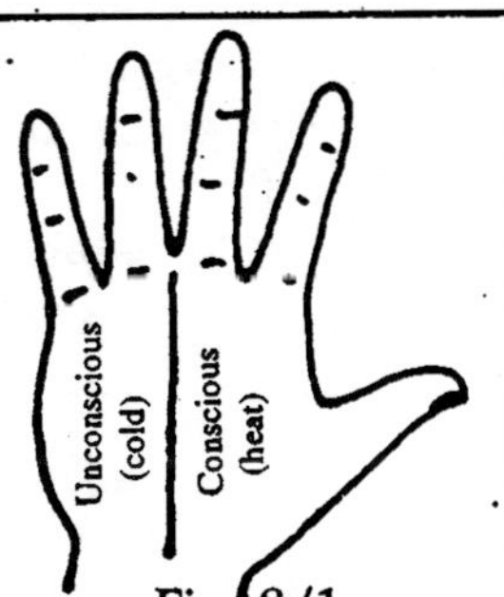

Fig. 8/1

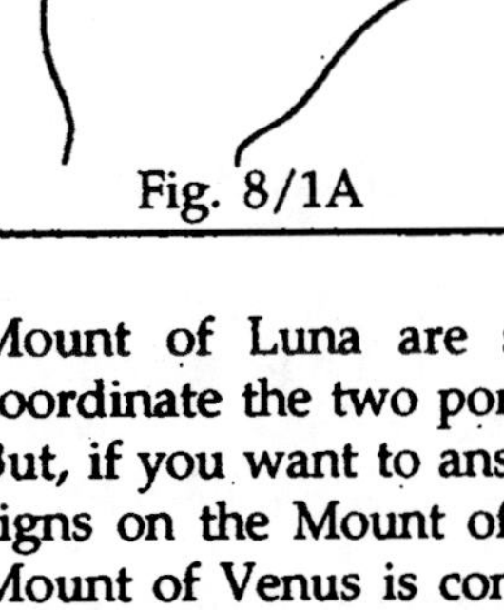
Fig. 8/1A

If you drew a line in the middle of the palm from the base of the fingers to the base of the wrist, the portion in which the thumb is situated would represent the conscious mind and the amount of heat in the body and the other one would be the part concerned with the unconscious and the amount of cold. (*See Fig. 8/1*)

Children and the family are a part of the conscious mind -- that is the half of the palm where the thumb is the one concerned with the progeny and the family of an individual.

In Western palmistry the vertical lines on the lines of sexuality (*See Fig. 8/1-A*) represent the progency of a person, but, according to the *Samudrika Shastra* that the portion around the thumb is the one, one must study if one has to answer questions regarding children and family of a client. The experience of the present author gives him reason to believe that the *Samudrika Shastra* is right in this context because the origin of life is concerned with the part of the palm where the index finger and the Mount of Venus are situated. The area concerned with the development of the mind is the one where the little finger and the Mount of Luna are situated. The bracelets/rascettes are the lines which coordinate the two portions of the palm. That is why they are also important. But, if you want to answer questions with regard to progeny you will find the signs on the Mount of Venus and the area around it. This is so because the Mount of Venus is concerned with sexuality.

The lines of progeny indicate a person's procreative powers. If either the man or the woman--one of them--has the procreative powers and the other is bereft of them, the lines become powerless. That is why one has to study the palms of both the husband and the wife to answer questions with regard to children. Only then can any forecast be made. If there are any defects in the lines, remedies must be suggested in such a way that one of the spouses is not able to blame the other for childlessness. Remedies must be suggested for both the spouses to save them from mutual recriminations.

The Question of Progeny

While answering questions about children the first thing to be studied is the line at the base of the thumb where there are islands and also the Mount of Venus. Next the shape of the rascettes should be studied and later the Line of Life, the Heart Line, the Head Line and the Line of Saturn.

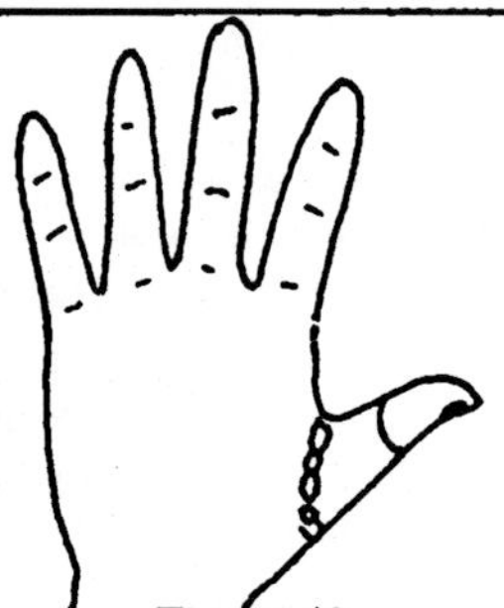

Fig. 8/2

The large islands at the base of the thumb (*See Fig. 8/2*) represent male progeny and the small ones girls. Study both the thumbs and if the number of islands is equal in both, a definite answer can be given. But, if the islands are only at the base of one of the thumbs you can say that so many boys/girls are a probability.

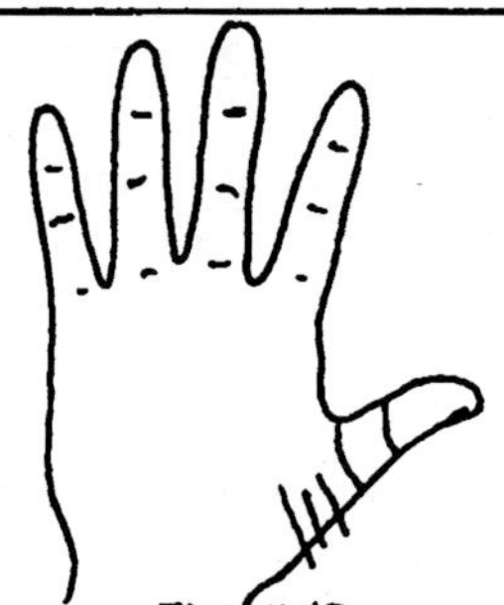

Fig. 8/3

The lines emanating from the outer edge of the base of the thumb which come towards the Mount of Venus near the base of the thumb (*See Fig. 8/3*) represent the number of children. Long lines represent boys and small ones girls. If the lines are without any faults the children are likely to be healthy or helpful to the parents. Defective lines represent unhealthy, short-lived or children who are not helpful to their parents.

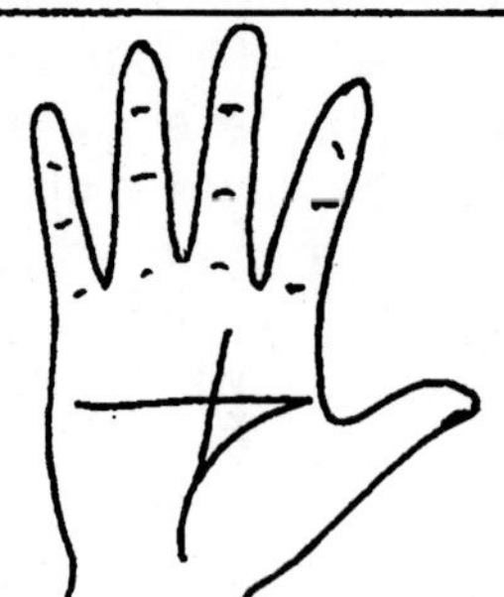

Fig. 8/4

If the Line of Life is semi-circular, the Line of Saturn emanates from it and the Head Line is without any defects (*See Fig. 8/4*) the children are lucky for their parents. To find the age at which a couple will have children calculate the age at which the Line of Saturn has emanated from the Line of Life. The time can be calculated according to the rules pertaining to calculation of age from the Line of Saturn.

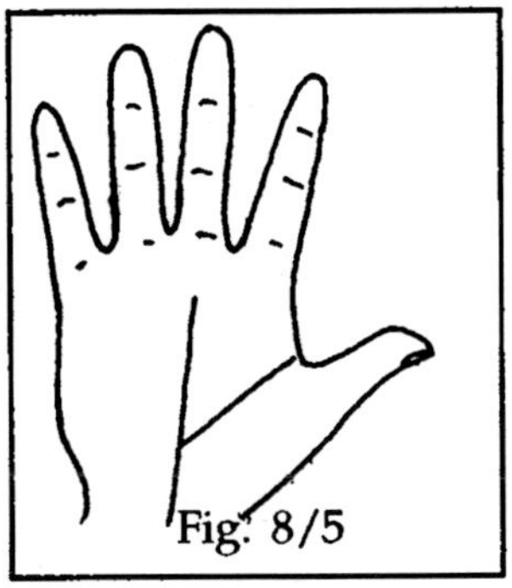

Fig. 8/5

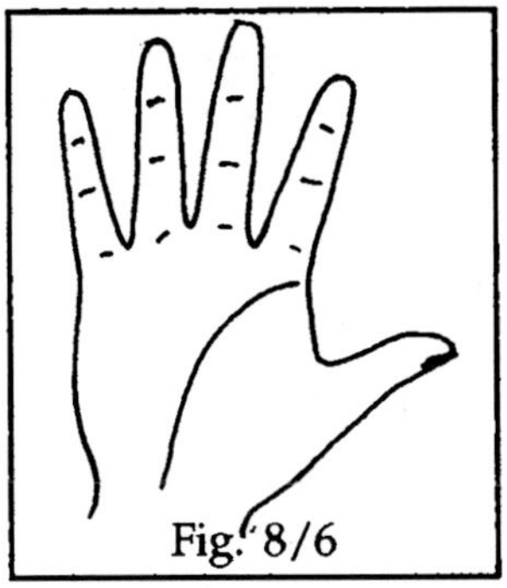

Fig. 8/6

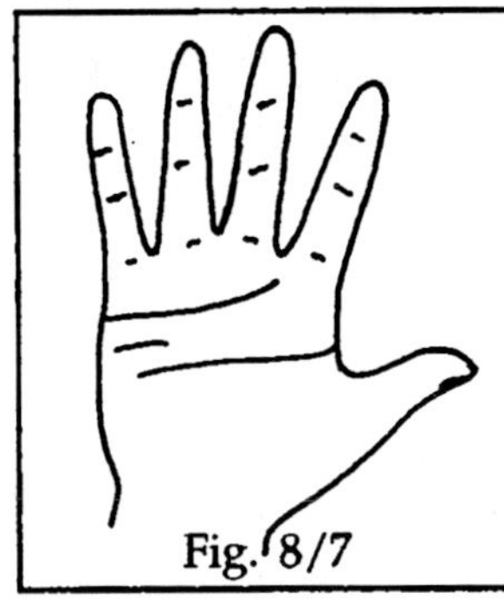

Fig. 8/7

If the Line of Life is straight, its defect is offset only when the Line of Saturn touches the Line of Life as it goes towards the middle finger. (*See Fig. 8/5*). This is the age at which the children are likely to be born. The age can be calculated from the point when the Line of Life comes near the Line of Saturn.

If the Line of Life emanates from the Mount of Jupiter (*See Fig. 8/6*) or if a branch of that line goes towards the Mount, the number of children is large.

A short parallel line between the Head Line and the Heart Line, which is on the Defensive Mars (*See Fig. 8/7*) also represents children.

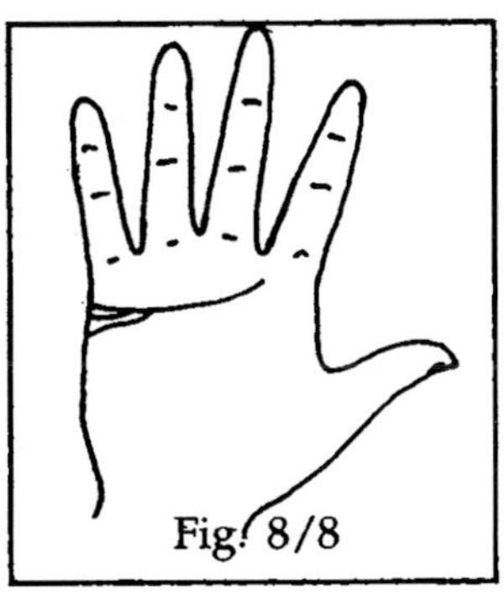

Fig. 8/8

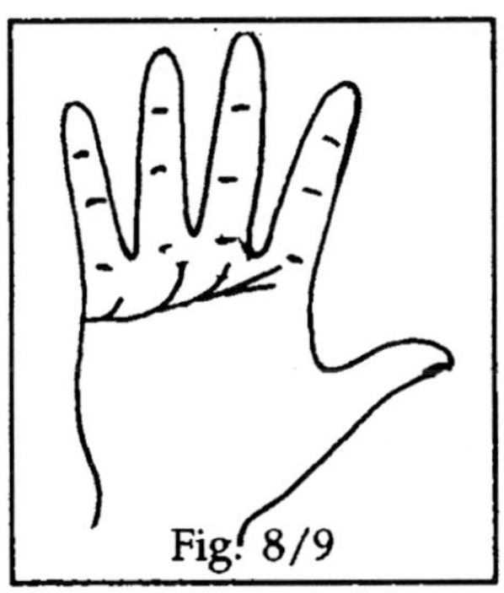

Fig. 8/9

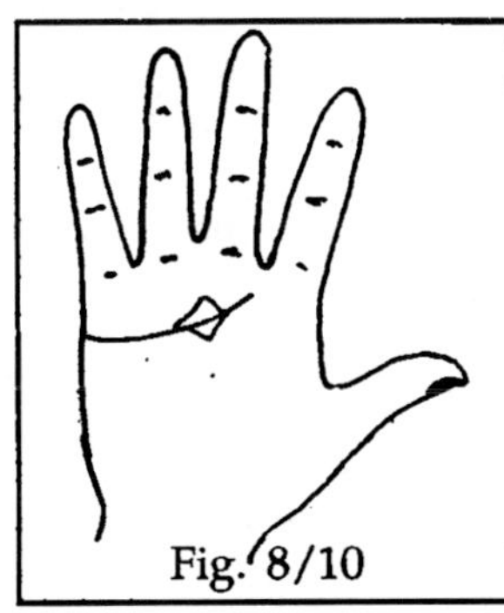

Fig. 8/10

If the Heart Line at its end, that is towards the Defensive Mars branches out in many directions (*See Fig. 8/8*) it is a sure sign of a couple having children.

If the branches of the Heart Line thin out as they go towards the fingers (*See Fig. 8/9*) children bring good luck to their parents.

If there are two triangles, one above and another below the Heart Line and both of them form a square (*See Fig. 8/10*) it is a sure sign of a couple getting children.

A thin Heart Line with branches in the palm of a woman is indicative of her being happy with her husband and children.

A good Line of Saturn and a good Heart Line with branches indicates happiness from children.

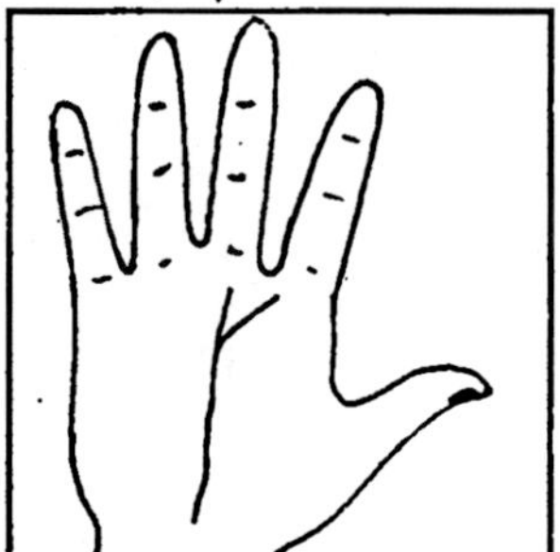

Fig. 8/11

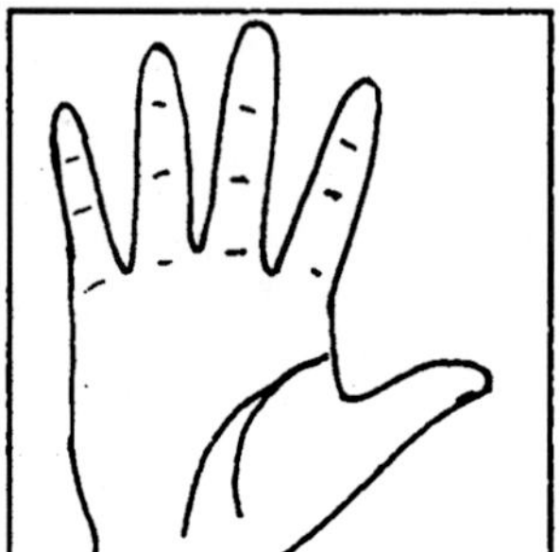

Fig. 8/12

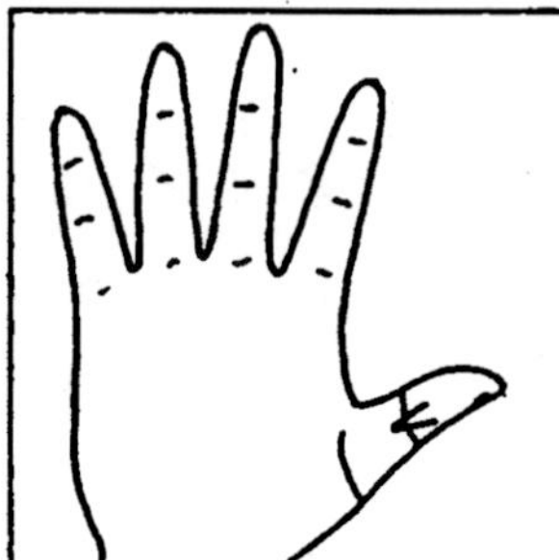

Fig. 8/13

If the Line of Saturn forks out in two branches as it reaches the Mount of Saturn and one of the branches goes towards the Mount of Jupiter (*See Fig. 8/11*), it is an indication of a person begetting children.

If a branch of the Line of Life enters the Aggressive Mars and runs parallel to it (*See Fig. 8/12*) a person is likely to have cordial relations with his children.

See, in addition to other signs, whether the Mount of Venus is firm because it indicates possibilities of children being born. If the Mount is under-developed, those possibilities lessen to the extent of its under-development. If there is a grill on an under-developed Mount of Venus, it has the same effect as a well-developed one. Other signs must, therefore, be consulted before any forecast is made.

Signs Indicative of Obstructing the Birth of Children

If there is a 'V' on the line between the two phalanges of the thumb (*See Fig. 8/13*) there are obstructions in the birth of children.

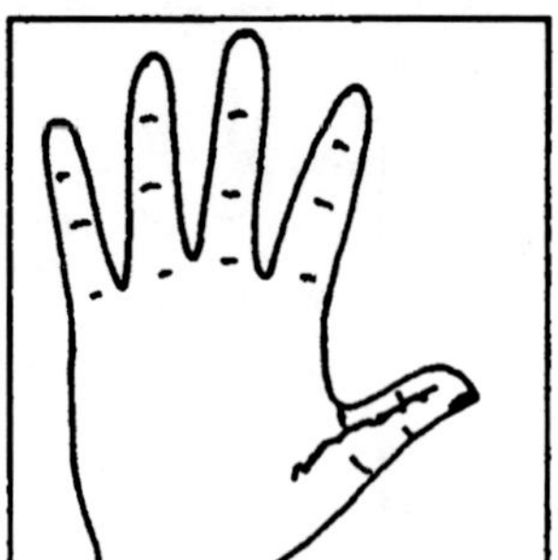

Fig. 8/14

If a twisted line of influence emerging from the first phalange of the thumb comes to the Mount of Venus (*See Fig. 8/14*) it is an indication of childlessness.

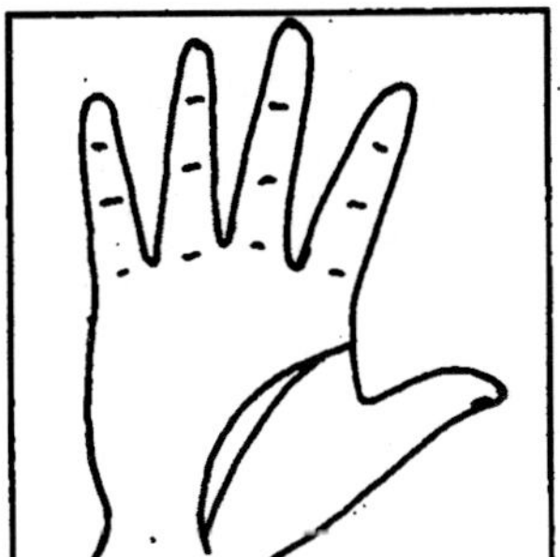
Fig. 8/15

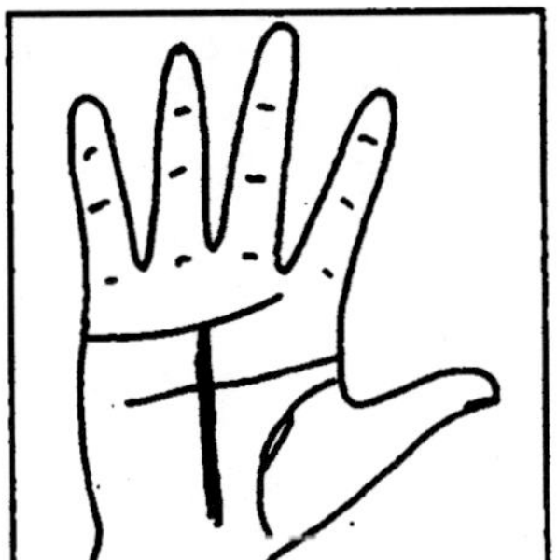
Fig. 8/16

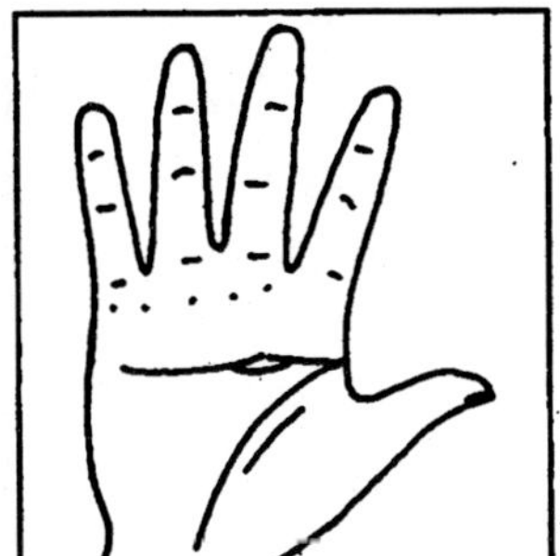
Fig. 8/17

If the Line of Life doubles itself and describes a large island (*See Fig. 8/15*) there is a possibility of a person having sickly children or an abortion.

If the Line of Life is full of islands, shortens the circumference of the Mount of Venus, a thick Line of Saturn stops at the Heart Line (*See Fig. 8/16*), it indicates obstacles in the way of having male progeny.

If there is an axe line with the Line of Life, and an island on the Head Line in the area of Saturn.(*See Fig. 8/17*) there would be obstacles to having children.

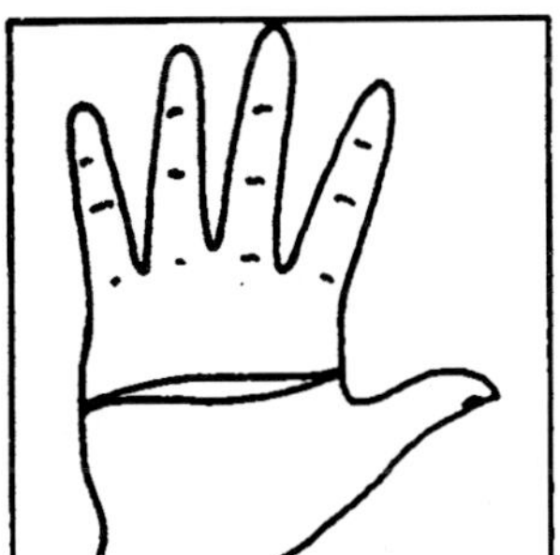
Fig. 8/18

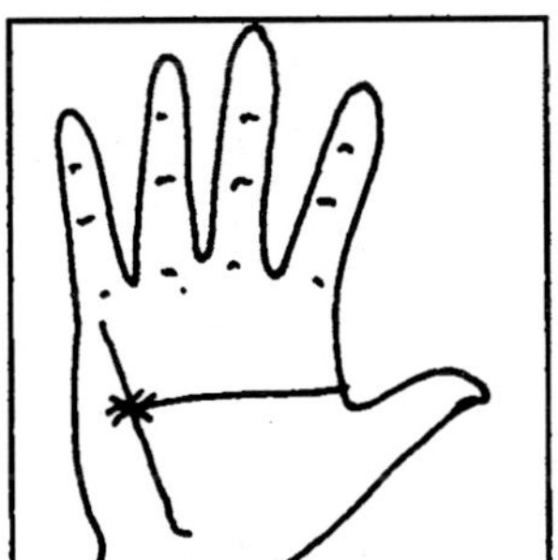
Fig. 8/19

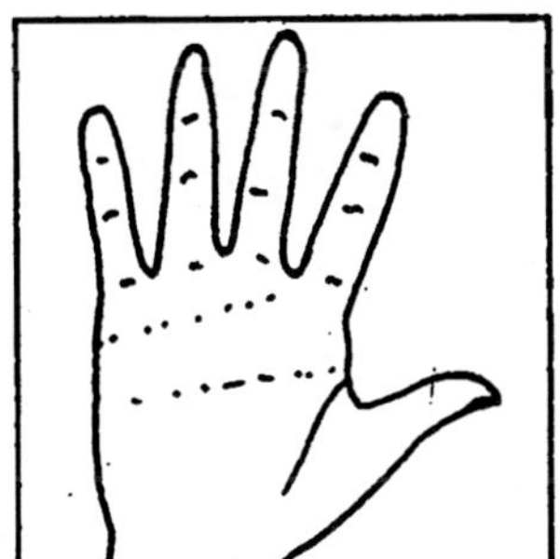
Fig. 8/20

If the ends of a double Head Line describe an island (*See Fig. 8/18*) there are obstructions to begetting children.

Similar is the effect of a star on the meeting point of the Head Line and the Line of Mercury on the palm of a woman (*See Fig. 8/19*). Same is the case when the Heart Line is without any branches.

If the Line of Life straightens and goes towards the Mount of Venus (*See Fig. 8/20*) it is an indication of childlessness.

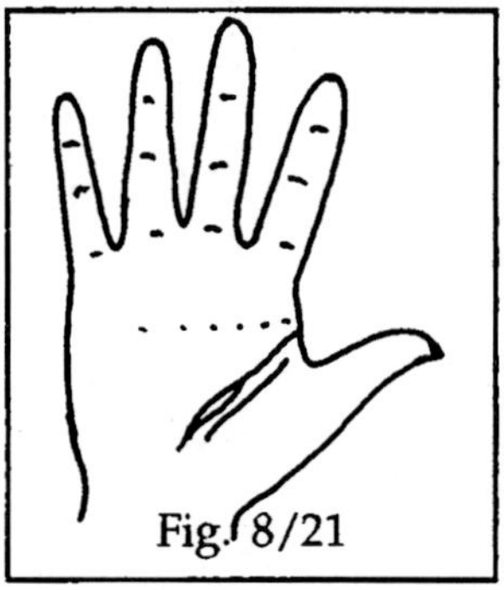
Fig. 8/21

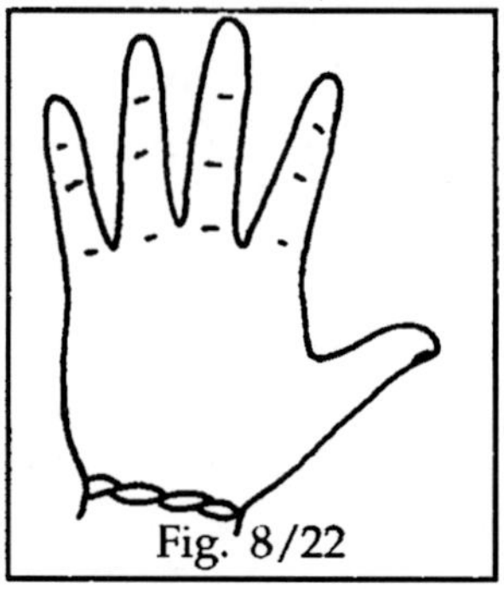
Fig. 8/22

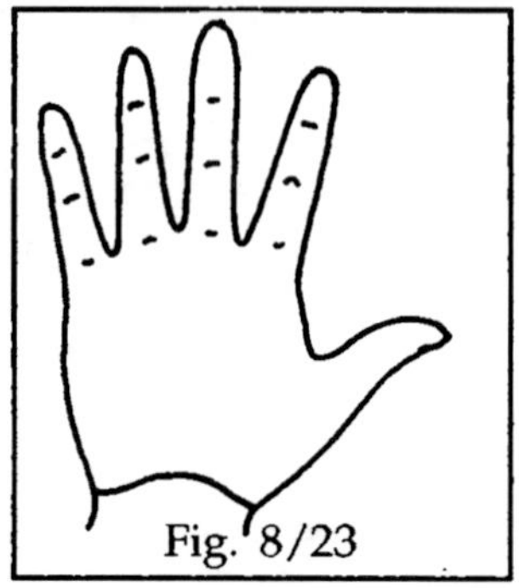
Fig. 8/23

If the Line of Life is straight, there is an island over it and also an axe line (*See Fig. 8/21*) there are obstructions to having children.

Similar is the effect of large islands forming the first rascette (*See Fig. 8/22*). But a chain of small islands is beneficial.

If the first rascette is circular and its protruding circular part faces the palm (*See Fig. 8/23*) there are obstructions to begetting children. If other signs are favourable, a child is born later in life.

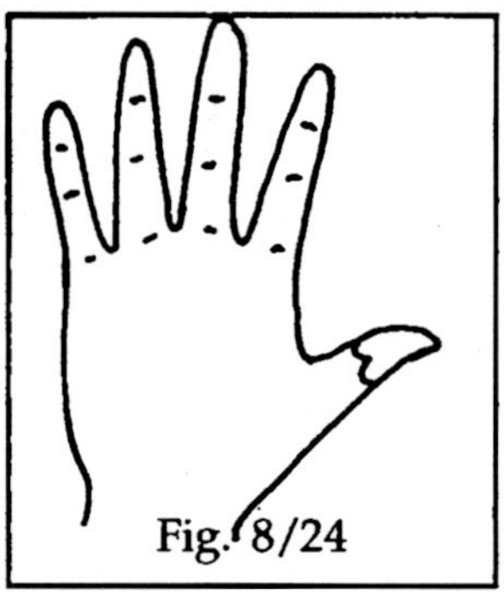
Fig. 8/24

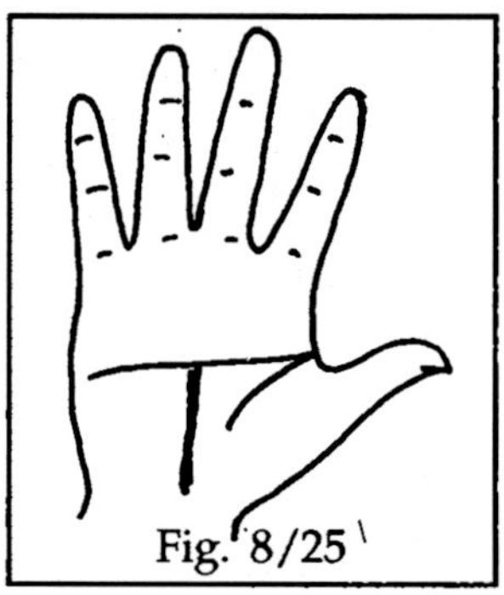
Fig. 8/25

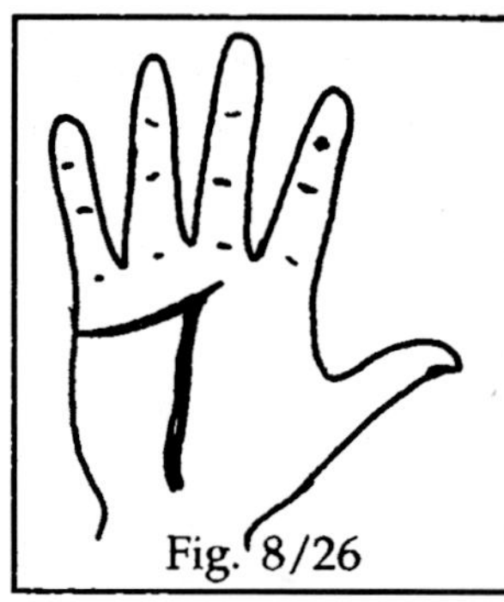
Fig. 8/26

Signs Indicating Progeny Who Will Cause Troubles

If there is a wavy line at the junction of the two phalanges of the thumb (*See Fig. 8/24*) one must not expect any happiness from his progeny.

If the Line of Life is incomplete and a thick Line of Saturn stops at the Head Line (*See Fig. 8/25*) progeny are likely to cause endless worries to their parents.

If the Heart Line is thick, starts from the Mount of Saturn and a thick Line of Saturn stops at the Heart Line (*See Fig. 8/26*) children would continue to cause worries to their parents.

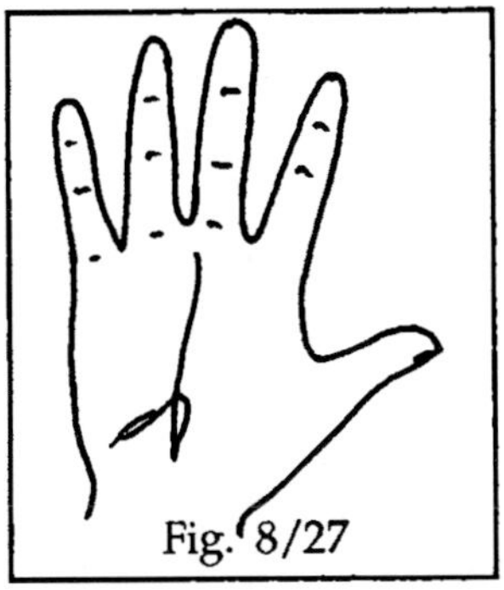
Fig. 8/27

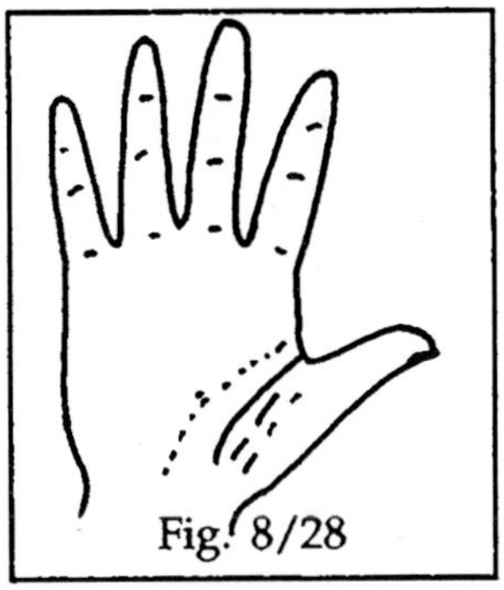
Fig. 8/28

If a line of influence from the Mount of Luna starts with an island, and meets the Line of Saturn which has island (*See Fig. 8/27*) there will not be much happiness from one's children. If there is a question with regard to marriage such a sign can be taken to mean that there are obstructions to marriage.

If the lines parallel to the Line of Mars on the Mount of Venus are broken (*See Fig. 8/28*) it is an indication of obstructions to any happiness from one's progeny.

Signs with Regard to Parents and Family

We have referred to the Indian *Samudrika Shastra's* dictum in Chapter VII to the effect that a man's Heart Line on the right palm tells you about his wife and the Heart Line on the left palm of the woman about her husband. Here we would like to add that the Head Line in the left palm of a man (*matri rekha*) indicates the state of health/longevity etc. of his mother-in-law and the Line of Life (*Pitri rekha*) about his father-in-law. Similarly, the Head Line on the left palm of a woman tells you about her mother-in-law and the Line of Life about her father-in-law. But this belief is still under investigation. Readers can study the palms of their friends and relatives to find the truth.

If the Line of Life emanates from the Mount of Jupiter, the person gets full affection/love from his parents/guardians. (*See again Fig. 8/6*). Similar is the case when a line emanating from the Mount of Jupiter touches the Line of Mars.

If a line of influence from the Mount of Jupiter touches the Head Line, a person gets the affection/love of his parents for a long time.

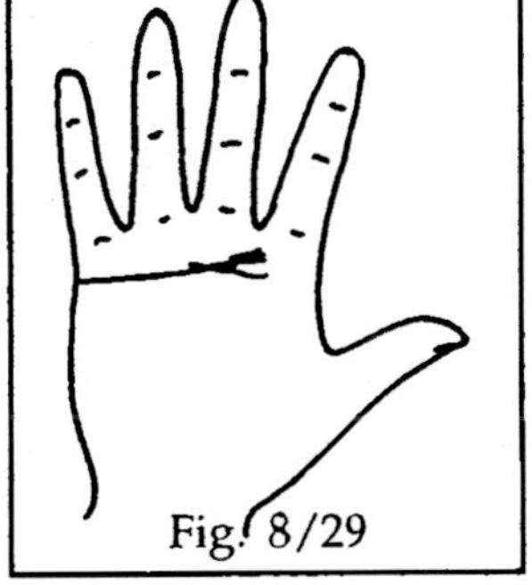
Fig. 8/29

If the Heart Line has many forks at its point of origin (*See Fig. 8/29*) the parents have a long life. You must remember that the Heart Line emanates from the Mount of Jupiter and ends at a point between the Mount of Mercury and the Defensive Mars.

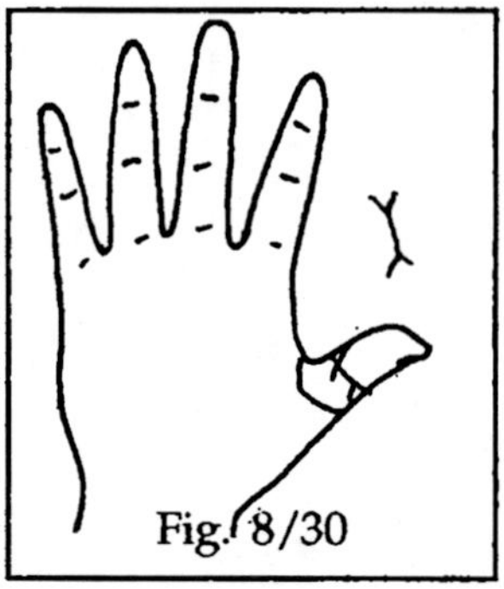

Fig. 8/30

If a line dividing the two phalanges of the thumb is forked (*See Fig. 8/30*) a person is deprived of his mother.

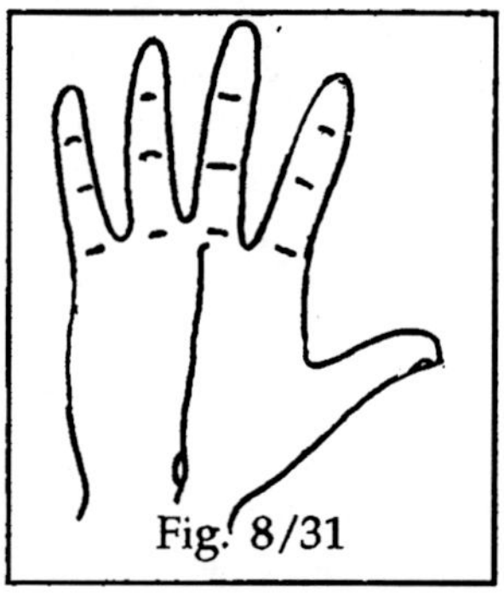

Fig. 8/31

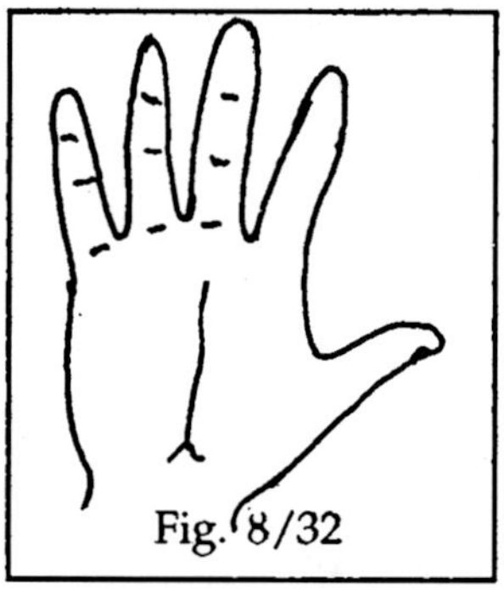

Fig. 8/32

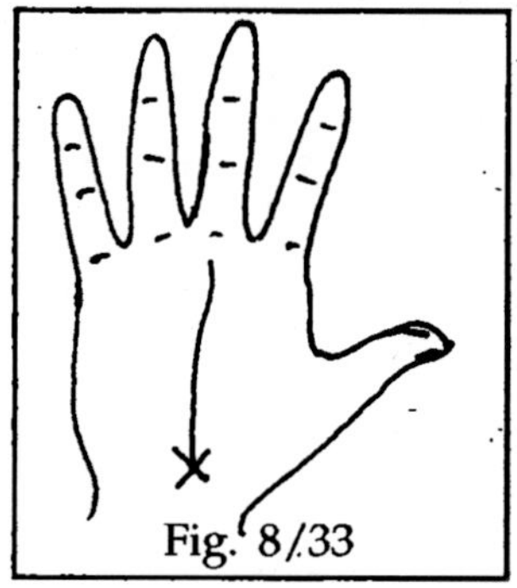

Fig. 8/33

If there is one island at the point of origin of the Line of Saturn (*See Fig. 8/31*), or there is a fork (*See Fig. 8/32*), or there is a cross (*See Fig. 8/33*), the person is deprived of his parents/guardians in his childhood.

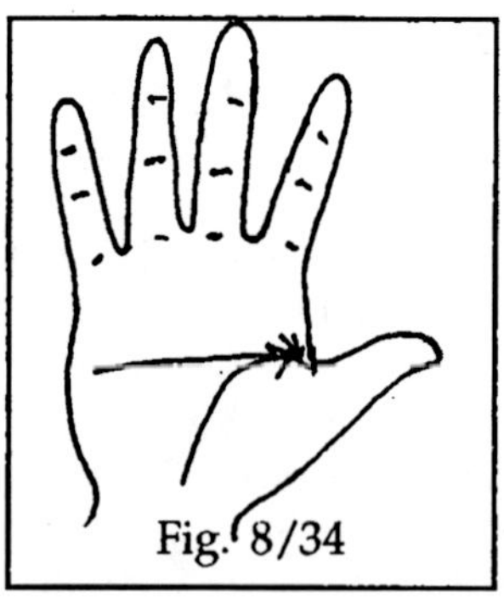

Fig. 8/34

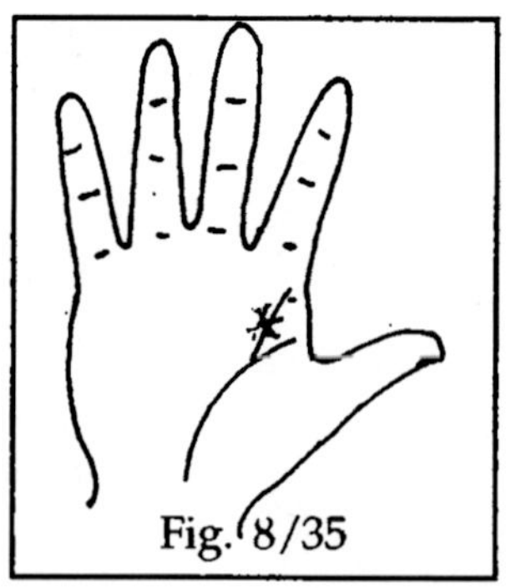

Fig. 8/35

If there is a star at the beginning of the Line of Life or the Head Line (*See Fig. 8/34*), a person faces many family tragedies during his childhood.

If there is a star on the branch of the Line of Life which goes towards the Mount of Jupiter (*See Fig. 8/35*), a member of the family meets with a tragedy.

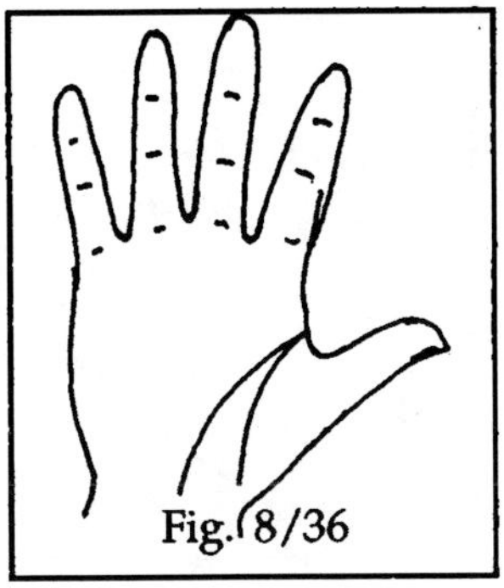

Fig. 8/36

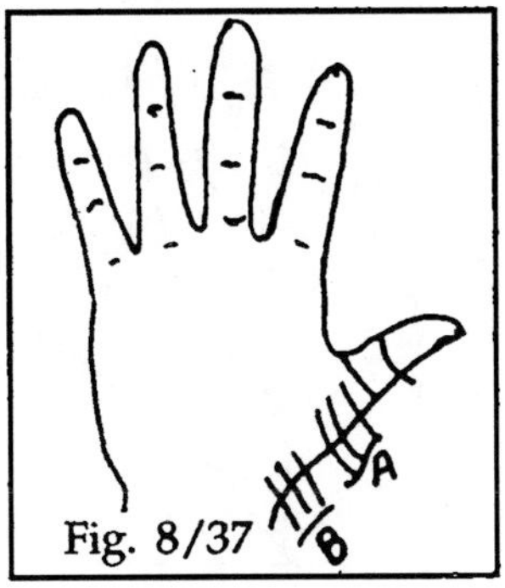

Fig. 8/37

If the Line of Life is forked in the beginning, one branch going to the Mount of Venus to encircle it and the other towards the wrist (*See Fig. 8/36*), a person is likely to be brought up during his childhood by persons other than his parents. Such a position also indicates the possibility of travel to foreign lands.

The Line of Mars, though parallel to the Line of Life, originates separately. But, if it starts, not independently, but as a branch of the Line of Life and encircles the Mount of Venus, a person gets the love/affection of his progeny. He is also likely to get the affection of his parents and also a share in patrimony (*Refer again to Fig. 8/12*).

Lines indicating progeny are found on the part of the Mount of Venus near the thumb (*See Fig. 8/37-A*), the lines on the part of this mount near the wrist indicate siblings (*See Fig. 8/37-B*). Those lines among them which are long are indicative of brothers and the short ones of sisters.

Signs Indicating Family Responsibilities

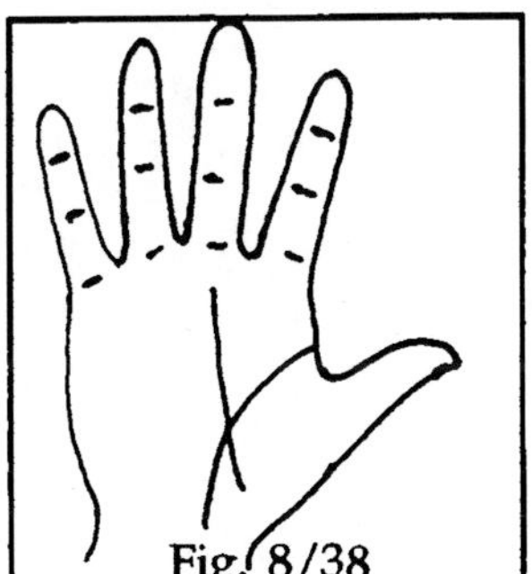

Fig. 8/38

If the Line of Saturn emanates from inside the Line of Life from the Mount of Venus, a man is burdened with family responsibilities. He can find respite from them only when the Line of Saturn separates from the Line of Life and enters the area of Saturn (*See Fig. 8/38*). If such a sign is found on the palm of a girl, she is likely to give up her comforts for the sake of the family. But, if other signs are unfavourable, she might even turn into what is known as a socialite or playgirl.

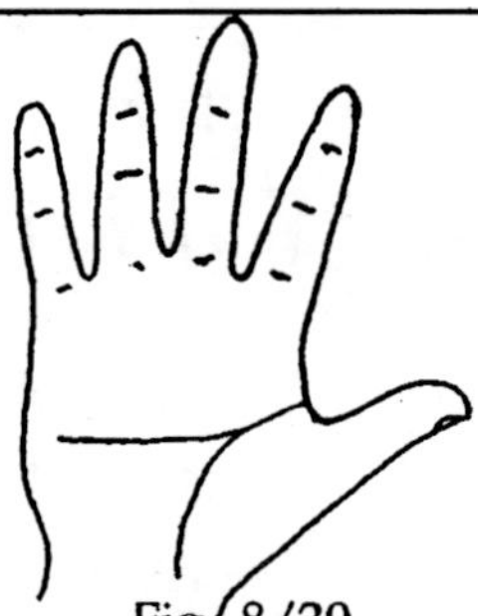

Fig. 8/39

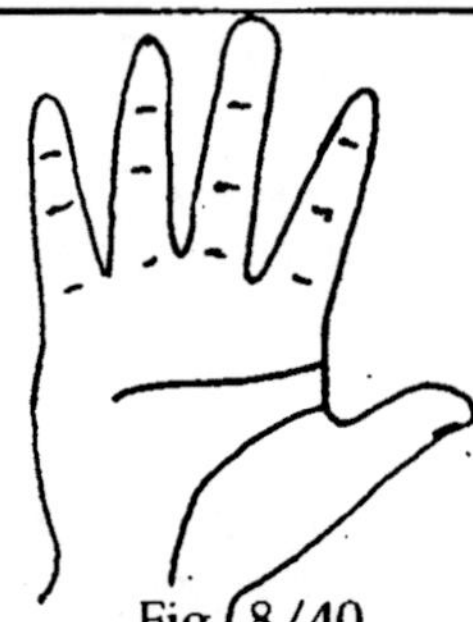

Fig. 8/40

If the Head Line hugs the Line of Life for a considerable distance, a person is burdened with family responsibilities. He gets a respite only when the two lines separate (*See Fig. 8/39*). The time when this would happen can be calculated according to the rules pertaining to calculation of age from the Line of Life.

If the distance between the points of origin of the Line of Life and the Head Line is considerable (*See Fig. 8/40*) a person is free from family responsibilities.

Fig. 8/41

Fig. 8/42

An island in the Line of Saturn adjacent to the Line of Life indicates a bad family situation at the time it occurs. The time can be calculated according to the rule pertaining to the Line of Saturn (*See Fig. 8/41*).

The age at which the Line of Saturn is near the Line of Life (*See Fig. 8/42*) is the time when a person is burdened with family responsibilities. If the Line of Saturn is thick this effect is accentuated.

If the three main lines of the palm are thin, deep and without any faults, the family is likely to be large, but finances tend to be sufficient to run the family.

Let it be said that the lines indicating progeny, siblings and parents arise only when a person has emotional attachment towards those persons or he heartily hates them. If there is no sense of attachment, family lines on a palm do not emerge. It is the most difficult thing to read such a hand. In such cases one must study the shape of the hand, the fingers and the thickness of the lines before one can make any forecasts about a person.

CHAPTER IX

SIGNS INDICATING HEALTH, DISEASE AND LONGEVITY

If a question is to be answered about a person's health, the first thing is to study the Line of Life and the Heart Line. Later, one must go to the Line of Mercury and the Head Line. The only indication that one can get from the lines is whether at a particular age a person's physical mental and emotional competence would be more or less. But they do not indicate any disease. The indicators of ill-health are the nails, mounts and the fingerprints.

Questions with Regard to Longevity

How long a person lives is in the hand of God and a palmist, must not, make any clear prediction about the time a man would die. The hand is only an indication of the vital force of a person -- his capacity to live. One must undertake practices which would add to that vital force. If a person is struck with cholera he cannot refuse to take treatment on the plea that he has a life line which indicates a long life. If one has considerable vital force it will keep him alive till medical aid is available, because his capacity to fight disease would come into play. Medical aid helps a person to survive, but if the vital force is low he might die till treatment for the ailment starts.

Experienced palmists would tell you that one cannot predict how long a person would live merely on the basis of his Line of Life. One must study other lines on his palm, because lines influence each other. It is just like a diabetic having a problem with his blood pressure. Hypertension tends to affect the other systems in the body. Similar is the case with the lines on your palm.

Sometimes circumstances conspire to make the vital force of no account. To take an example, if a train in which a person with a faultless Line of Life, Heart Line etc. is travelling, is attacked with explosives by terrorists, or two trains collide head-on or an earthquake hits that area, he is liable to be killed. This is what a palmist must always keep in mind. You must, as a palmist, use your discretion about what is to be told to the client in such matters.

It is because of the above that a palmist must never predict about death and the time when it would strike the questioner or client. If the signs on the palm indicate that a person is likely to die at a particular age, he should be told that he is liable to fall victim to a fell disease. He should be advised to take steps to augment his vital force; remedies should be suggested so that hope continues to inform such a person and he is able to augment his vital force to maintain good health. If the signs indicate that a person is liable to suffer from a particular disease, he should be warned to take precautions.

If you study the Line of Life in handprint No. 9-A in Part IV of the book you could predict the death of the owner of that hand print in his 63rd year, but the time at which that person came to me for consolation he was 67 years old. The lines indicated a bad family situation at the age of 63 and not death. That is why I would reiterate that one must be very careful in predicting death.

Signs Indicating Longevity

If the Line of Life, the Head Line and the Heart Line is short in both the palms of a person calculate the age at which a crisis is likely to develop and tell him that he is likely to suffer from a fatal disease. He should be advised to practise digital postures calculated to augment the vital force, the heart and the brain. These postures are dealt with in Part III. If the above lines are short in one palm and of normal length on the other, the danger of death at that particular age is lessened.

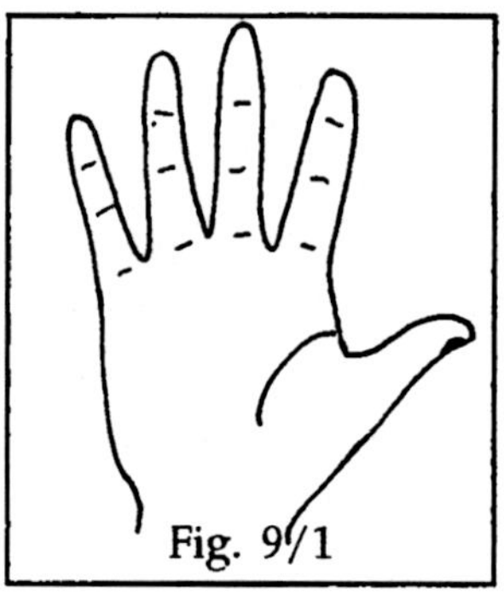

Fig. 9/1

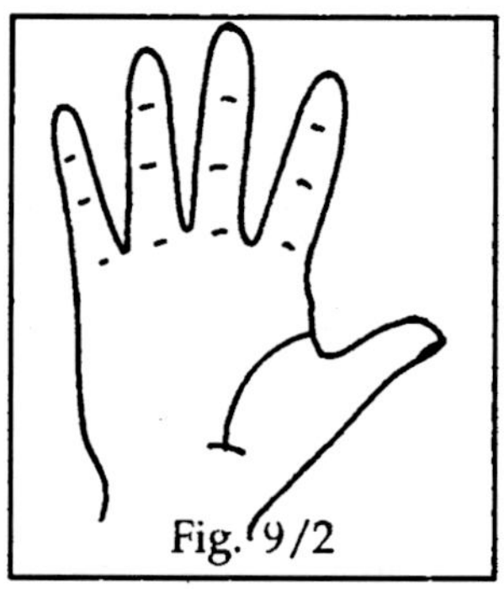

Fig. 9/2

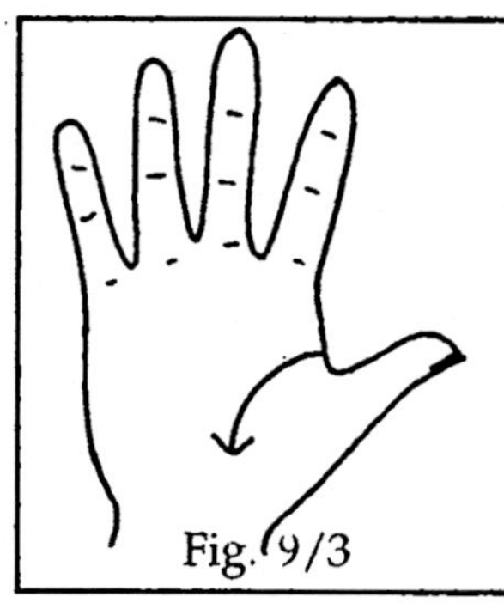

Fig. 9/3

If the Line of Life is short it might also indicate financial troubles or family problems (*See Fig. 9/1*). If the end of the Line of Life is intersected by an horizontal line (*See Fig. 9/2*) or an inverted bracket (*See Fig. 9/3*) it bodes ill for the life of a person. If the Line of Life continues after that point of intersection, a tragedy is averted after that age.

A star or a cross at the point where the Life Line ends, is harmful, but if the line continues beyond that point, evil is averted after that age.

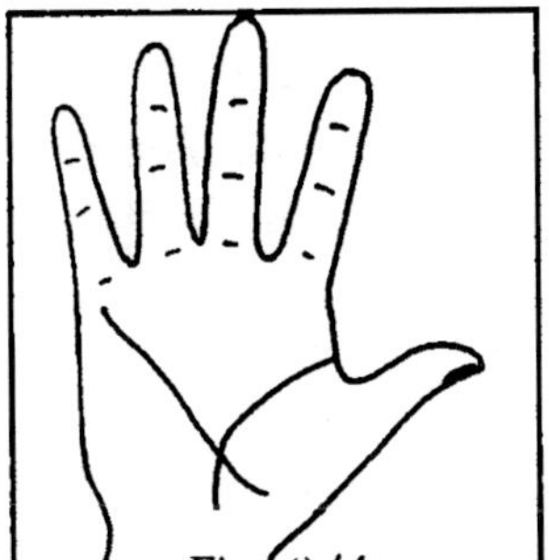

Fig. 9/4

Palmists of old used to predict death at an age when the Line of Mercury intersected the Line of Life, (*See Fig. 9/4*) but, what one should see is whether the Line continues after that point of intersection. One should predict that the person is likely to suffer from an intractable disease at that age. If the Line of Life ends at that point, you should see both the palms and then predict that your client is likely to suffer from a fell disease at that age. If the Line continues you should say that there are chances of the client surveying the attack of that disease.

India's ancient science, *Samudrika Shastra*, calls the Heart Line as the Line of Longevity. It is true because life continues so long as the heart continues to beat. That is why you must see the position of the Heart Line after you have found a fault in the Line of Life. Similarly, see whether the fault in the Heart Line is confirmed by a similar fault in the Line of Life. If it is confirmed, there is a strong probability of death intervening; otherwise, it is a mere possibility.

If both the Heart Line and the Line of Life are deep and full a person is likely to live long and maintain his health till the day he dies.

If the Line of Life and the Heart line are short or there are faults in them, but the Mount of Venus is well-developed, chances of ill-health are reduced.

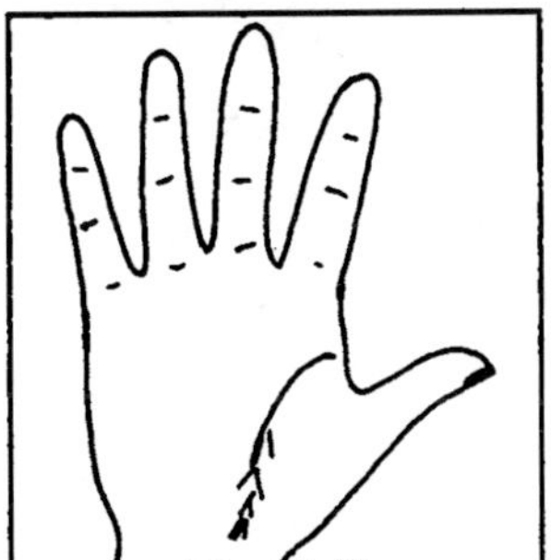

Fig. 9/5

If there is a tassel at the end of the Line of Life (*See Fig.9/5*) a person's vital force is much reduced in old age.

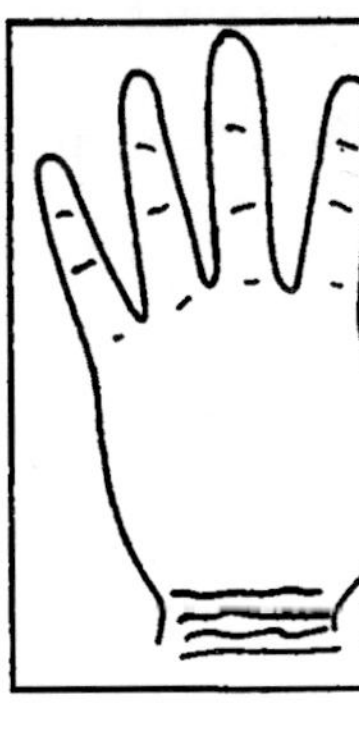

Fig. 9/6

According to *Samudrika Shastra* four well-defined rascettes indicate an age of 120 years (*See Fig. 9/6*). Each rascette represents a life span of 30 years and the life span of any particular individual can be calculated according to this rule. An incomplete rascette indicates ill-health. But the new Western palmistry does not depend on rascettes alone. The rascettes are consulted, no doubt, but so are the other lines. If the other lines are without any fault, the effect of the faulty rascettes is much reduced.

Other Signs Indicating Health

If there are too many lines on the palm it is an indication of depression and tension. Persons suffering from tension should go for a regular check-up of their blood pressure. When you come across a hand with too many lines, refer to Handprint Nos. 3 and 15 in Part IV of this book.

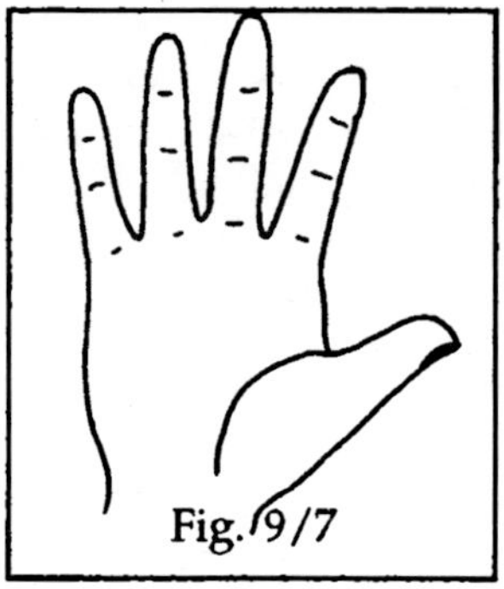

Fig. 9/7

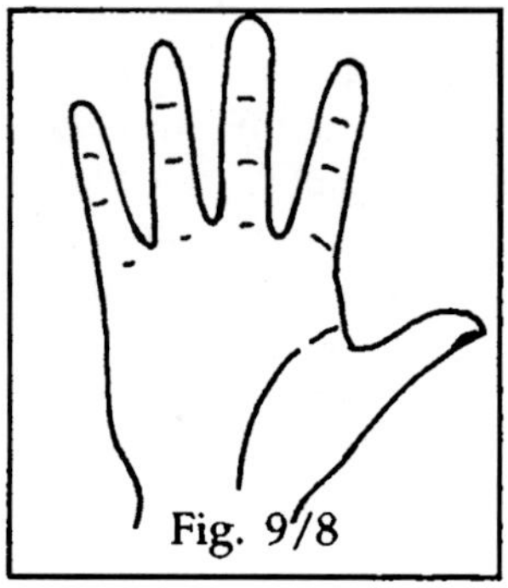

Fig. 9/8

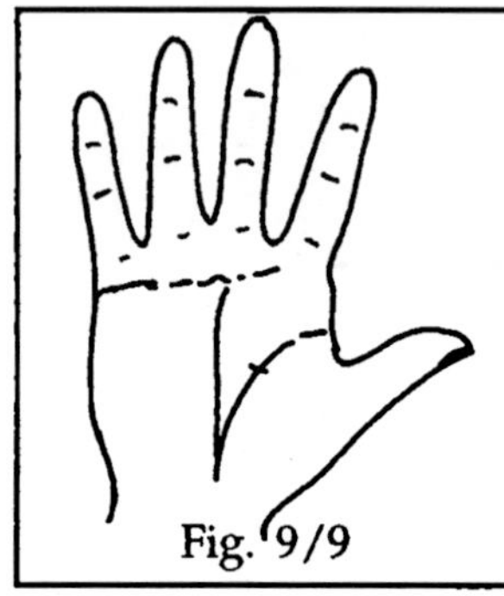

Fig. 9/9

If the Line of Life emanates from the Aggressive Mars (*See Fig. 9/7*) a person is likely to suffer from hyperacidity.

If the Line of Life breaks under the Mount of Jupiter (*See Fig. 9/8*) there is a possibility of diseases of the intestines.

If the Line of Life is thick at places and thin at others, a person is easily susceptible to disease.

If the Line of Life is good and the rascettes resemble a chain a person is likely to enjoy good health.

If the Line of Life is defective and the Line of Saturn stops at a defective Heart Line (*See Fig. 9/9*) a person is liable to suffer from a heart ailment.

A person with a defective Heart Line should get his blood pressure and the heart checked up regularly after he crosses 35 years.

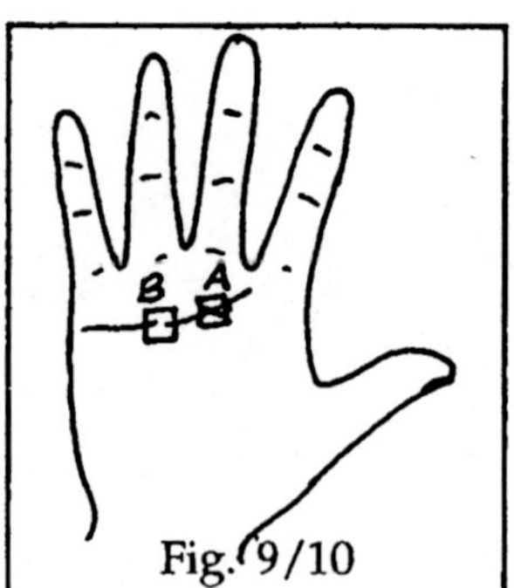

Fig. 9/10

If there is a rectangle at the place where the Heart Line is defective (*See Fig. 9/10-A,B*) it presages that the person would recover even if he suffers from any heart ailment.

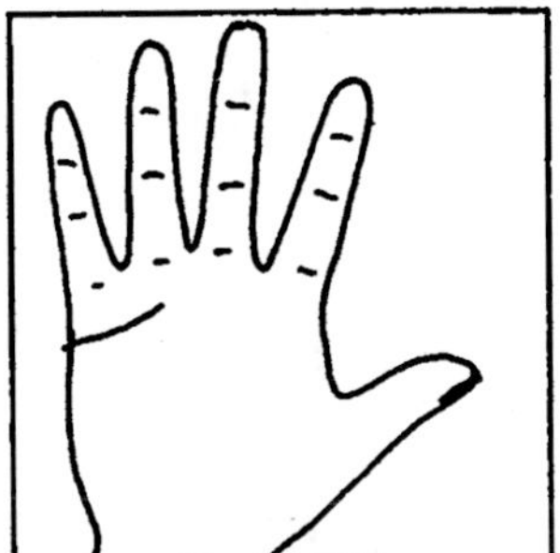

Fig. 9/11

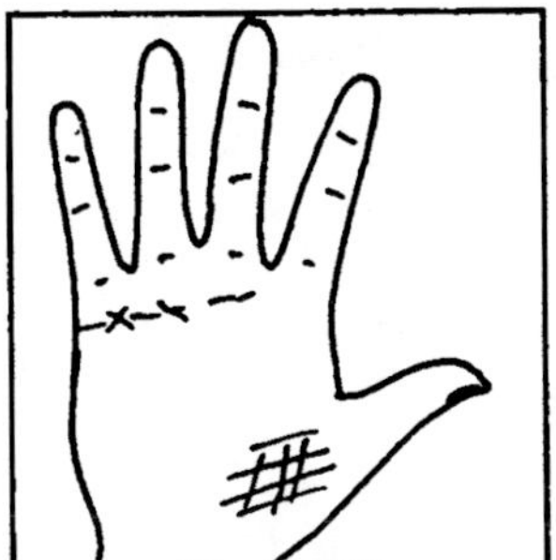

Fig. 9/12

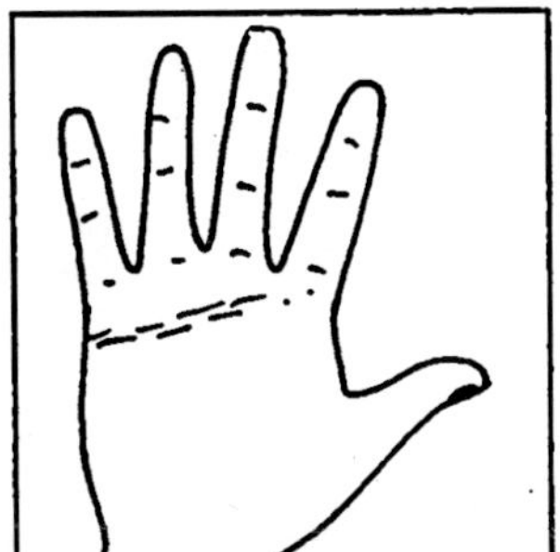

Fig. 9/13

If the Heart Line emanates from the Mount of Apollo (*See Fig. 9/11*) there is possibility of a heart ailment. But this also indicates financial and marital difficulties. What a particular line indicates would depend on the question your client is asking you. If there is a query regarding health, you should study the Line of Life and the Heart Line together. If the question is with regard to financial problems, the Line of Saturn could give an answer. If you are answering question with regard to marital relations the line of sexuality and the Line of Mars should also be studied alongwith the other lines.

If the Heart Line is broken at many places it indicates possibility of a heart ailment.

If there is a grill over the Mount of Venus alongwith a defective Heart Line (*See Fig. 9/12*) a person's blood pressure is bound to be abnormal.

If the pieces of a broken Heart Line overlap each other (*See Fig. 9/13*) health is likely to be affected due to an emotional trauma.

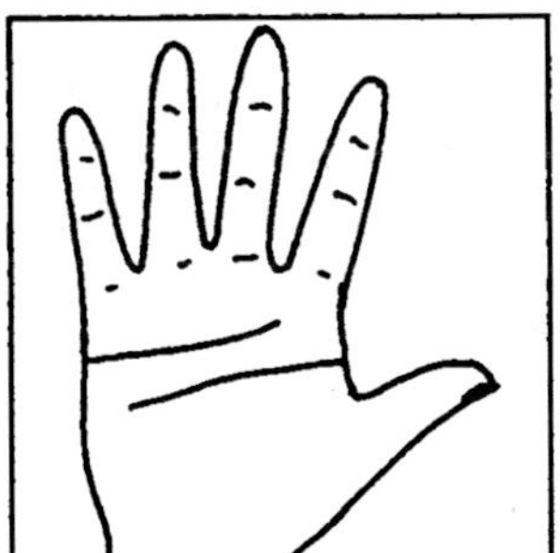

Fig. 9/14

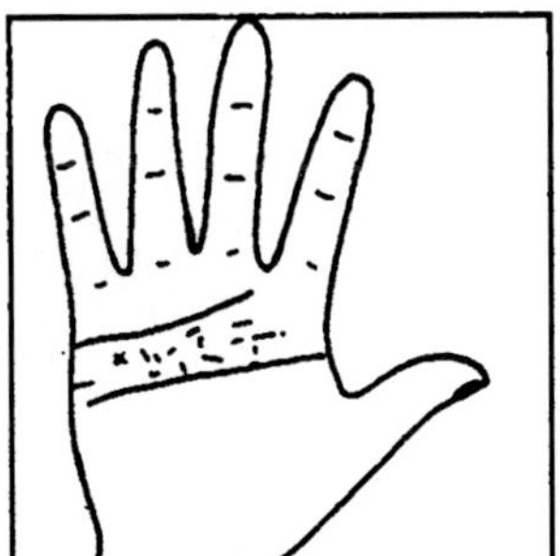

Fig. 9/15

Persons whose Heart Line is near the Head Line (*See Fig. 9/14*) should not over strain their minds.

If these two lines are near each other and the Line of Mercury is broken, one is likely to suffer from asthma.

If there is a quadrangle between the Heart and the Head Line over which there are short lines *(See Fig. 9/15)* a person is never at peace with himself. Tension thus created can lead to a heart ailment.

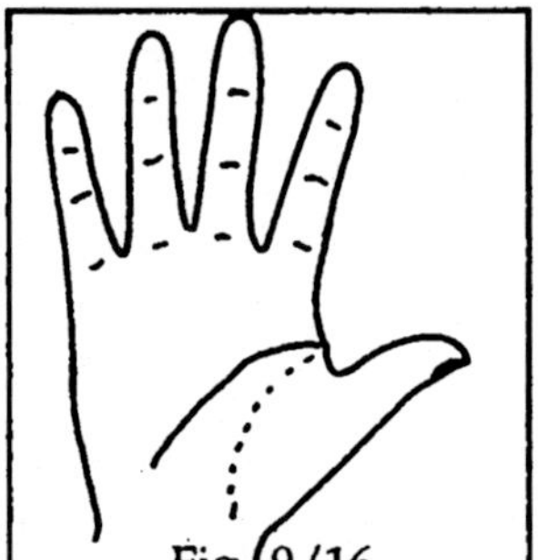

Fig. 9/16

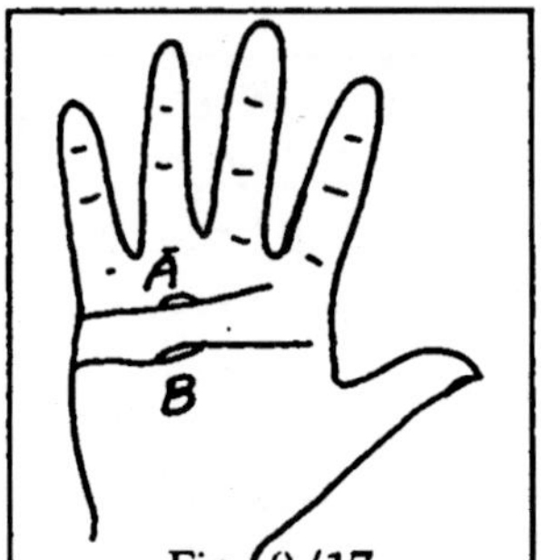

Fig. 9/17

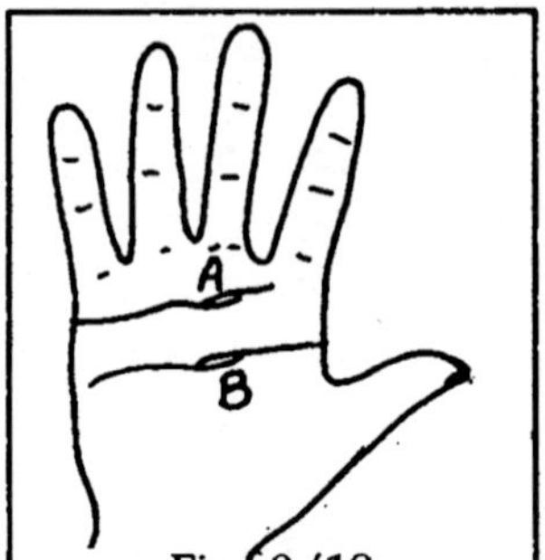

Fig. 9/18

If a woman's Head Line leans towards the Mount of Luna (*See Fig. 9/16*), the Mount of Venus is developed and the thumb makes an acute angle with the rest of the fingers, she is liable to suffer from hysteria.

If there is an island on the Heart or the Head Line under the Mount of Apollo (*See Fig. 9/17-A,B*) there is a likelihood of ailment of the eyes. If such a position is found on both the palms the occurrence of such an ailment is a certainty.

If there is an island on the Head Line or the Heart Line under the Mount of Saturn (*See Fig. 9/18-A,B*) there is a danger of flatulence, diseases of the teeth or the bones. It also means that a person might suffer from pain in the joints, might run a risk of paralysis and suffer from excessive wind in the stomach.

If a broken Head Line is intersected by short lines, it indicates headache and a weak memory.

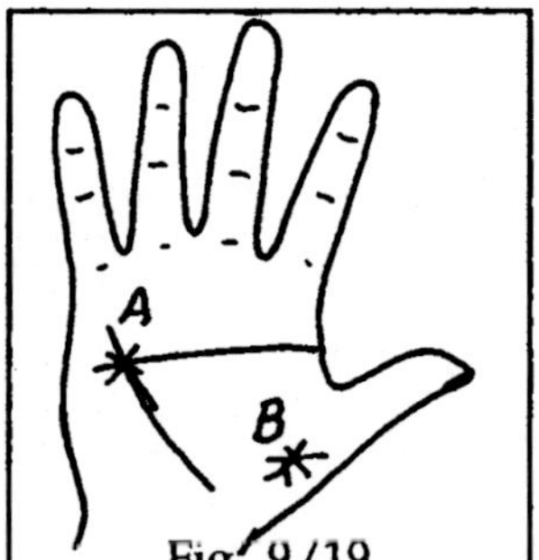

Fig. 9/19

If there is a star at the junction of the Head Line and the Line of Mercury (*See Fig. 9/19-A*) it is a sign of diseases of the genitals. If there is a star on the Mount of Venus too (*See Fig. 9/19/B*) the occurrence of such ailments is a certainty. If these signs are found on the palm of a woman, it is indicative of a difficult labour.

If the Line of the Sun is thin at the point of origin, but thickens as it nears the Mount of Apollo there are possibilities of diseases of the chaste or the heart.

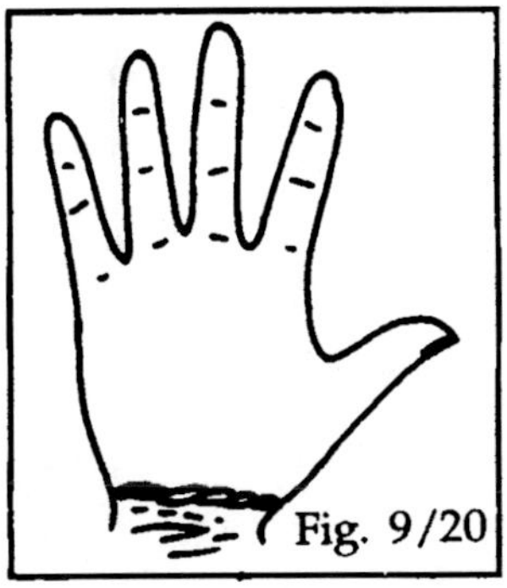

Fig. 9/20

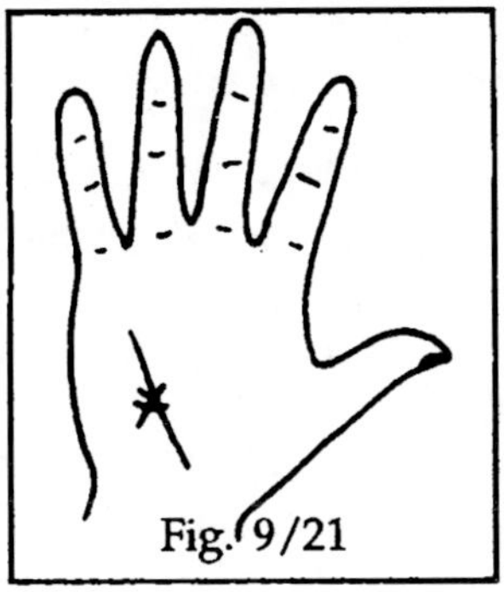

Fig. 9/21

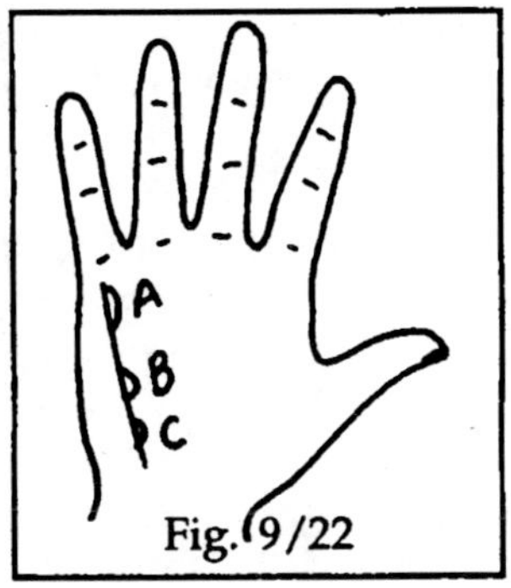

Fig. 9/22

If the rascettes are broken, ill-health is indicated. If the first rascette is composed of a chain of small islands (*See Fig. 9/20*) health tends to improve as one nears middle age.

A good Line of Mercury indicates a good memory. If the Head Line is defective, but the Line of Mercury is good it tends to remove the faults of the Head Line.

A star on the Line of Mercury (*See Fig. 9/21*) is indicative of ailments of the stomach.

If there is an island on the upper part of the Line of Mercury, it indicates diseases of the upper organs of the body (the Mount of Mercury controls the upper part of the body), if such islands are found in the middle, hyperacidity is indicated. If there is an island in the lower part, organs below the navel are likely to be affected (*See Fig. 9/22-A,B,C*).

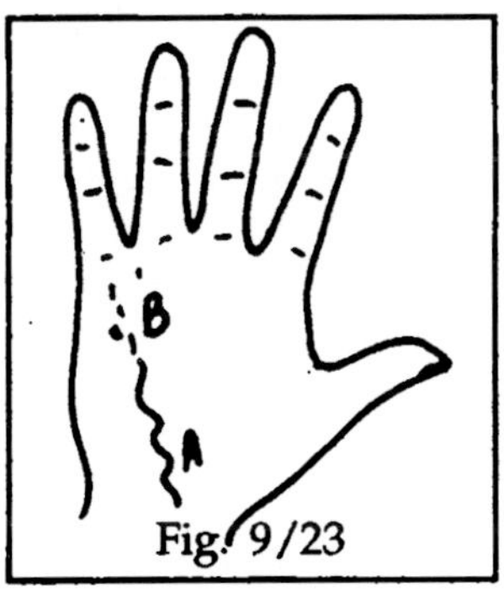

Fig. 9/23

If the Line of Mercury is wavy (*See Fig. 9/23-A*) or is fragmented (*See Fig. 9/23-B*) diseases of the liver and a weak digestion is indicated.

If the Head Line suddenly descends to the Mount of Luna (*See again Fig. 9/16*) suicidal tendencies are indicated.

Mounts as Indicative of One's State of Health

If there is a fault in the Line of Life, the following Mounts should be studied to find which ailment one is likely to suffer from.

If the Mount of Jupiter is well-developed, diseases of the digestive system are indicated.

If the Aggressive Mars is well-developed, paralysis is indicated.

If the Defensive Mars is well-developed, diseases of the nervous system are a possibility.

If there is a cross or oblique lines on the lower part of the Mount of Luna, there is danger of diseases of the parts below the navel, if the fault is in the middle, diseases of the stomach are indicated and a fault on the upper part of the Mount signifies diseases of the chest or the throat.

If the Mount of Venus suffers from a fault, venereal diseases are a possibility.

If there is a fault in the Mount of Saturn or the area covered by it a person is in danger of suffering from diseases caused by *Vata dosha*, diseases of the bones and the teeth.

If there is an island on the Mount of Apollo or under it, there is danger of diseases of the eyes.

A star on the Mount of Luna is indicative of an emotional trauma.

Diagnosing Diseases from the Nails

The nails start growing from the base of the first phalanges of the fingers to their tips. It takes about five months for a nail to renew itself. If there is a fault near the base of the nail, the disease indicated by it is likely to manifest itself within about one month, if it is in the middle, the disease might take two and a half months to strike the person and if it is near the end of the nail, the ailment might become apparent within 4 months.

Large, bright nails, with a pinkish hue indicate excellent health.

If there is a small depression in the middle of a nail, it is indicative of an emotional trauma. The time when it would manifest itself can be calculated keeping in view the fact that a nail takes about five months to renew itself.

If the depression is deep and gives the nail the appearance of a spoon, there is a danger of skin diseases, syphilis and influenza.

If the middle of the nail is raised like the back of a tortoise it presages ailments of the lungs and the person concerned should undergo a medical check-up.

Vertical stripes or white spots on the nails presage tension. If the nails are blue, the danger of tension increases.

Horizontal strips on the nails indicate constant mental trauma.

People with white nails are conceited and act hastily.

A pale nail indicates a diseased liver.

It is natural for girls to have blue nails in the beginning of their menstruation. If their nails are blue at any other time or, if men have such nails, it indicates a possibility of the lungs being affected.

A person with short nails is more susceptible than others to diseases of the nervous system and emotional tensions. If there are vertical stripes on the nails, it presages increased tension and possibility of diseases of the intestines.

A long nail, which has a short width indicates low physical strength. Such a person is liable to tire easily and diseases of the nose, ears, throat, eyes and chest are more likely to attack him. Such persons are also liable to suffer from ailments of the backbone.

Reading Health from Fingerprints

If the number of whorls on the first phalanges of the fingers are more in number, there is possibility of a heart ailment. The reason is that such persons are obstinate and when they do not get their way they become subject to tensions.

If the number of arches on the fingers is more, a person is likely to be short on tolerance and is liable to ailments of the nervous system.

People with tented arches have a weak digestion.

If the number of loops or double loops are in majority there is likely to be too much pressure on the nervous system.

Palm, Thumb and the Fingers as Indicators of Health

If the thumb is rotated and it bends completely backwards and the fingers are very pliable, a person runs the risk of suffering from paralysis.

A child with spatulate fingers should not run or take violent exercise because he is likely to have a weak heart. If the upper part of the fingers is bluish, the danger of a heart attack is more in such children.

A person with abnormally long fingers is likely to have an under-developed pituitary gland. Since this gland controls the functioning of other glands, including the gonads, an under-developed pituitary is likely to have an adverse effect on the metabolism and such persons cannot undertake much manual work.

If the palm is red and hot, it indicates an elevated blood pressure. Persons with such palms are also in danger of suffering from diabetes.

A colourless or pale palm which is also cold is an indication of anaemia.

A palmist is like a physician. A doctors prescribes medicines for a physical ailment, but the palmist has to treat the mind which is more difficult than treating the body.

-- The Institute of Palmistry

CHAPTER X

SOME MORE IMPORTANT QUERIES. AND HOW TO ANSWER THEM FROM THE HAND SIGNS

A palmist's clients want to know a variety of things. This chapter dealt with some hand signs which can help a palmist to answer some very important questions which most clients ask. We now come to some more signs which would help you to answer some more questions.

Let it be repeated that unless four or more signs favour a particular possibility, a palmist should not make any predictions if the number of signs is less than four, you can only indicate a possibility of something happening. If only one or two signs indicate something, you should keep quiet about it. But, each decision would have to be taken on the merits of each case.

Travel

The main sign to be consulted to answer questions about whether a person would undertake any journeys is the Mount of Luna. Among the lines, the Line of Life, the Sun Line, the Line of Mercury and the lines of influence on the Mount of Luna should be studied. If the Mount of Luna is well-developed the desire to travel is intense. If the lines are favourable the desire is fulfilled.

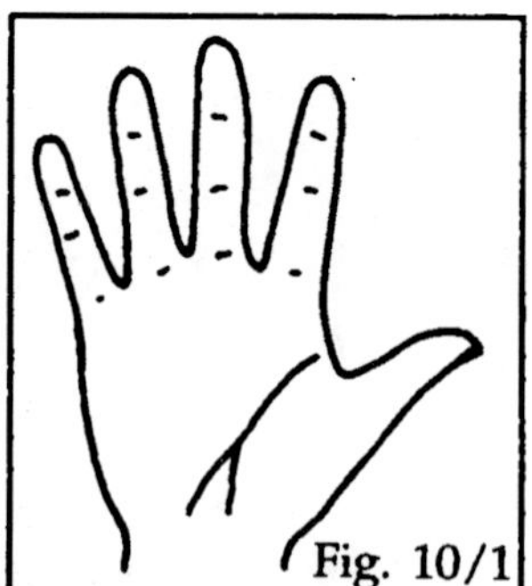

Fig. 10/1

If a branch of the Line of Life goes towards the Mount of Luna (*See Fig. 10/1*) there are possibilities of travel.

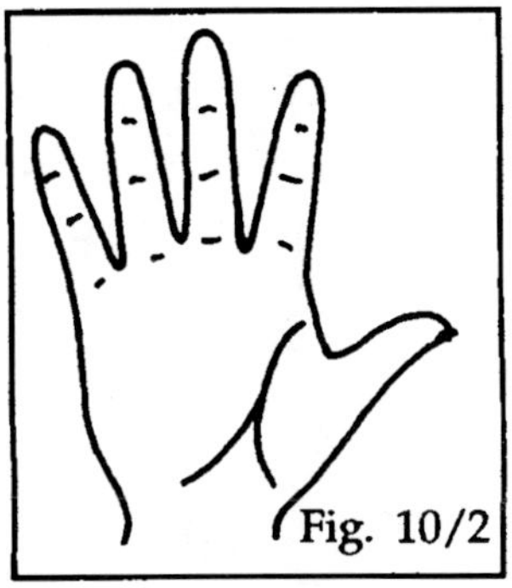
Fig. 10/2

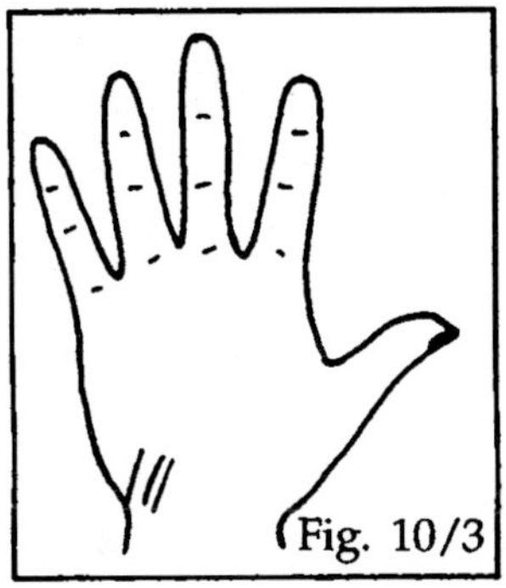
Fig. 10/3

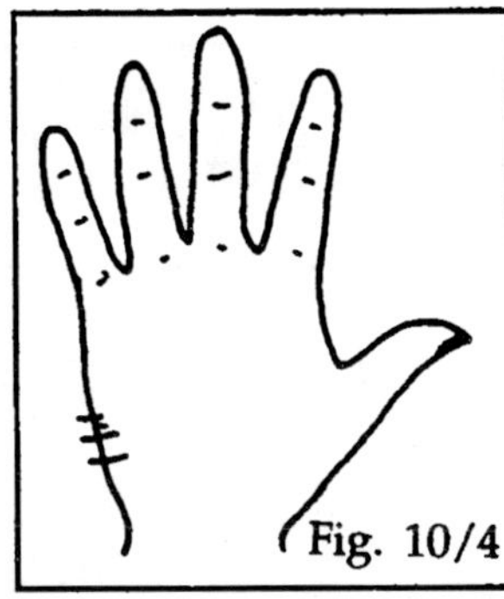
Fig. 10/4

If the Line of Life has branches, one encircling the Mount of Venus and the other goes towards the Mount of Luna (*See Fig. 10/2*), a person travels extensively. The deeper of the two branches has the greater effect. If the branch encircling the Mount of Venus is deeper, a person goes on a journey, but ultimately returns home, but, if the branch going towards the Mount of Luna is deeper, a person is likely to go on a journey and will settle abroad.

Lines going from the wrist to the Mount of Luna (*See Fig. 10/3*) indicate travel.

Lines going from the percussion towards the Mount of Luna (*See Fig. 10/4*) indicate short journeys.

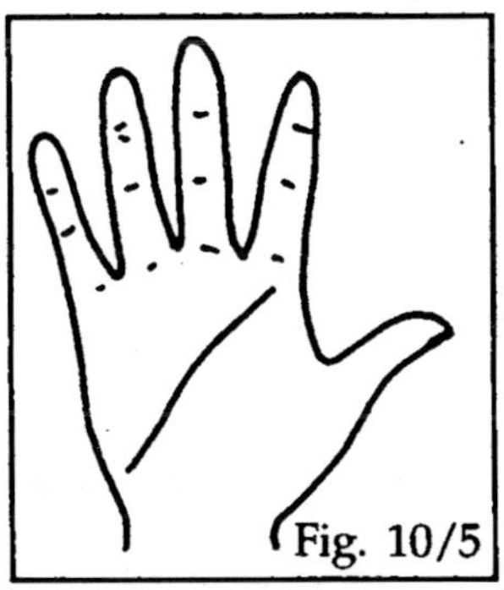
Fig. 10/5

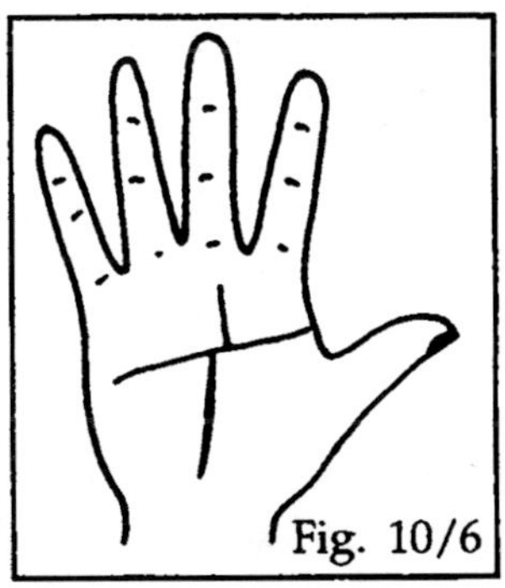
Fig. 10/6

A line emanating from the Mount of Luna which reaches the Mount of Jupiter (*See Fig. 10/5*) indicates a long and fortunate journey.

If you want to know when or at what age a person will undertake a journey see when the Line of Saturn turns thin after being thick in the beginning, or when it is freed from its fault, or when the branch of the Line of Life going towards the Mount of Saturn emanated, or the age at which the Line of the Sun arose. Answer the question after studying the favourable signs amongst the ones enumerated above.

If a thick Line of Saturn stops at the Head Line and thin Line of Saturn emerges from the other part of the Head Line (*See Fig. 10/6)* a person is likely to go on a journey at that age.

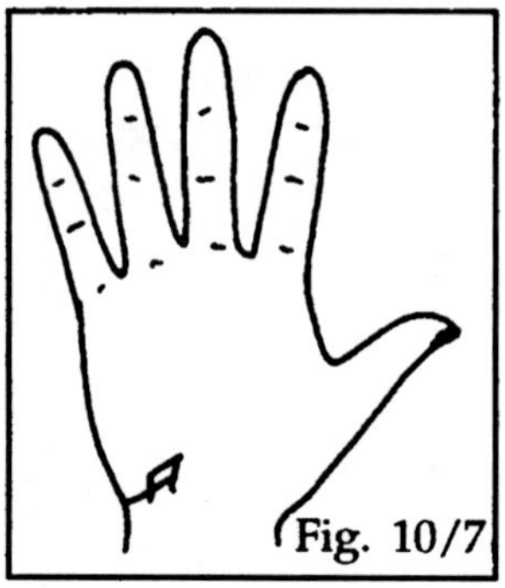

Fig. 10/7

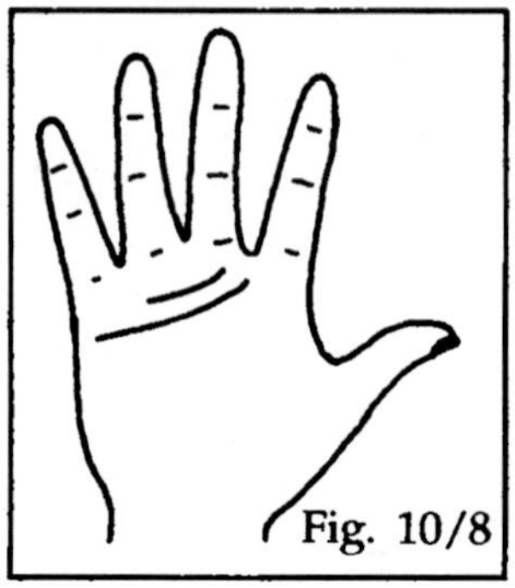

Fig. 10/8

A well-developed Mount of Luna and clear Line of Mercury indicates travels.

If there is a sign of the fish on the Mount of Luna (*See Fig. 10/7*) a foreign travel is indicated.

If there is a line parallel to the Heart Line and Mount of Luna is well-developed (*See Fig. 10/8*) there are possibilities of many journeys.

It should be remembered that if the lines indicating travel are faultless, the journeys are fortunate or lucky. A defective line or its defective branch presages problems and difficulties during travel. It should also be made clear here that there are no lines or signs in the hand indicating travel undertaken suddenly during an emergency. The signs only indicate travel undertaken for pleasure or for employment.

Education? How Much?

If there are only three main lines (the Line of Life, the Head Line and the Heart Line) on the palm, a person is not likely to take interest in studies. Such a person should not waste his time in higher studies but take up employment according to his capacity or taste. The hand signs indicating the profession or vocation which suits the different types of individuals have been commented upon in Chapter VI.

Persons with a sign of the fish on their palm are scholars. Scholarship, let it be said, does not signify getting academic degrees, but gathering of knowledge because of a person's inherent desire for it. One might be a scholar without any formal eduction, as the great poets Tagore and Kabir were.

If the Line of Life emanates from a faultless Head Line and if there are other lines in addition to the main three lines, and the hand is pliable and soft one should continue one's education. The point from where the Line of the Sun emanates is a guarantee of success in this field.

If both the Line of Saturn and the Heart Line are thick, a person is not likely to complete his education.

A person with long fingers is interested in studies. The time of life when he would achieve success can be known from the position of the Sun Line.

A straight index finger is indicative of a studious nature. If there is a vertical line on the Mount of Sun a person achieves success in this field.

If the fingers are long and knotty a person is likely to be interested in mathematics, science and philosophy. If long fingers have soft knots a person is more suited to literature and fine arts.

One should note here that a person should choose a field of study which suits his nature. If he chooses another because it is more in demand, though opposed to his natural choice, he is not likely to be at peace with himself.

Interest in Religion and the Occult

See the following signs if you want to know whether a person has interest in spiritualism, *Yoga, Tantra, Mantra* and *Yantras*, palmistry, psychology and desires to renounce the world. If you find four or more signs favouring a possibility, that is sure to turn into a certainty. It is the Sun Line which is a sure sign of success in these fields.

A long middle finger or a developed Mount of Saturn

Knotty fingers.

A triangle on the Mount of Saturn

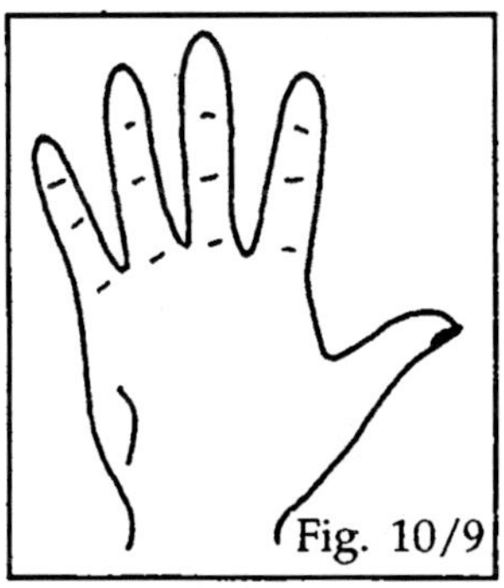
Fig. 10/9

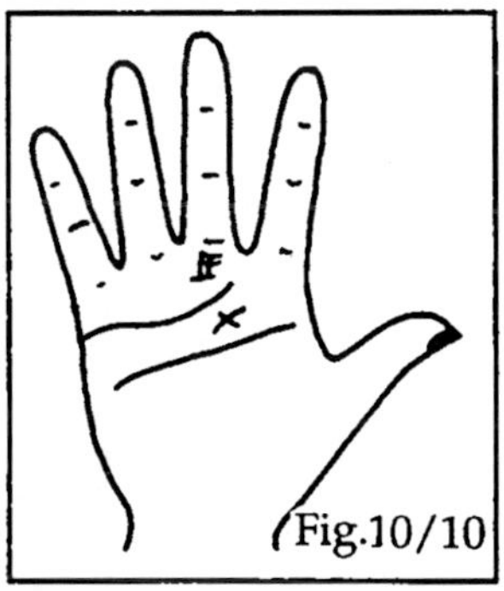
Fig.10/10

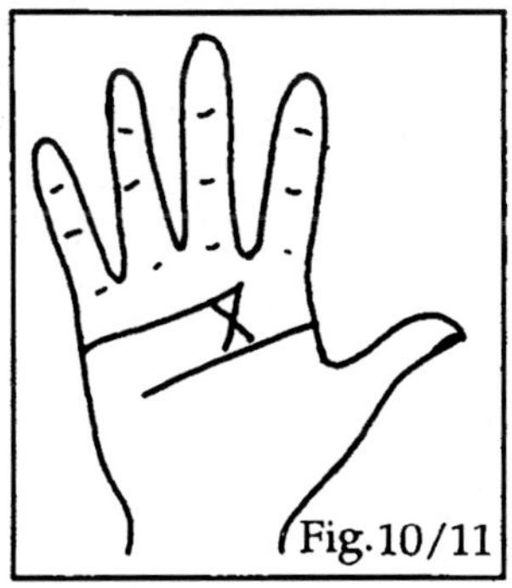
Fig.10/11

A clear Line of Intuition (*See Fig. 10/9*)

A quadrangle on the Mount of Saturn or a mystic cross under the Mount of Jupiter or under the Mount of Saturn in the great quadrangle (*See Fig. 10/10*).

A sign of *damroo* on the great quadrangle (*See Fig. 10/11*)

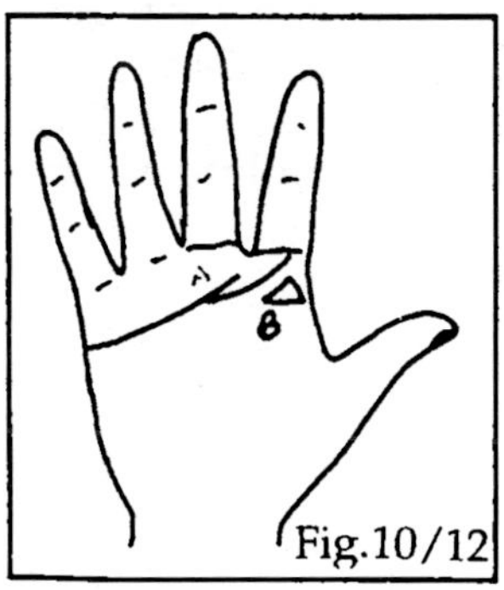
Fig.10/12

A triangle on the Heart Line or the Mount of Jupiter (*See Fig. 10/12-B*) or a branch of the Heart Line going towards the index finger (*See Fig. 10/12-A*)

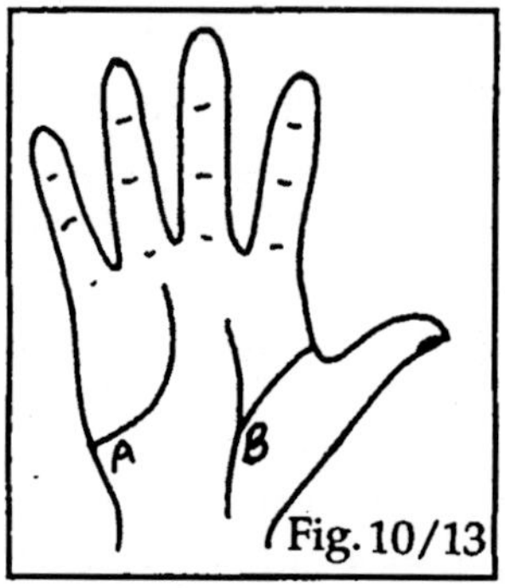

Fig. 10/13

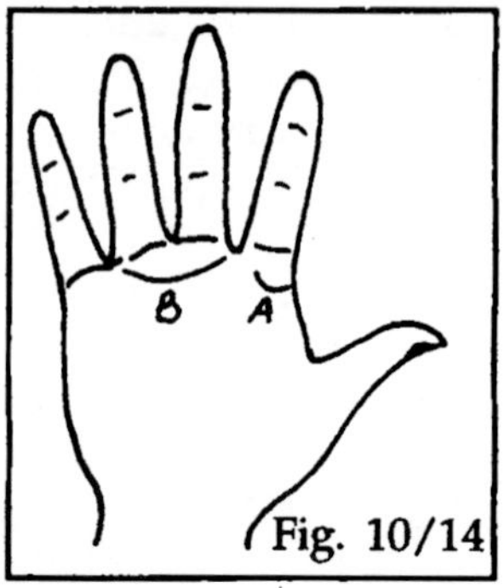

Fig. 10/14

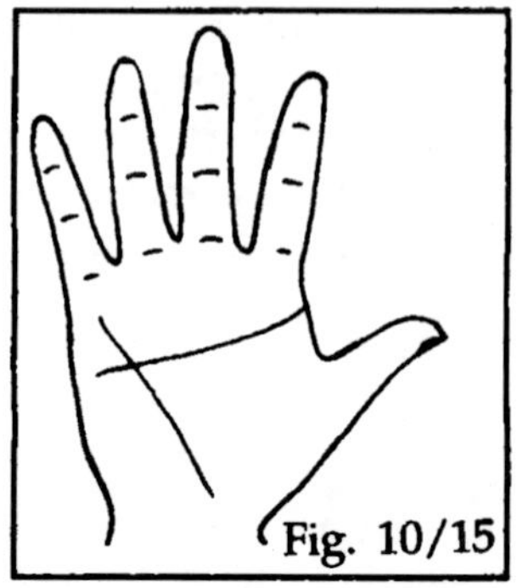

Fig. 10/15

A sun line emanating from the Mount of Luna (*See Fig. 10/13-A*)

A thin Line of Saturn emanating from the Line of Life (*See Fig. 10/13-B*)

A ring of Solomon (*See Fig. 10/14-A*) or a Girdle of Venus (*See Fig. 10/14-B*)

A well-developed Mount of Luna and an under-developed Mount of Venus.

A cross is formed at the junction of the Head Line and the Line of Mercury. (*See Fig. 10/15*)

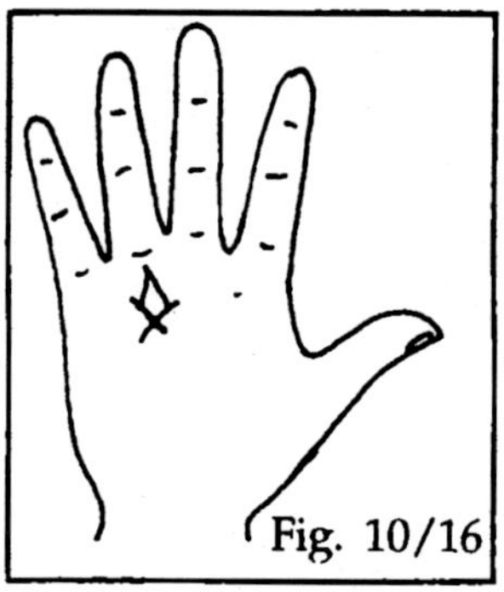

Fig. 10/16

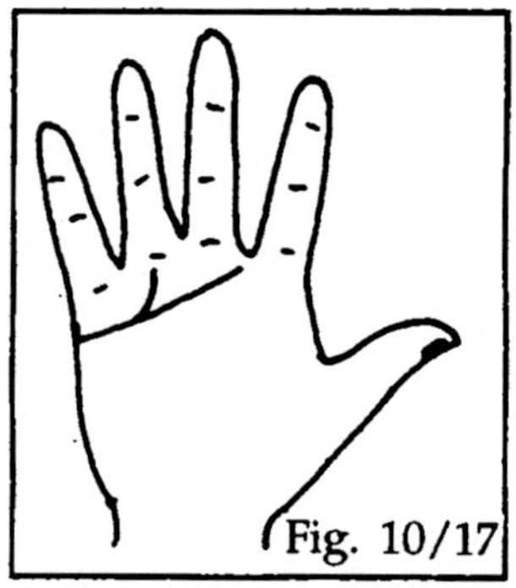

Fig. 10/17

The sign of the fish of the Mount on Apollo (*See Fig. 10/16*).

A branch of the Heart Line goes towards the third finger (*See Fig. 10/17*).

While interpreting the above signs it should be borne in mind that a well-developed Mount of Saturn and/or long fingers motivate a person to renounce the world. The third finger and a well-developed Mount of Apollo encourages a man to remain worldly and to gain fame and honour. Even though these areas encourage spirituality, the signs mean something different according to their nature. If a person has a developed Mount of Mercury and a long little finger, he might be spiritual but even then he seeks worldly gain.

Hand Signs Indicating a Violent Nature and a Conspiratorial Tendency

If, the hand is heavy, red and wide, the Aggressive Mars and the Mount of Venus are well-developed, or there is a cross on it, the thumb and the fingers are short and thick, there are only the main lines on the palm and they are deep, a person is likely to turn violent when angry.

If the hand is thin, white and cold, the fingers long, the mounts of Mercury and Saturn are well-developed, there is no Heart Line or it is short, the hand is long, a person is likely to conspire to visit violence on others. If the Head Line is long and goes towards the Mount of Mercury, such a person does not get caught after such a conspiracy towards violence.

Hand Signs Indicating Nobility of Character

If a person has a developed Mount of Apollo and the Mount of Jupiter, there is little likelihood of his taking to evil ways. Even if he takes to something immoral, he gets a good name instead of disgrace. Other hand signs indicating nobility of character are the following :

A person with rounded nails is loyal toward his friends.

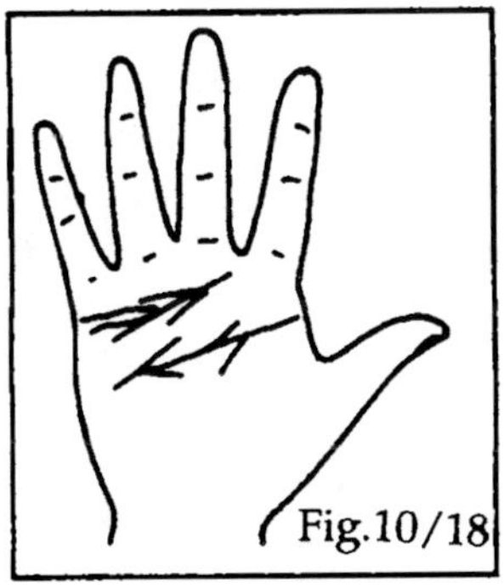
Fig.10/18

If the Head and the Heart Lines are forked, but their branches do not touch each other and there is sufficient distance between the two (*See Fig. 10/18*).

The lines are thin and without any fault.

The Line of Mars is thin and away from the Line of Life.

If there is a Ring of Solomon, or there is a cross on the Mount of Jupiter or an oblique line over it or a vertical line.

If the fingers are straight and long and resemble a Japanese fan when extended and are inclined outward from the palm.

A pink palm and a soft, pliable skin (Let it be noted that in a dark-complexioned man a skin with a deep tan has the same effect as a pink one).

Signs Favouring Disrepute

Persons with a well-developed Mount of Mercury or a long, thick little finger, or a little finger which is not straight are cunning and there is greater likelihood of their taking to wicked ways. If four of the following signs are found in a hand of such persons they come into disrepute.

If there are spots or depressions in the Line of the Sun or there is a cross over it, a person would get a bad name in that age signified by the position of such a fault over the line. If the line continues beyond that point, a person might be mentally disturbed but, later on, there is no ill-effect.

If, along with other faults, the Line of Mercury is wavy or there is a grill over the Mount of Mercury or a star over it.

If the index finger is short and the Mount of Jupiter is depressed.

If the hand is thin.

If the Line of Saturn is thick or faulty.

If the Line of Saturn enters the third phalanges of the middle finger it

presages disrepute in old age.
If the Head Line is defective.
If the Heart Line is not there in the palm or is short.

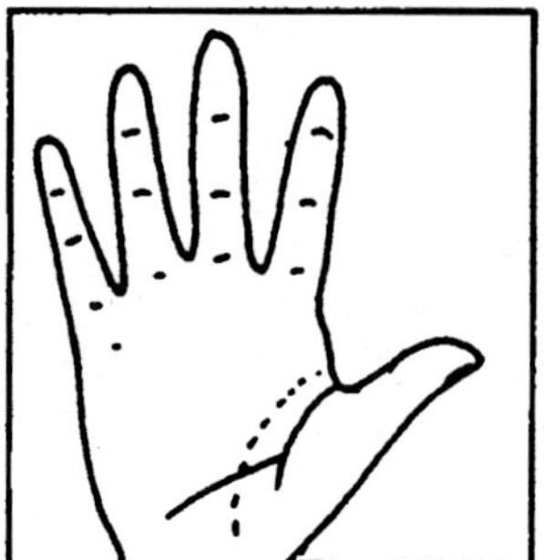

Fig. 10/19

If a branch of the Line of Mars enters the Mount of Luna (*See Fig. 10/19*) and the hand is thin or flabby, there is a tendency towards taking of narcotic drugs. If, along with these signs, the hand is heavy and hard, a person is likely to be an inveterate lecher.

Signs Favouring an Accident

There is a general belief that if there is a cross on the Head Line it is indicative of a head injury and a cross or any obstruction on the Line of Life signifies physical injury in an accident. But, it would be unwise to predict an accident merely on the basis of these signs. One must also study the mounts and the fingers to make any such predictions.

If the Aggressive Mars is very well-developed and any of the three main lines -- the Head Line, the Heart Line and the Line of Life -- is broken there is a possibility of a person being involved in a road accident.

But, if in addition to the broken main lines you find that the Aggressive Mars is under-developed or the area along the length of the palm towards the little finger -- the Mount of Mercury, the Defensive Mars and the Mount of Luna -- is developed, a person does not suffer injury in a road accident. Here the broken Head Line indicates headache, the fault of the Heart Line presages an emotional trauma and the fault of the Line of Life indicates family or financial problems.

Persons with a heavy palm are violent and take hasty decisions in anger. They should not drive a vehicle when under the influence of anger or emotional upsets.

A long ring finger encourages a person to take risks in every field. If along with this sign the palm is heavy and wide the tendency to take risks is accentuated. In conjunction with these signs, the faults of the Head Line and the Line of Life presage an accident.

In order to find the age at which a person would meet with an accident, one should see at what age the Line of Saturn or the Line of Life become faulty. There is no rule under which one can calculate the time on the basis of a study of the other lines.

PART III

Remedies to Remove Ill-Effects of Inauspicious Signs

CHAPTER XI

THE REMEDIES ARE SCIENTIFIC

Once I happened to meet H.C. Ganguli, a professor in the Psychology Department in the Delhi University who told me that it was not the in-thing in our country to take to psychoanalysis for dealing with psychological problems. He said that people in the USA and Europe went to their psychoanalysts or psychiatrists for consultations.

I told him that what the psycho-analyst did in the USA and Europe is the domain of the astrologer and the palmist.

What I said was based on my long experience of the subject and a deep study of physiology and psychology. Let me deal with them before I prove that the remedies suggested for dealing with the defects of the hand lines do have a scientific basis.

Psychology and Physiology - Some Facts

Modern physiology believes that emotional states like those of fear and anger are a danger signal for the human system. Many physiological changes take place when emotions hit a person. For example, when the cause for anger arises, the rate of breathing increases, which provides more oxygen to the human body. The heart rate also increases so that more blood can be pumped into the muscles. The spleen which stores blood become more active so that the number of red blood corpuscles increases and the face becomes red. These changes in the system are a result of the secretion of a harmone *Norapinephrine* into the blood stream.

When fright strikes a person his heart rate and breathing increases, but the face becomes wan or pale. This is caused by the harmone, *epinephrine*.

The flow of these two harmones, though caused by different factors, comes from the adrenal medulla into the blood stream. But the signal which activates this gland comes from the Sympathetic Nervous System.

The Causes of Emotions Like Fear, Anger and the System Which Counters Them

Fear and anger both arise when a person is faced by an unwanted person or situation. When a person feels that he can chase away the unwanted person or vanquish him, he feels angry. And when he is sure that he will not be able to face that individual or situation he is struck by fear.

The symptoms created by the stimuli which engender fear and anger are different. In both these emotional states various parts of the body need more energy. It is needed to fight, when one is angry and to flee when one is afraid.

"Vengeance" and "animosity" are two different facets of the emotion of anger. If we take the emotion of fear, "worry" and "despondency" are its two constituents. Both these emotional states are situations of a crisis for the human system. And the extra energy which the body needs to counter these two states does not come from outside but from the body itself. Some parts of the body reduce their level of activity so that more energy could be funnelled to the organs that need it. For example, when a man is angry there is more energy in his muscles, but the capacity to think and the digestive powers are reduced. The same happens when a person is afraid -- his power to think and to digest is reduced considerably. Tension increases which affects sleep too.

A doctor would prescribe tranquillizers to counter tension and depression and to bring on sleep. But the effect of these drugs is temporary. After their effect wears off, repeated doses are needed and the patient is likely to become addicted to them.

What Can a Palmist Do in Such a Crisis?

When a person is in trouble or worried he thinks of an astrologer or a palmist. It should be endeavour of both to remove the worries and tensions their clients complain of. In a situation of deep anxiety or tension a person is enmeshed in circumstances which do not leave any escape route for the stricken individual. The reason is that a person loses his capacity to think and he becomes incapable of solving the problem that confronts him. If at such a time he gets an assurance that there is a remedy which can help him counter his personal crisis, he is able to rid himself of the tension. His capacity to think returns and he can find a solution to his problem.

As we have said in the beginning, the tranquillizers prescribed by a physician are only temporary in their effect on the tensions and depression. But the palmist prescribes some remedies to counter the tension and if they are applied faithfully they have a salutary effect on the mind. The centres of the brain start producing *serotonin* which has a tranquilizing effect.

According to researches in physiology if sufficient amounts of serotonin continue to be produced in the brain, the chemical protects the heart during trauma and the stricken one is able to have a restful sleep. But, according to the reasoned belief of the present author, it is the mind which leads to the production and flow of the hormones like aphinephrine, norepinephrone and serotonin. It is the Sympathetic Nervous System, driven by the mind, which activates the glands to produce these secretions.

A psychiatrist, working according to his own methods, gives a fillip to the mental capacities of the patient and motivates him to face and solve the problems in which he is enmeshed. A palmist on the other hand, strengthens the mind of his client by suggesting a regimen of fasting, prayers and rituals. Such remedies are certainly beneficial if a person has faith in them.

Faith is the Key

Special emphasis must be placed on faith because without it no remedy would succeed. Remember that if you have faith in a doctor even a placebo administered by him would put you on the road to recovery and 50% of your troubles would be over. Conversely, if there is no faith in the doctor or the drugs prescribed by him even the best of medicines would be totally ineffective. The question arises that if an individual does not have any faith how can he get out of the clutches of a problem which bothers him?

No, it is just not possible for a man to have faith in nothing and nobody. Everybody has faith in something or the other. If a person does not have any faith in *mantras,* fasting, prayer and rituals he may be a believer in science and may place faith in that. It would become necessary, in that case, to suggest scientific remedies.

If a person has faith and takes recourse to remedies suggested to him, his morale is enhanced to such an extent that he can convert misfortune into good fortune. The reason for this is that after a person gets rid of the tensions that bother him the energies released are utilized to solve the problems that caused the tension. It is necessary, therefore, for a palmist to suggest remedies to his client according to his psychological state and his faith.

One must take into account the financial position of the client while suggesting remedies. If you suggest the wearing of a topaz to a man who is pining to get a job which will pay him about a thousand rupees a month, it is merely adding to his tension because he can ill afford to spend a sum of five thousand rupees to buy a topaz ring. Even a copper ring would do in his case.

Remedies to convert the inauspicious into the auspicious are suggested in the next chapter according to the beliefs and the financial positions of the various kinds of clients who consult the palmists.

Palmistry does not tell you what business or employment you are at any particular time, but it can tell you what you are suited for best

-- The Institute of Palmistry

CHAPTER XII

SOME YOGIC REMEDIES

Examine Your Breath

Gautam the Buddha had discovered during his meditations the *Vipashyana* method about 2500 years ago. This is an unfailing remedy to quieten your mind and to go into a state of meditation. If one wants to enter the state of deep meditation one has to stay in camps organised by Vipashyana Vidyapeeth, Igatpuri, Maharashtra, but everybody does not have time enough to enter a camp or an ashram to practise this method of watching your breath.

The early stage of Vipashyana method, if exercised properly, can rid a person of all his tensions. Preliminary exercises are easy to do and one can undertake them at home, during travel, in one's office or shop and anywhere else which is convenient to one.

But you must understand the method before you start practising it.

Breath is the basis of our life because you live only so long as you breathe. But hardly anyone pays any attention to the process of breathing.

Close your eyes and concentrate your attention on the breath that comes through your nostrils. Experience the intake of air through the breath; also the air which leaves your lungs through your nose. You have only to take notice of the air that is entering your body and is leaving it after having oxygenated your blood. One does not have to stop the breath like Pranayama and not quicken the process or to make the breath deep. Just experience the speed with which breath comes and goes out of your nostrils.

When you start practising this method your attention would wander. But do not be disappointed. When you feel that your mind is wandering to other subjects like your business, your job, your friends and enemies and your past and future, pull back your attention to the process of breathing which your body is undergoing.

A person with a highly developed Mount of Luna has a rich imagination. The moment he closes his eyes his mind wanders to other subjects because his imagination has full play. This interferes with the process of concentrating on your breath. Such persons can practise watching their breath even when their eyes are open. This process gives peace to the mind; it is diverted from the problem which reduces the tensions.

This should be practised for fifteen minutes in the morning and for an equal time in the evening. It gives you peace of mind. If you feel tense or worried during the day you can repeat this process several times. It would remove the anxieties and you would be able to find a solution to the problem causing tensions.

But everybody is not able to undertake all kinds of practices. Some other remedies are, therefore, suggested here.

Digital Postures

If you look at statues of the sages of old, you would notice that they sat in meditation with their fingers in certain peculiar positions. Why they did it, dawned on me while I was studying physiology. Before suggesting digital postures as remedies let us take some physiological facts into consideration.

The somatosensory area of the brain controls the various functions of the bodily organs. A major part of this area is responsible for the movement of hands and fingers. About 25% of this region is concerned with the movement of the thumbs and the fingers and the rest of the 75% area controls the movement of the other organs of the body. This fact has been commented upon in detail in my book ALL THE SECRETS OF PALMISTRY.

I have studied the subject of digital postures and their beneficial effects and have also sat at the feet of scholars who are experts in this field. As a palmist I have experimented on my clients the use of digital postures to remove the evil influence of defects in the lines and the Mounts. I have seen that such postures do give relief and would recommend the following to my readers.

Digital Posture Designed to Strength the Heart

This posture consists in joining the tips of first three fingers with the tip of the thumb, leaving the little finger away from them. If the Heart Line is defective, the Mount of Apollo is over-developed and the Mount of Luna under-developed, this posture definitely helps.

Persons suffering from hypertension and those who have had a heart attack should practise this every day to find relief from their troubles.

Digital Posture to Strengthen the Brain

This posture consists in joining the tips of the index finger and tip of the thumb. In Yoga it is called the *Chinmudra* (digital posture for the mind). If the Head Line is defective or the Mount of Jupiter either over-developed or under-developed, this posture helps.

Digital Posture to Bolster the Vital Force

This posture consists in joining the tips of the third and the little finger with that of the thumb. It removes the defects of the Line of Life and the Line of Mercury. If your Mount of Venus is under-developed or the Aggressive Mars is not fully developed this posture should be practised both in the morning and the evening.

Digital Posture to Remove the Defects of the Line of Saturn

Bend your index finger so that its tip touches the Mount of Venus and press the base of the finger with the tip of your thumb. The other fingers must be kept apart from this combination. If the Line of Saturn or the Mount of Saturn have defects this posture definitely helps. It should be practised for fifteen minutes in the morning and an equal time in the evening. If you are suffering from paralysis or gout or any disorder caused by the *Vata Dosha* this posture should be used for more time than indicated above.

Digital Posture to Remove the Defects of the Mercury

This posture consists in the touching of tip of the index finger of the left hand with the joined tips of the index and the middle finger of the right hand. If both the Line of Mercury and the Mount of Mercury are defective, this posture should be tried with both the hands turn by turn. If there is flatulence this posture can be used as a part of the curative process.

A Digital Posture Popular in Ancient China

In ancient China, it was a common practice to rotate a small copper ball with the tips of fingers. It is supposed to strengthen the brain. Looking at it from the point of view of modern physiology there is some truth in this belief because a large part of the somatosensory area of the brain is concerned with the movement of fingers. It is axiomatic to state that a wrong decision taken by your brain could mar your future and a good decision make your luck or fortune. I generally advise my clients to rotate a walnut with the tips of their fingers. This tends to activate the areas of the brain concerned with the movement of the fingers. As a consequence of that, a major part of the brain is strengthened.

How to Use Digital Postures?

All these postures should be tried with both the hands for fifteen minutes with each of them turn by turn. Even if there is no defect in any of the lines of the palm, if these postures are tried for two minutes at a stretch, the possibility of any of the defects arising or diseases striking a person is reduced. Indirectly it exercises the various centres of the brain.

If at the time of exercising these digital postures you remember your favourite or family deity, the beneficial effects are enhanced.

CHAPTER XIII

GEMS AND METALS TO DEAL WITH THE MALEFIC

Astrologers study the horoscope of their clients and advise them to wear specific gems to deal with the malefic effect of their stars. Their aim too is to strengthen certain centres of the brain through the effect of the gems on the fingers. In palmistry too the present author has seen the beneficial effect of metals and gems, the details of which are given below.

Astrology believes that there are nine planets which affect a man's destiny. Various gems are supposed to strengthen the effect of these planets : *ruby* is for the Sun, *pearl* for the moon, *coral* for Mars, *emerald* for Mercury, *topaz* for Jupiter, *diamond* for Venus, *blue sapphire* for Saturn, *pyrope* for *Rahu* and *cat's eye* for *Ketu*.

Mounts and Gems

Most of the writers on palmistry have named the mounts on the palm, seven in number, after seven planets. They are : Jupiter, Saturn, Sun, Mercury, Mars, Moon and Venus.

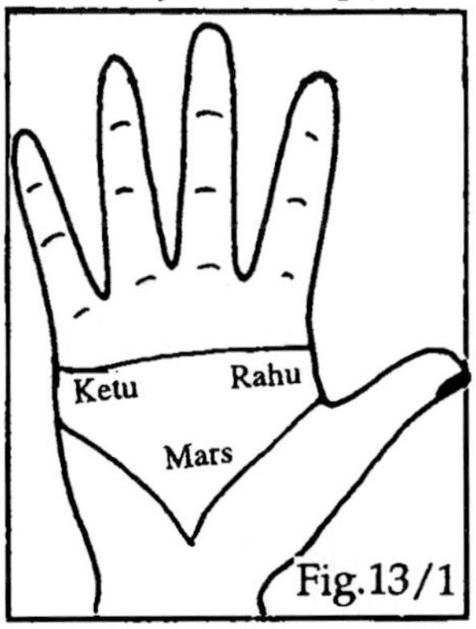

Fig.13/1

Some of them call Aggressive Mars as the *Rahu sthan* and the Defensive Mars as the *Ketu sthan* (*See Fig. 13/1*), but most of the palmists have the area of Mars into the following three divisions :

The area between the Mount of Mercury and the Mount of Luna or the Moon has been called upper Mars, but the present author has described it, according to its peculiarities, as the Defensive Mars. The area between the Mount of Jupiter and the Mount of Venus is called Lower Mars, which I have because of its peculiarities, called the Aggressive Mars.

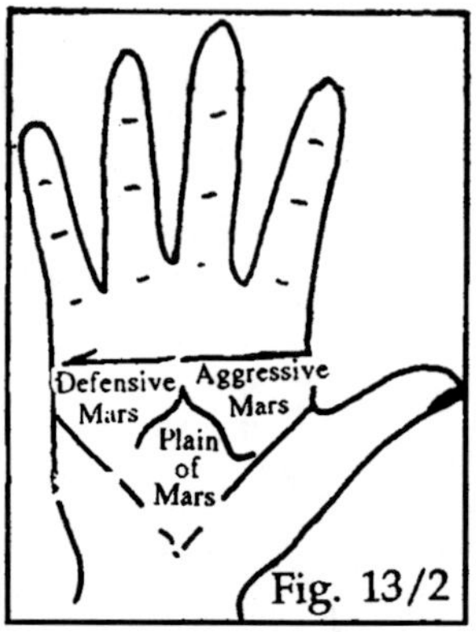

Fig. 13/2

The area in the middle of the palm is called the Plain of Mars (*See Fig. 13/2*). I feel that this is the proper division of the area of Mars because it takes into account the peculiarities of the planet.

Rings with various gems help to strengthen the mounts of the palm, because of their auspicious effect, but wearing a blue sapphire is not without risk. I advise my clients to wear emerald instead because the emerald and the blue sapphire both have an element of *Vayu*, but there is no danger in wearing the former whereas the blue sapphire is not without risk of harm.

For the under-developed mounts of the palm the following gems should be worn, as explained in the succeeding paragraph.

If the Mount of Jupiter is under-developed or the index finger is short, a topaz should be worn in a ring. But for a defective Saturn, an emerald is the right stone.

It must be stressed here that the Mount of Saturn is generally depressed, but the finger connected to it, the middle one, is usually long. The depressed mount should be considered a developed one. If the middle finger is long and the Mount of Saturn is developed it should be taken to be over-developed.

If the Mount of Mercury is under-developed or the little finger is short, an emerald should be worn, an emerald again if the Defensive Mars is under-developed; if the Aggressive Mars or the Plain of Mars is under-developed , a coral, if the Mount of Luna is under-developed a pearl and a coral if the Mount of Venus is under-developed; a ruby if the Mount of Apollo is under-developed.

Astrology believes that a diamond should be worn to accentuate the effect of Venus, but according to the theory of *pancha tattavas* (five basic elements of the universe) a diamond has *jal-tattva* (water) as its dominant element. But according to palmistry the Mount of Venus is connected with one's sexuality which is connected with the *agni tattva* (fire element). Coral has the fire element as its dominant constituent which is more appropriate for strengthening the Mount of Venus.

I have suggested that emerald and diamond should be worn in place of the blue sapphire because my experience of palmistry supports the view that these are better stones than the blue sapphire. The reason why this should be so has been explained above. An astrologer can say what stone you should wear after he has studied your horoscope and you should follow his advice.

One can ask the question that in case many mounts on the palm are under-developed should one wear many stones to offset their effect? The answer is that one should wear not more than two stones. If more than two mounts are defective, one should wear coral to strengthen the mounts which are fundamentally hot and emerald to strengthen those which are cold in nature.

Hot and Cold Mounts

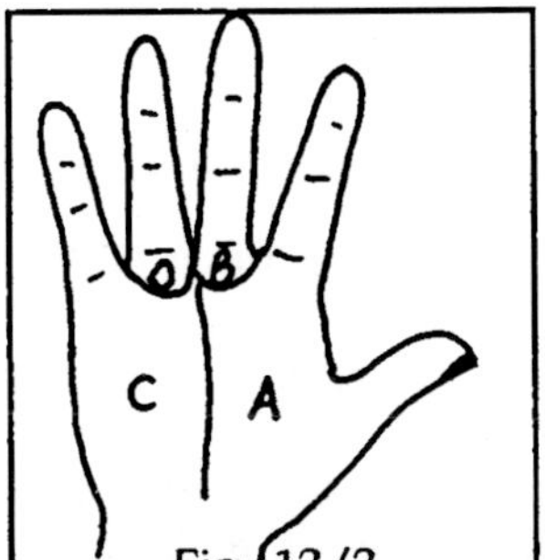

Fig. 13/3

If you draw a vertical line on the palm to divide it into two parts, the one towards the thumb represents the element of heat (*See Fig. 13/3-A*). The only area in this part which represents the element of cold is that of the Mount of Saturn (*See Fig. 13/3-B*) and that comprises only a small percentage of this part of the palm.

The half of the palm towards the little finger represents the cold element (*See Fig. 13/3-C*), but a small portion of it, occupied by the Mount of Apollo or the Sun (*See Fig. 13/3-D)* represents the element of heat.

The area with the element of heat represents the conscious. In other words it is connected with action and the area with the element of cold is concerned with thought (sub-conscious). In other words, persons whose half of the palm towards the thumb is more developed, are better suited to manual action and those whose other half of the palm is more developed are more given to thinking. They are adept at making plans.

Weight of the Stones to be Worn

According to the division of the hand into two parts, as explained above, if one of the mounts in the area represented by heat is under-developed, a stone weighing about 500 mg. should be worn -- a topaz for the Mount of Jupiter, a coral for the Aggressive Mars, the Plain of Mars or the Mount of Venus and a ruby for the Mount of Apollo or the Sun.

If two of the hot Mounts are under-developed, a coral weighing 700 mg. should be worn; in the case of three such mounts a coral weighing 900 mg. and for four a coral with a weight of 1200 milligrams.

If only one of the cold Mounts is under-developed a stone weighing 500 mg. should be worn to offset the defect. If the Mount of Saturn, the Defensive Mars of the Mount of Mercury is defective, an emerald and a pearl in case the Mount of Luna is under-developed, should be worn. If more than one cold mount is under-developed, an emerald weighing 700 mg should be worn. If more than two mounts are involved, the same stone weighing 900 mg. and if four are involved, one weighing 1200 mg. should be worn.

If you wear a stone to strength the planets, it should so set in the ring and its posterior touches the skin of the finger on which it is worn.

The Touch of Metals

Precious stones being costly, not every one can afford to wear them. The touch of metals can, in their place, offset the evil influence of the hand lines or mounts.

It is an old belief that the touch of iron has a cooling effect and copper heats up. If, therefore, hot mounts are under-developed, one should wear copper rings in place of coral, ruby and topaz. If, on the other hand, a cold mount is under-developed, an iron ring is the thing to wear.

Finger on Which Gem/Metal is to be Worn

If only one gem is to be worn it should be worn in the ring finger of the active hand. If two gems are indicated, hot gems or copper should be worn in the middle finger of the active hand and gems with a cold effect or iron should be worn in the ring finger of the active hand.

Let it be repeated that those who write with the right hand have that hand as the active one and those whose writing is done by the left hand have the left as the active hand.

Auspicious Day on Which a Gem or Metal Should be Worn

The day connected with the mount which is under-developed is the day on which the person concerned should wear the appropriate stone/metal after having prayed to his favourite deity. For example, a person with an under-developed Mount of Apollo or the Sun should wear the ring on a Sunday. For one with an under-developed Mount of Luna or the moon should wear the ring on a Monday. Likewise for the rest of the mounts.

Those who do not want to wear a ring, should wear a copper bangle to increase the effect of the hot planets and iron bangle to give a fillip to the cold planets.

Balance is the Key

A person whose all the mounts are developed need not wear any gem/ metal. If all the mounts are not developed, a balance should be maintained by seeing that all the mounts are equally developed. A balance between the power of the mind and of the body leads to good fortune. Such persons can take to the use of digital postures to remove the defects of the lines of the palm.

Fingerprints do not change, but the lines of the palm do. On this basis we can say that we are subject, to some extent, to our destiny, but we make our own luck to some extent.

-- The Institute of Palmistry

CHAPTER XIV

REMEDIES LIKE PRAYERS AND RITUALS

Prayers and Recitation of Mantras Etc.

Some superstitious persons are always apprehensive that somebody bearing them a grudge is engaged in rituals to do them harm. They should be advised to pray and recite *mantras* to ward off all evils. This would bolster their morale and evil would be warded off. One must, however, discourage people from undertaking any rituals which might harm others. Bearing ill-will against others or to think of harming them only vitiates your own mind which pushes you towards ill-luck and misfortune. One must, therefore, pray to God that He be kind to one and all. As an ancient *mantra*, so favourite of our forbears, says :

Sarve bhavantu sukhinah sarve santu niramayah
Sarve bhadrani pashyantu, ma kaschit dukhbhaga bhavete

सर्वे भवन्तु सुखिनः सर्वे सन्तु निरामयाः ।
सर्वे भद्राणि पश्यन्तु, मा कश्चित्, दुःखभाग भवेत्।।

If you recite this *mantra* morning and evening your mind is cleansed of all evil thoughts and you are at peace with yourself. Any prayers or rituals performed with peace in your heart grant you more benefits than you think is possible. This *mantra* should, therefore, be recited before any regimen of prayers or worship.

The Significance of Yantra, Mantras and Tantras

Meaning of words tend to change with time and place. At one time *Vaishanava* meant a devotee of Lord Vishnu, but now the word understand for vegetarian, regardless of the deity he worships. India's ancient texts prescribe the use of *yantras, mantras* and *tantras* for removing obstacles that one encounters in one's life.

A "*yantra*" connotes the removal of obstacles through the use of specific techniques. Taking recourse to medicine by a childless couple comes under the heading of "*yantras*".

A "*mantra*" is a system of syllables or words arranged in a specific manner, the recitation of which produces results. The *mantras* tend to influence the inner system of the body.

A "*tantra*" refers to the inner system of the body, represented by the central nervous system. From *kundalini* to *sahasrara* it is composed of six chakras or centres. *Kundalini* which is at the base of the most important of those *chakras*, the *muladhara* remains dormant. *Hathayoga* practices aimed at awakening it, it reaches the seventh chakra, *sahasrara* in the base of the brain, having passed through *muladhara, swadhishthana, manipoora, anahata, vishudha* and *ajnachakra*. When it does one is suddenly confronted with *Brahma*. That is the point when a person is totally bereft of any desires.

The use of *tantras* must be undertaken under the guidance of a competent *guru*, but for the recitation of *mantras* you only need faith and a sense of commitment. If one recites the *mantras* with a sense of commitment and faith in their effectiveness evil is warded off.

Mantras for the fulfilment of various desires are indicated in this chapter. Also given are the *yantras* or techniques to be used for specific purposes. It is like a doctor telling you what to eat and what to avoid when you are sick. When one has diahorrea, milk should be avoided, but the eating of curd helps you to recover. If dietary instructions are not followed, any medicines prescribed for a malady would not have the effect they should. An example is the advice to avoid the use of ice when one has a cold.

Medicine and Diet : Two Examples

A youngman of 22 years came to consult me. He wanted to marry a very beautiful girl. The youth had been left large properties by his deceased father, but he did not have any qualities which might persuade a man to give his daughter's hand in marriage to him. The reason was that he looked pale and wan, his clothes did not show any sense of dressing properly and there was a five-day old stubble on his face. His hair was long and unkempt because he had forgotten to use a comb. He had come into this bodily state because he had been busy in some religious rituals which prohibited him from having his hair cut on many days of the week.

I did not stop him from continuing the rituals, but advised him to have his beard trimmed on the day of the week on which there was no prohibition on these things. I told him to give attention to his personal appearance regardless of the rituals and that unless his personal appearance improved no beautiful girl would consent to marry him merely because he had lots and lots of money, and that a girl would normally marry a youngman out of love and not for money.

A woman did not get along with her husband. She was sick of the constant quarrels and had come to consult me. I studied her palm and told her that her husband was stubborn, not likely to be intimidated and that the quarrels continued because he did not listen to her. She accepted the truth of my reading of her palm. I had reached this conclusion because there was quite a distance between the points of origin of the Line of Life and the Head Line. She had short nails, to boot. This made it apparent that she was wayward. Had her husband been of a pliable nature, some kind of a compromise could have been reached. But he was a man with a will of his own and his wife had to come for consultation with me.

Only the recitation of some *mantras* could not have given her relief and I told her, therefore, that in addition to recitations she should inculcate a spirit of toleration which would result in the improvement of her relationship with her spouse.

Having said this by way of introducing the subject, we give below some of the *mantras* which should be recited every day for attaining some of the desired results. Each *mantra* should be recited 108 times (in other words one round of the garland of holy beads).

A *Mantra* for Children

Childless couples desiring children should recite the following *mantra* :

Om shri hri klin glaun Devaki suta Govinda Vasudeva Jagatpate.
Dehi may tanayam Krishna twamhamam sharanam gatah.

ओं श्री ह्रीं क्लीं ग्लौं देवकी सुत गोविंद वासुदेव जगत्पते।
देहि मे तनयं कृष्ण त्वामहं शरणं गत: ।।

This *mantra* should be recited every morning. Childless couples should worship their favourite deity on the seventh day of the bright fortnight of *Bhadra* month and fast on that day.

Couples who have only daughters throw to the winds all considerations of a planned family and go on producing children, all of them female. They should take it that God does not want them to have any boys and should remain content with daughters only. But, if they give alms on *Bhishmashtami* day every year, God might grant them their wish and they might have sons. Even if they do not get any sons they are saved from the disadvantage of not being cremated by their sons as the scriptures prescribe and there is no need for their *shraddha* ceremony in which sons offer oblations to their manes. The *Bhishmashtami* falls on the eighth day of the bright fortnight of *Magha* month of the Hindu calander.

Mantra For a Happy Marriage

Girls who face obstacles to their marriage or married women who do not get along with their husbands should keep fast during Navaratras every year and should recite the following mantra every day :

Hay Gauri : Shankarardhanagini yatha twam Shankar priya,
Tatha Maam kuru kalyani kant kanta sudurlabhava.

हे गौरि शंकरार्धाग्नि यथा त्वं शंकर प्रिया।
तथा मां कुरु कल्याणि कांत कांता सुदुर्लभाव।।

For men, the proper *mantra* to recite for this purpose is the following :
Om, Namah Shivaye

ओं नमः शिवाय ।

Mantra for Wealth, Strength and Knowledge

Om Shri Hrim Kleem Namah

ओं श्री ह्रीं क्लीं नमः ।

"Om" in this mantra is the symbol of God, the Maker of the Universe. "*Shri*" is the name of the goddess of wealth, Lakshmi, "*Hrim*" stands for Durga, who gives strength and "*Kleem*" is the name of Goddess of knowledge, Saraswati. The three deities represent the majesty of God in His various forms. The recitation of this *mantra* leads to the worship of all the above forms of the Maker of this Universe.

Mantra to Ward Off/Solve Crises

If a crisis faces you, like indebtedness, involvement in some litigation or a serious disease, you should keep fast on *Chaturthi* (the fourth day of each half of the lunar month) and recite the following *mantra* every day :
Om Ganeshaye Namah

ओं गणेशाय नमः ।

Other Beneficial *Mantras* and Remedies

A person usually benefits from the recitation of a *mantra* dedicated to his favourite deity (in whom he has faith). Those who have faith in Hanuman should recite the *Hanuman chaleesa*. We are giving below mantras for those who believe in other deities and religious beliefs.

Mantra for the Jains

Namo Arihantanam
Namo Siddhanam
Namo Aayeeryanam
Namo Uvajhayanam
Namo Loye Savva Sahunam

णमो अरिहंताणं
णमो सिद्धाणं
णमो आइरियाणं
णमो उवज्झयाणं
णमो लोए सव्व साहूणं

A short form of this *mantra* is :
Om Asiaoosa Namah

ओं असिआउसा नमः ।

Mantra for Sikhs

Ek Onkar satinamu Karta Purakhu, Nirbhau, Nirvaire Akaal murti
Ajooni sai bhanga Guru Prasadi

एक ओंकार सतिनामु करता पुरखु निरभउ निरवैरि अकाल मूरति
अजूनी सै भंग गुर प्रसादि ।

Mantra for devotees of Lord Rama

Rama Rameti Rameti Rame Rame Manorame
Sahasra Naam Tattatulayam Rama Nam Varanane

राम रामेति रामेति रमे रामे मनोरमे ।
सहस्र नाम तत्तुल्यं राम नाम वरानने ।।

Mantra for devotees of Lord Krishna

Om Namo Bhagwate Vasudevaye

ओं नमो भगवते वासुदेवाय ।

Mantra for devotees of Lord Vishnu

Shantakaram Bhujangashayanam Padmanabham Suresham
Vishwadharam Gagansadrisham Megha Varna Shubhangam
Lakshmikantam Kamalanayanam Yogibhirdhyanamnaganyam
Vande Vishnum Bhavabhayaharam Sarvalokayeknatham.

शान्ताकारं भुजंगशयनम् पद्मनाभं सुरेशम्,
विश्वाधारं गगन सदृशं मेघ वर्ण शुभांगम् ।
लक्ष्मीकान्तं कमलनयनं योगिभिर्ध्यानगम्यम्,
वन्दे विष्णुं भवभयहरं सर्वलोकैकनाथम् ।।

The Gayatri *Mantra* which Gives All Kinds of Happiness

Om Bhurbhuva Swaha; tat saviturvaraynyam. Bhargo devasya dhimahi. Dhiyo yo naha prachodayat.

ओं भूर्भुवः स्वः । तत् सवितुर्वरेण्य भर्गो देवस्य धीमहि । धियो यो नः प्रचोदयात् ।

Mantra for devotees of Durga

Om Hrim Dun Durgae Namah

ओं ह्रीं दुं दुर्गायै नमः ।

A person benefits from worshipping the deity of whom he is a devotee, according to his beliefs, dogmas or faith. Those who do not have faith in the efficacy of *mantras* cannot get any benefit if they recite them. They should, instead, take to the use of the digital postures described in Chapter XII.

Other Remedies

Just as looking at yourself in the mirror every day tends to improve your looks, examining your palms every day tends to improve your fortune. While you look at your palms, remember your favourite deity and seek his blessings. It would bolster your morale and the evil effects of defective lines are softened, if not substantially reduced.

Some astrologers advise their clients to feed the birds. If a person does this with a sense of faith (that it would give him good results) his morale improves and this tends to affect his luck beneficially. If there is no faith, you cannot expect any gain from these remedies. But the digital postures, stones and metals do have their effect.

●

POVERTY AND RICHES ARE COMPARATIVE TERMS

Persons whose hands show auspicious sings might appear to us to be poor whereas those who appear to be very rich might have inauspicious signs on their palms. That throws my students into confusion.

In fact, poverty and riches are comparative terms. A person born in a family too poor to afford a pair of shoes might be called rich in the context of the standard of living of his family if he is able to buy a bicycle, but an influent man, who owns a car made in India is forced to consider himself poor if those who move in the same social circles in which he does, own imported limousines.

If the lines continue to improve the process of a rich man getting richer and richer continues, whether he owns a bicycle or a car.

Poverty and riches can also be measured with reference to one's assets and liabilities. The difference between one's income and expenditure is another measure you can use to gauge whether a man is poor or rich. If a person earns Rs 1,000 a month, but limits his expenses to Rs 900 per month, he is rich, but, if a man has an income of Rs 1,00,000 per month but spends 1,25,000 per month, he must be considered to be poor.

Property or wealth, in the eyes of some, is only immoval property, but money in the bank, share and stocks, insurance policies, houses and cash are other forms of wealth.

It is usual for large businessmen to borrow. If a person's liabilities are less than his assets his palm would show signs of wealth. Any obstruction in the cash flow for a businessman might represent a temporary difficulty. A problem might also result from the fact he is not spending in one direction but in another, but this situation improves if his assets are more than his liabilities. If remedial action is taken at that time one can avoid the tensions cause by tha state of affairs.

— AUTHOR

PART IV

Some Hand Prints; Their Study and Interpretation

CHAPTER XV

HAND READING WITH 20 CASE STUDIES

Reading a hand is like delving into the deep sea which is bottomless. Some palms have a multiplicity of lines and the palmist does not know from where to begin and some have so few lines that he finds it difficult to answer the questions that the client wants answers to. This is a difficulty which every palmist faces in the beginning, but with constant practice and experience he is able to overcome it.

Here we give twenty pairs of hand prints of men and women from various fields of life. We have dealt with the lines of the palm in the first and second parts of this book and you would find a composite picture of those lines in these handprints. Some of the persons whose handprints are given here are prominent and famous persons in their respective fields, but their names have been withheld. We have only identified them by saying that so and so is a prominent industrialist or that the handprint belongs to a woman entrepreneur.

The readings of the handprints are for the benefit of the readers and those who seek training from the author in the science of palmistry. How much of the reading is to be told to the client depends on the palmist's discretion at the time of giving it.

The descriptions accompanying the handprints identifies the fingerprints, nails and mounts wherever such identification was necessary. It is pointless to go into details of all the signs on a palm.

The reading is given by keeping in mind the need to consider the active hand as the main palm. Where clear indications are not available on the active hand, support is sought from the signs on the inactive hand.

The author hopes that the handprints and their readings would help the readers to understand what the lines on the palm signify and they would be able to give independent readings of their clients' hands.

Handprints 1-A, B

These are the handprints of a 37 years old businessman. The hand is heavy and large. The thumb is shorter than normal and its first phalange is almost equal to the second. The little finger is long but in a low setting. The Mount of Venus and the aggressive Mars are developed, but the Mount of Luna is under-developed. The other mounts are displaced. There is the island on the joint of the two phalanges. There is a clear and well-defined island in the left thumb.

1-A, The Right Hand
There are three vertical lines on the Mount of Apollo on the right palm which resemble somewhat a trident.

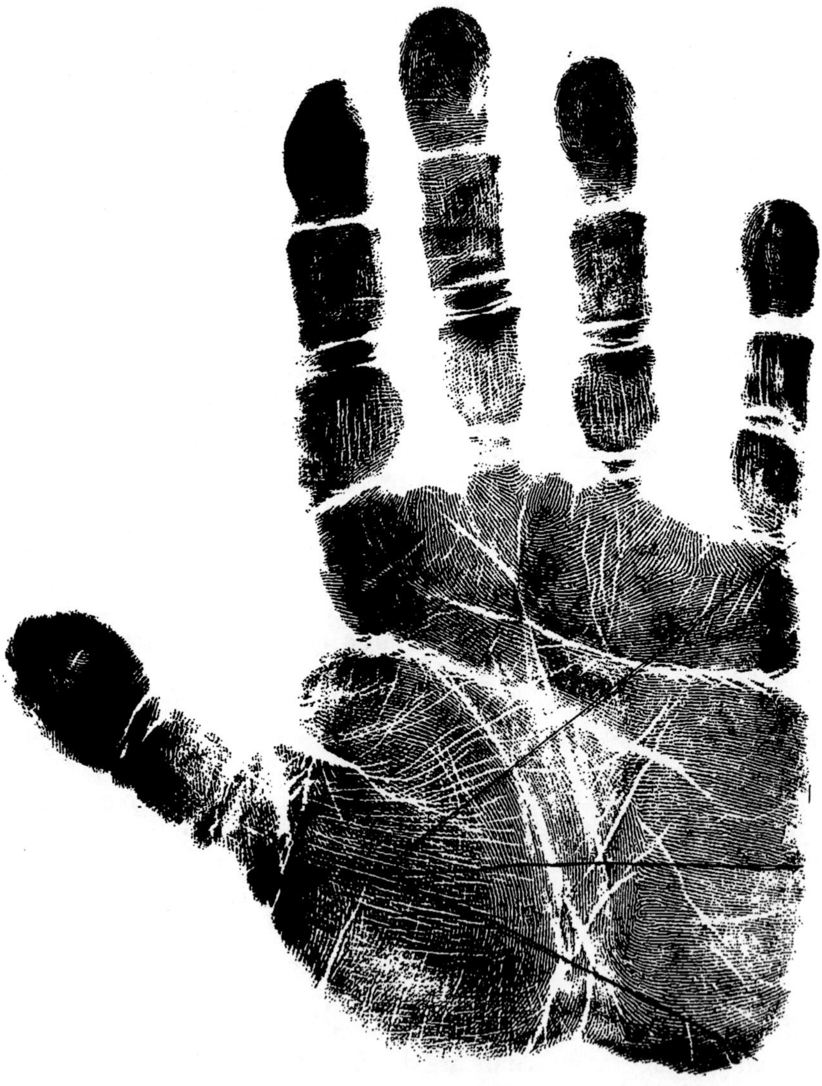

1-B, The Left Hand
A clear Yava between the two phalanges of the thumb. A Yava resembles an island.

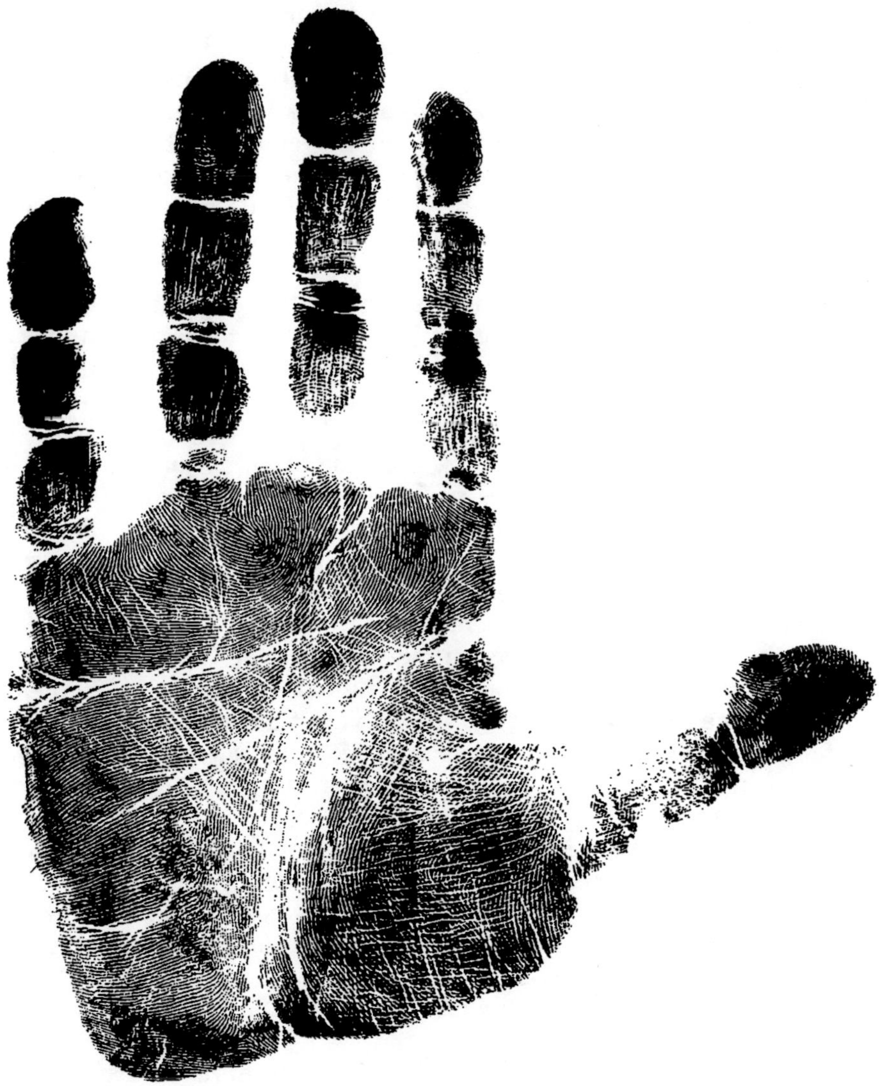

At the base of the thumb there is a line resembling a chain. There are two lines of sexuality: the upper one is long and thick but the one below is short. The right hand is the active one.

Thumb of a normal length indicates that the person is possessed of normal intelligence, but the long little finger is an indication that he is very wise in so far as his own personal interest is concerned. But, because of the low setting of the little finger he is not able to express himself clearly.

The hand is heavy: it means that the man is courageous. The large hand is an indication of the fact that he wants to go into details of things. The fact that the two phalanges of the thumb are equal in length indicates that there is a balance in the capacity to think and the power to act. A well-developed Mount of Venus is proof that he has a fair amount of vitality and also sexuality. The developed state of the Aggressive Mars is an index of an angry nature. Taken in conjunction the developed state of the Mount of Venus and the chain-like line dividing the thumb from the palm indicate that there is a good possibility of children being born. A clear line on the Mount of Venus near the base of the thumb shows that one of his children will live long. The end of the Heart Line is forked, an indication of excellent progency.

If there is a clear and well-defined island on the line dividing the two phalanges of the thumbs, it presages good luck. But, here the island on the right hand is broken, but, in the left, it is clear and well-defined. It means that he would get the benefit of one and a half islands. This person will never face financial stringency.

Let us now take the lines of the palm. The Line of Life is circular; it is thick at places and thin at others, which is an indication of fluctuations in relations with the family members and also in business. But the fact that the line is circular reduces its fault to some extent. The lines of influence from the Aggressive Mars intersect the Line of Life till the age of 38, which indicate obstacles placed in his way by the members of the family. But these lines have not reached the Mount of Saturn which means that in spite of obstacles there will be success in earning money. The lines of influence do not intersect the Line of Life after the age of 38 years, but the line is thick at this point which indicates that the family obstacles would continue after 35. This thickness of the Line of Life continues upto the age of 48, which means that these obstacles would vanish after that age.

The Line of Mars is very indistinct. It means that there is no hope of any cooperation from any quarter, nor is there any tendency on the part of this individual to cooperate with others. Since the hand is heavy and the Aggressive Mars is strong, the man will not admit defeat in the face of any difficulties.

The Line of Life in the left hand is thick throughout and the lines of the right hand are better than those of the left which means that the man has the capacity to improve himself.

A branch of the Line of Life goes to the Mount of Luna, which speaks of foreign travel. According to the Line of Life, the time when this is possible is the age of 52 years, but for a correct assessment look at the Line of the Sun or Apollo which starts at the age of 40 years. The person is likely to undertake a journey to foreign lands sometime around age 40. At the age of 60 the Line of Mercury emerges from the Line of Life and proceeds towards the Mount of Mercury. But this does not reach beyond the Mount of Luna, and, instead a line of influence from the Mount of Luna intersects the Line of Mercury and forms a cross. It means that the person is likely to fall ill at the age of 60. These lines tend to form a square near the Line of Life which indicates possibility of recovery from that illness.

At age 26, the Line of Saturn emerges from near the Line of Life and at age 29 the Line of Mercury starts which, without touching the Line of Life proceeds towards the Mount of Mercury. This line is indistinct till the age of 36 years. A segment of the Line of Saturn has emerged from the Mount of Luna at age 24 and stops at age 32, beyond which it does not go. There are two crosses on this segment of the Line of Saturn, one at age 25 years and the other at 30 years. The Line of Saturn which has started at the age of 26 is thin in the beginning, thick in the middle and has again thinned out at age 37 after some obstacles. The combined effect of these lines is that from 24 to 37 years the man would have many sources of income open to him, but there would be obstacles in his way. After the age of 37 the obstacles would diminish. After age 40 a group of lines from the Sun starts emerging which means that the man would get the benefit of the efforts put in by him till that age.

The Head Line is thick which is an indication of family problems. The time when these problems would cease is the time of the emergence of the Line of the Sun at the age of 40.

We have referred to the island in the middle of the thumb as an indication of the financial status of the man. The other good feature is the existence of an extra luck line, which lies from the Mount of Jupiter till the base of the middle finger above the Heart Line. Four vertical lines on the Mount of Mercury signify profit in trade. All these signs taken together mean that after the age of 40 the man would have money and fame.

There is a vertical line on the Mount of Jupiter in the left hand and in the right there is a light Ring of Solomon which points to the desire for prestige and ambition. That would be fulfilled after the year 40 when the Sun Line emerges on the hand.

The Heart Line is away from the base of the fingers and near the Head Line. It shows that the man has a pragmatic outlook and a desire to earn money rather than any sentimentality.

At age 62, the Line of Life touches the Line of Mercury and continues beyond that point. A parallel line (parallel to the Line of Life) emerges at age 62 which is helpful. It appears to go upto the wrist. That is why the man is likely to live beyond the age of 75 years.

The palm towards the Aggressive Mars is developed which points to a lot of vitality and an angry nature. The man was advised to wear an iron ring to

2-A, The Right Hand
Count the Lines of Saturn in this hand and identify.

2-B, The Left Hand
There are only a few lines in this hand. The Line of Life is straight in both the hands.

offset this evil effect. That would help him to control his temper and success, which is indicated in the year 40, come nearer.

Handprints 2-A, B

The handprint belongs to a young unmarried woman of 22 whose active hand is the right one. The nails are short, the index finger long and the ring finger and the little finger are inclined towards the middle finger. The mounts of Jupiter and Mercury are well-developed, the second phalange of the thumb is long and the knots of the fingers are soft. There are two lines of sexuality in the right hand, the upper one is longer and inclined downwards, that is towards the Heart Line. The line of sexuality in the left hand is straight.

The number of lines on the left palm is limited and they are not faulty. In comparison, the lines of the right hand have more faults. They are broken or are thick at places and thin at others. It is clear that the girl has herself spoiled her luck. This could be due to many reasons. For example, the short nails point towards a wayward nature which insists on having its own way. Fingers without knots and the second phalanges of the thumb being longer point towards less of action and more of imagination in the person. Such a person is given to making plans which cannot be implemented. The developed Jupiter and the long index finger means that the person wants prestige, which, if unavailable, tends to spoils the lines.

The active hand is the right one that is why we must first study it. The Line of Life is straight and its beginning is faulty. This indicates that till the age of 16 to 17 years there would be problems created by the family and the health would be indifferent. The fault of a straight Line of Life is removed when the Line of Saturn touches it and goes towards the fingers. The Line of Saturn emerging from the wrist intersects the Line of Life at age 28 and goes straight to the Mount of Saturn. This is the time when some special achievement is indicated. It could be marriage.

A line of influences coming from the Mount of Venus intersects the Line of Life at 28 touching the Line of Saturn and proceeds towards the Mount of Apollo. It means that the girl would be free from the shackles of the family at 28 and would march towards success. But, this line of influence becomes thicker and then vanishes. This could mean that she would have to struggle for success in a more pronounced manner. Good works and remedies might result in the line appearing again.

Another Line of Saturn emerges from the Mount of Luna at age 23. This is intersected by lines of influence at ages 26 and 28. The time when this line emerges, that is 23 years, might be the year when she would get married, but obstacles are likely to be experienced. Since this line is broken at many places and the line of sexuality is downwards, the best time when she should get married is 28 years of age. After that age obstacles would cease. Even though after the age of 28 the second Line of Saturn becomes indistinct, re-emerging at

35, but this fault if offset by the fact that the Line of Saturn which emerged from the wrist continues.

The third Line of Saturn emerges from the Defensive Mars at 31. This line is without any faults and at 35 it is supported by the Line of Saturn emerging from the Mount of Luna and the other starting from the middle of the wrist. This goes till the age of 50 and touches the Heart Line. It is also distinct and later on merges with the Heart Line and proceeds towards the Mount of Saturn like the steps of a ladder. This means that the time between the ages of 31 and 50 is the best time of life for this girl. After the achievement at 28 a struggle continues for three years but that would cease at 31. Till the age of 50 the period would be full of happiness -- from the point of view of family as well as from a financial point of view. She need not worry about what would happen after the age of 50 because there is sufficient time and the situation can improve considerably.

The Head Line is short and faulty which presages financial and family troubles. The time when these difficulties would have to be faced has been indicated while discussing the lines of Saturn and Life. There is a line of influence forming a bridge between the Heart and Head Line. These two lines appear in the shape of one Head Line. It is an indication that the person is self-centred who would think only of her own interests. There is little room for sentiment in the life of such a person. The desire for profit is stronger which might vitiate the marital relations and the person might find herself alone. Marital relations are referred to in this context because one of the lines of sexuality is inclined towards the Heart Line. Even so there is no danger of anything deleterious because there are many squares near the point of intersection of the Head Line and the Heart Line which tend to reduce the faults.

Faulty horizontal lines on the middle part of the Mount of Luna point towards disquiet and stomach troubles. She should pay attention to her digestive processes and try to get mental peace.

The Line of Mars runs parallel to the Line of Life from age 21 to 40 years. During this period the girl will continue to get support and sustenance from parents, siblings, guardians or her husband. The Line of Mars stops at age 48 when cooperation from the relatives might reduce. Remedies to improve the situation should, therefore, be undertaken expeditiously.

The last part of the Line of Life has merged with the Line of Saturn. A line of Mercury which has emerged from the Mount of Venus intersects this joint line at age 50, which presages physical troubles in that age. Later on, the Line of Life continues till the age of 70 which means that those troubles would cease and the person would live till 70. The Line of Saturn and the Line of Life which have become one are inclined towards the Mount of Luna which shows travel. It is likely to be undertaken at the age of 31.

All in all, this is the handprint of a disturbed personality. The time of achievement for her begins at age 28 and the period between the years of 31 and

3-A, The Right Hand
A hand full of many lines. Such a hand indicates Hyperactivity of the man's mind.

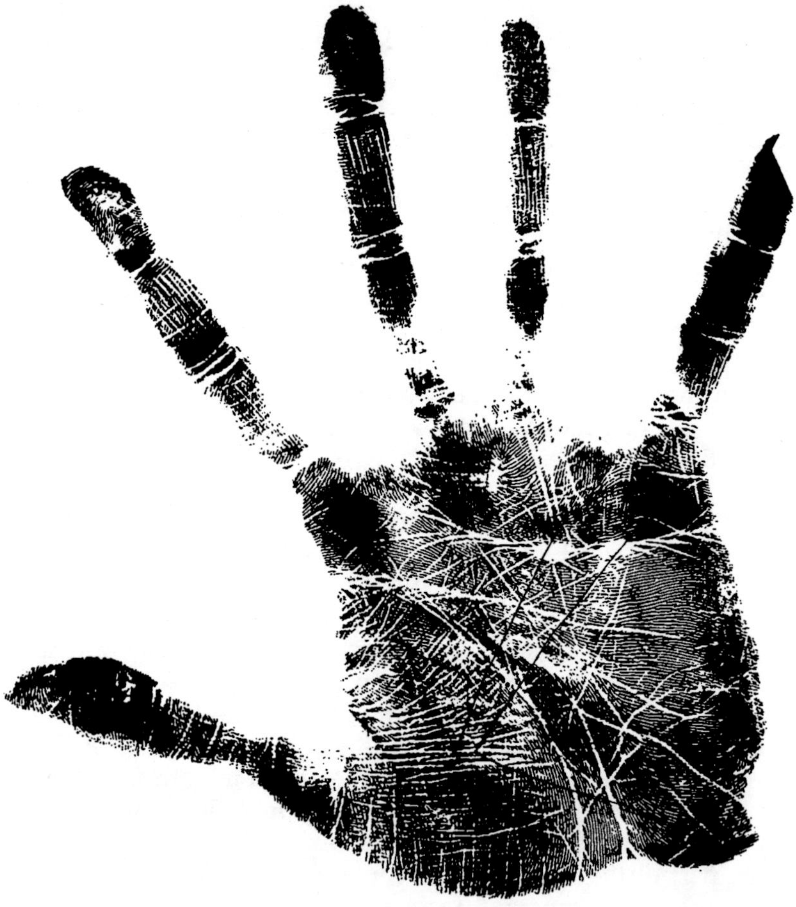

3-B, The Left Hand

The depressed portions in the middle of the Line of Saturn are particularly noteworthy.

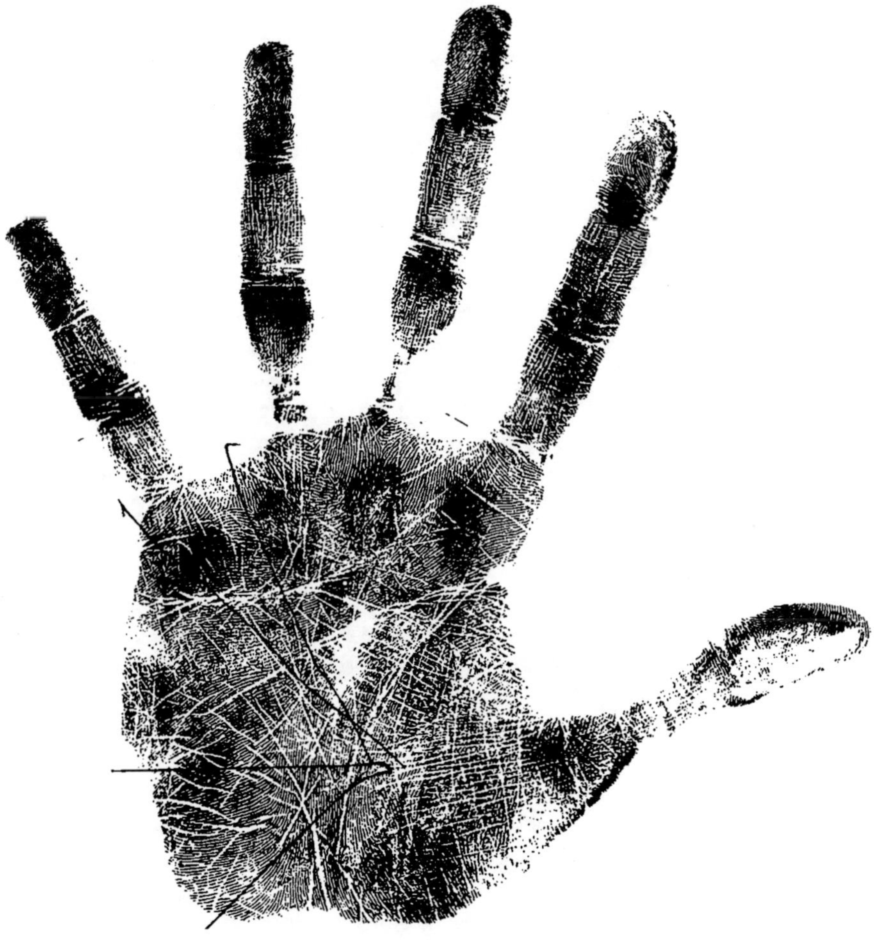

50 is the best period of life. Remedies should be undertaken now to ward off the bad times after that. She should practise the digital posture designed to increase the power of the brain vitality and the digital posture which would strengthen the Mount of Mercury. For removing disquiet she should undertake exercises which consist in studying one's own breathing processes. She should study her palms on waking up and should pray to her favourite deity to give her wisdom. She should also wear both iron and copper. This would help her to have a nice time for the first 28 years of life and better life after the age of 50.

Handprint 3-A, B

This handprint belongs to a rich, 30-years old woman whose active hand is the right one.

The fingers are asymmetrical--in other words they are not placed in a straight setting. The little finger is short, is in an inferior position and inclined backward. It is separate from other fingers and to some extent it might be called a crooked finger.

The second phalange of the thumb is longer, the Mount of Venus is developed, with the other mounts being normal. There are two lines of sexuality in the right hand. One of them has two forks, one of which is inclined towards the Heart Line.

Too many lines indicate a mercurial temper. The result is that she thinks too much and has no peace. The lines of the right palm are better than those in the left, which means that there is a tendency towards improvement.

The branches of the Heart Line go towards the Head Line which presages the greater force of the brain. The little finger is crooked which is a sign of a person who thinks only of his own interest. The line of sexuality has two forks which presages differences of opinion with the spouse. The non-existence of the Line of Mars supports this theory. All the signs point towards a person who would think only of his own self-interest. The Line of Life and the Head Line is combined for the first 18 years and is twisted like a rope. The Head Line is defective till age 21.

Till the age of 21 years the woman must have suffered from an inferiority complex and financial troubles. This view is supported by the first section of the Line of Saturn which has emerged from the middle of the wrist. This line is forked near the wrist which shows a deprived life in childhood. The Line of Life is double till the age of 28 and describes an island. It is an indication of physical and family troubles.

The incomplete Girdle of Venus is a sign of mental disquiet. The main trouble from which she is suffering is connected with the highly sensitive nervous system. There are many Lines of Saturn. The main Line of Saturn has emerged from the middle of the wrist and is forked in the beginning. We have already interpreted the significance of this. The second Line of Saturn emerges from the lower part of the Mount of Luna and merges with the main line at the age of 28. The Line of Mercury emerges from this junction of the two lines. This indicates some achievement in the business field at the age of 28. The woman started taking active part in the family business at this age.

The third Line of Saturn has emerged from the upper part of the Mount of Luna. This meets another line of the same name at the age of 30 and from their junction emerges the Line of Sun. That is why this period is a period of special achievements. At the age of 35 two branches of the Line of Life start towards the Mount of Saturn. Because they are too close their effect is that of an axe line (*kuthar rekha*). It means that there would be profit or benefit, but there would be problem too. Between the ages of 40 and 50 there is a depression in the Line of Saturn on the left palm. Since the lines in the right palm are without any blemishes in this period, the fault of the depression is lessened. Even so some financial problem would tend to persist during this period. That is why attention to this aspect should be paid right now. There is possibility of some remarkable changes between the ages of 50 and 55 because some lines stop at the Heart Line at that point of time and three vertical lines show themselves on the Mount of Sun. Short horizontal lines intersect these lines which is an indication of the fact the heart's desire would be fulfilled after some obstructions.

The branches of the Heart Line tend towards the Head Line, which indicates that the person is possessed of a strong mind. The result is that she is more pragmatic than sentimental. The branches of the Heart Line in the beginning and at the end indicate that the person is likely to have considerable patrimony and good progeny. Two children have been born which is clear from the vertical lines on the base of the thumb.

At the age of 65 there is a line of influence which intersects the Line of Life and then goes towards the Mount of Luna. This is an incomplete line of intuition. This means that the person has the capacity to understand what is in the minds of others. This line has met the Line of Life at its end and has formed a triangle close to the Line of Life. This shows acquisition of property at the age of 65. This line of influence forms a triangle with a branch of the Line of Life going towards the Mount of Luna and another Line of Saturn. The triangle lies in the area of Saturn. The time when this triangle has been formed is between the ages of 22 and 28 according to the rules applicable to the Line of Saturn. Other lines of influence and the Line of Mercury describe many triangles when they meet the other Lines of Saturn during the period between 25 and 30 years. These presage acquisition of property in some form or the other. Let it not be forgotten that a bank balance or a vehicle are also other forms of property. Because of these triangles the woman has been able to acquire considerable amount of property, but she has been facing troubles too.

The Line of Life indicates an age of 75 years. The non-existence of a Line of Mars is an indication that she has less resistance to disease than normal. She must be careful about her health. The depressions in the Heart Line also send out their warning signals.

4–A; The Right Hand
Notice the three Rings of Solomon and the Line of Life which begins from the Mount of Jupiter. The hand is an excellent example of such a Line of Life.

4-B, The Left Hand
Compare the Heart Line in the right and the left hands.

To sum up, the hand shows a good financial position, but also the existence of worries and troubles. She should practise the digital postures calculated to increase the strength of the brain and also vitality. More strength should be given to the Mount of Jupiter so that the fault represented by a crooked little finger is reduced. She should best wear a topaz. That would remove the faults of the Sun Line during the period after middle age and obstacles to success would be reduced.

Handprint 4-A, B

The handprint belongs to a 41-year old trader whose right hand is the active one. There is a double loop in the print of the left thumb and nine whorls in the rest of the fingerprints. The little finger is in low setting . The Mount of Mercury below its base is under-developed, but the other mounts are developed in a normal manner. The thumb is of normal length with the second phalange larger. There is an island on the joint between the two phalanges of the right thumb. The island in the left thumb is bisected. There are two lines of sexuality in each hand. The upper line has two forks and one of the two forks is inclined towards the Heart Line.

We would interpret mainly the lines on the right palm.

The Line of Life has emerged from a point near the Mount of Jupiter which shows overweaning ambition, but there are delays in the fulfilment of desires because the other lines are not helpful for that happy outcome.

The Line of Life encircles the Mount of Venus and tends to go towards the Mount of Luna which indicates a great amount of vital force and the desire to travel. From the high point of the Mount of Luna you can see lines of influence entering the mount, which points towards a tendency to travel, but the Line of the Sun is not helpful to that tendency.

One Line of Life ends at the age of 60 years; another starts from the year 59. That shows that the period between the ages of 58 and 62 years is the time of changes in the family. This might result in a break-up of the family, or, it might result in change of residence, but the change would not be a happy one. The Line of Life which starts at 59, goes upto 80 years on a parallel course, which means that the life span might be of 80 years.

The Head Line is good and inclines towards the Defensive Mars. It points towards a pragmatic nature and a good financial position. Let us also take into account the effect of the islands in both the thumbs. The island on the right thumb is well-defined, but the one on the left thumb is broken. We can, therefore, say that the benefit would be that of one and a half islands. It is a good hand from the financial point of view, but we would also study the Line of Saturn to get confirmation of the financial state of affairs.

The main Line of Saturn separates from the Line of Life at age 28. This is the age when this man has gained on his own without support of his family. This is the time when he should get married too. It is at this point of time that an indistinct Line of Mercury has started emerging, which means that the man might go in for business. But, since that line is short, indistinct and broken up there would not be much profit in a business venture. Another Line of Saturn has emerged at age 24 from the Mount of Luna, which means that the time is ripe for going in for partnership in business. An oblique line intersects this line at age 29 which might mean that his partner in business has cheated him at this age. This line ends at age 33, but before it does a parallel line supports it. This parallel line ends at age 34. A new line emerges from that point and goes towards the middle of area between the Mounts of Apollo and Mercury. Another line goes towards the Mount of Apollo in this age. There is an indistinct cross on the Line of the Sun. This is the time when fortunes fluctuate and the tendency is more towards fame than money.

In the midst of these fluctuations the island between the two phalanges of the thumb and the circular shape of the Line of Life helps to preserve finances. He has been advised to wear an emerald to offset the shortcomings of the Mount of Mercury and also digital postures to remove the faults of this mount. There are indistinct vertical lines on the Mount of Apollo which point towards interest in various fields. One vertical line instead of many on the Mount of Apollo is more beneficial. This person should undertake exercises to watch his breathing process so that he can concentrate on things. One single line on the Mount of Saturn indicates that the man would be free from financial worries after middle age.

The Heart Line in the right hand is defective. It is like a rope made of short strands. Such a line indicates that the person would be constantly subjected to emotional traumas. This man never met again those on whom he showered his love/affection. There is an island in this line between the mounts of Apollo and Mercury, which speaks of possibility of diseases of the heart and the eyes. The time when these maladies would trouble him would be between the ages of 58 and 60, because the Line of Life in this period is faulty. He must constantly keep an eye on his blood pressure and should use the digital postures calculated to strengthen the heart. The triangle under the Mount of Apollo is towards the Head Line which is good for his finances.

The horizontal lines on the Mount of Venus and the Aggressive Mars speak of obstructions caused by the members of the family. But the lines in the areas of Mars and Venus below, parallel to the Line of Life point towards the removal of those obstructions. One of those lines, the Line of Mars is very near the Line of Life which portends a restless nature. The second Line of Mars is broken, which is supported by the two-forked line of sexuality. It means either differences of opinion with the wife or her indifferent health. Let us look at the fingerprints for the reason behind this state of affairs. There is only one double loop on the others there are signs of a whorl. It means that the man is not clear about what he wants, but is determined to have his way. He must do a bit of introspection. That would lead to improvement of his relations with others. Along with a broken parallel line there is one clear Line of Mars in this hand which points towards somebody in the family who offers cooperation to the man. It also offsets the fault of the broken line.

5-A, The Right Hand
A depression in the middle of the palm. The handlines had to be drawn with a pen.

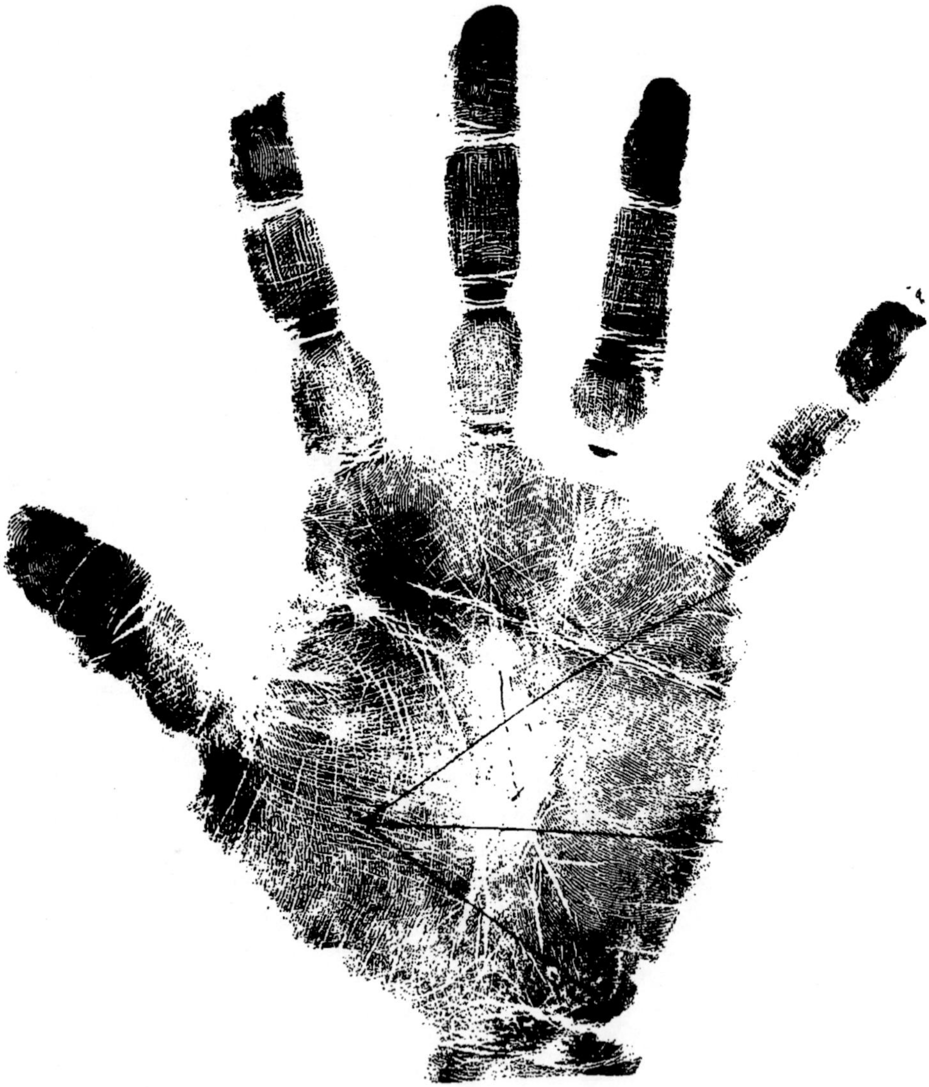

5-B, The Left Hand
There are many influence lines on both the hands.

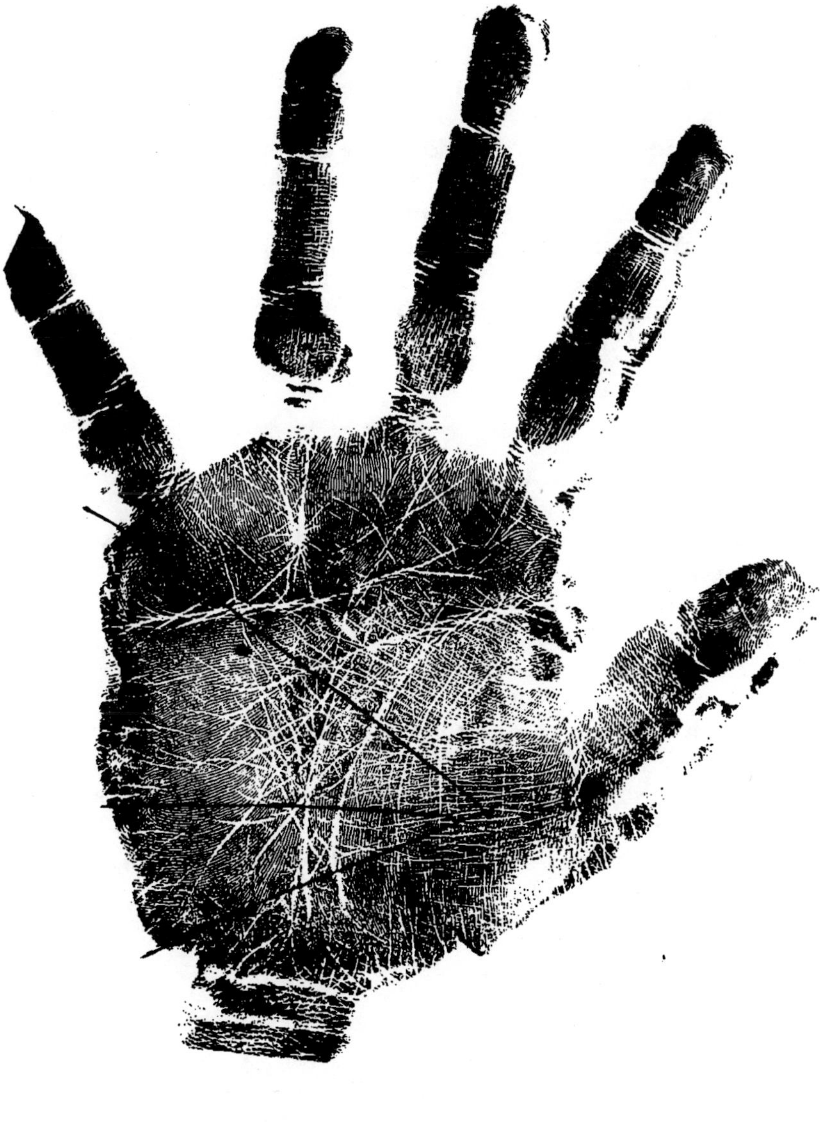

There are as many as three Rings of Solomon which point towards interest in spirituality and the occult. There is a tendency towards religion but it would come into play after the age of 50, because the Line of Saturn is well-defined in that age. There is a large island at the base of the right thumb, a twisted line in the left and also one long and one short line on the Mount of Venus near the base of the thumb. It signifies many children, one of whom would cooperate with the man till the end of his days. Many lines at the end of the Heart Line also indicate multiplicity of progeny.

The upshot of the foregoing is that it is a good hand which shows a comfortable financial position after middle age. But for this he would have to struggle hard. He should concentrate on one field instead of many if he wants to get recognition and fame. That would result in improvement in the lines on the Mount of Apollo. The remedies have been indicated above. For the improvement in the Heart Line he should do good to others but not expect anything in return. Remembering the good that one does leads to disappointments because one does not get the expected return or response from those for whom one has done something. That leads to a psychological trauma. He should constantly keep his blood pressure and the eyes under medical supervision.

Handprint 5-A, B

This handprint belongs to a young woman of 24, who works for a firm, but wants a change for better service prospects.

The mounts of Luna, Venus and Aggressive Mars are underdeveloped. The other mounts are normal. The little finger is short and is in low setting. There are islands on the area between the phalanges of the two thumbs and a chain at the base of the thumb. There is one line of sexuality in the right hand which is inclined towards the Heart Line. In the left hand there are three short lines of sexuality.

Since her active hand is the right one, we should concentrate on that.

The Line of Life is defective till the age of 21 and has emerged from the Head Line. Till that time she has suffered from an inferiority complex and has kept indifferent health. The Line of Life ends towards the Mount of Luna, which points towards travel abroad. To know when that would become a possibility look at the fact that the Line of Saturn emerges at age 31 as a branch of the Line of Life. That is the time when her wish to travel to foreign lands would be fulfilled.

Between the Mounts of Venus and Luna, a small line has emerged towards the Mount of Saturn. The time when it emerged was the age of 21 years. That was time when she got the job. Between the ages of 24 and 26 there is an indistinct island on this line. The upper part of the island touches the Line of Saturn. Another Line of Saturn has emerged from the Mount of Luna at 22 years, the time when this lady got married. Because of the second Line of Saturn the fault caused by the island on the first one has been removed which means that there is financial gain between the ages of 24 and 26 but with some difficulties.

From the under side of the Line of Life, that is from the Mount of Venus, a combined Line of Mercury and Sun has emerged. The period when it intersects the Line of Life is between 55 and 60 years of age, calculated according to the length of the Line of Life. There is an island adjacent to the Line of Life, which means loss of health during that period, but the line continues upto 70 years which means that her health would improve and she would live upto 70, in full health.

The time when this Line of Mercury/Sun has emerged from under the Line of Life is 18 years, according to the rule of the Line of Saturn. From 18 to 23 years this line remains within the Line of Life. This is the period of pressures of the family. After 24 this line separates from the Line of Life and upto age 35 it is distinct and goes towards the Mount of Mercury. Her business sense is strong during this period which means that she can occupy a high place in a business organisation. After that age the line is broken up and goes towards the Mount of Mercury. She must be careful about fluctuations in her health and particularly disease of the middle of her body, especially the stomach. A look at the Line of Mercury one should answer this lady that the time has come for her to change her place of service if she wants better prospects, because during this period the Line of Mercury separates from the Line of Life and a line of Saturn emerging from the Mount of Luna is well-defined and distinct between the ages of 23 and 24. This line supports the Line of Mercury. Between the ages of 24 and 35 there are crosses, squares and triangles between the Line of Saturn and the Line of Life. The combined effect of this is that financial sources would become available, but worries would also persist. Even so she is being advised to take up a new career.

In order to see the area of difficulties, have a look at the line of sexuality and the Line of Mars. A broken Line of Mars and a downward line of sexuality points to marital problems. After the age of 35, the two lines of Saturn merge into one. After that there is an axe line which points to financial gain but the persistence of family troubles. The reason for that is the interference by some outsider in the marital relations of the lady. But, it would be better not to tell her this at this stage.

The area in the middle of the palm representing the age between 28 and 36 years is depressed and has not come out clearly in the handprint. The lines have, therefore, been drawn with a pen. Two lines of Saturn and one Line of Mercury passes through this area. Because of the depression in the palm the favourable effect of the lines is reduced by half. The result is that this lady would have marital problems but also benefit financially.

The Heart Line is defective and is near the Head Line, which means that the lady is less than normally sentimental. She has a pragmatic outlook and knows which side of the bread is buttered.

A defective Heart Line points to bad health. On the area above the Line of

6-A, The Right Hand
Many of the branches of the Line of Life going upwards.

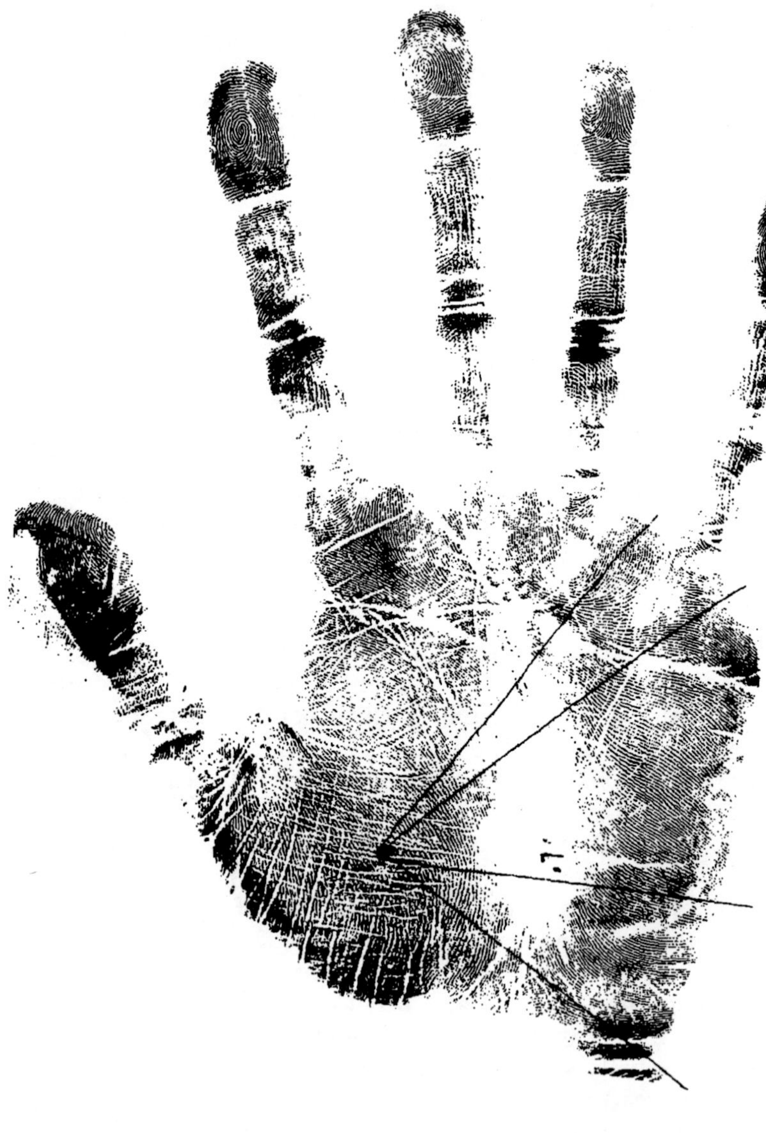

6-B, The Left Hand
The Ring of Solomon in the left hand is distinct, but in the right it is broken.

Heart, near the base of the fingers, the mounts are criss-crossed with broken lines which point towards problems to be faced after middle age. If remedial action is taken now, the evil effect of this state of affairs can be modified.

On the upper and the middle part of the Mount of Luna there are broken oblique lines which should make this lady beware of disorders of the chest and stomach. We have already pointed towards the fault in the Mount of Mercury.

Too many lines on the palm point towards the hyperactivity of the nervous system which might lead to insomnia and hypertension. She should take to meditation and watching her breath and keep her blood pressure under medical check-ups.

There are many lines of progeny on the Mount of Venus near the base of the thumb, but they are not distinct, but there are three well-defined islands on the wavy line at the base of the thumb which point towards the fact that she can have three children.

The island between the two phalanges of the thumb reduces the virulence of Saturn; in other words, opportunities for financial gain would continue to be available. The upshot of the whole thing is that this is the hand of a disturbed woman. In spite of financial resources, there will not be any happiness in life. If she takes to the remedies suggested she would get peace of mind. The opportunities for progress would, of course, arise in her life.

Handprint 6-A, B

The handprint belongs to a 36-years old, prosperous businessman. His active hand is the right one.

Fingers when spread remain closer to each other than they normally do. The little finger is long and the mounts of Mercury and Defensive Mars are under-developed. The Mount of Venus is over-developed, the state of development of other mounts being normal. There is an island between the two phalanges of the thumb. There are three lines of sexuality in each hand which are long and they incline towards the Heart Line.

The fact that there is not much distance between the fingers shows that the man does not easily change his views. The Mount of Mercury is under-developed, but the length of the little finger offsets that defect. The Line of Mercury which has emerged from the Line of Saturn supports this view. He has a good business sense.

The Line of Life has many branches; they are all inclined towards the Mount of Jupiter. The multiplicity of lines points to overweaning ambition, but it also shows lack of concentration of any one objective which rarely leads to the achievement of any of them.

A branch of the Line of Life goes towards the Mount of Luna at age 42. It has an island. This is an indication of change of place which will not be happy because of the island.

In the right hand the main Line of Saturn starts in the 22nd year of life: it could be a time of marriage or entry into business.

The Line of Mercury emerges from the Line of Saturn in the 30th year of life. It goes towards the middle of the area between the mounts of Mercury and Apollo. This is good both for business and fame. Going a little further the line vanishes into many small lines which are bunched together and then becomes indistinct. This indicates the possibility of diseases caused by flatulence or those of the stomach and the intestines.

Another Line of Saturn emerges out of the Line of Life as its branch in the 35th year. After that year an axe line runs with the earlier line of Saturn and continues till the 50th year. Because of a line parallel to the Line of Saturn, the fault caused by the axe line tends to be reduced. It shows progress but with some struggle.

Another Line of Mercury emerges from below the Line of Life, (towards the Mount of Venus) cuts across the Line of Saturn and then stops. This line intersects the Line of Life in the 60th year and later, the latter line is broken. But another segment of the line of Life covers this break and it continues till the 70th year. It means that in the 60th year there would be a change but that would not be happy. It seems that the man will live beyond the 70th year.

The Line of Saturn coming from the Mount of Luna, the second Line of Mercury and the Line of Life going towards the Mount of Luna form a triangle between the Line of Saturn and the Line of Life. This triangle lies in the area of Saturn and according to the rule applying to this line for calculating the age, it occurs between the 22nd, the 30th year which means acquisition of wealth and property in that period. The Head Line is good and is inclined towards the Mount of Luna. It shows that the man would use his imagination in business. A good Head Line shows that he should have wealth and the island between the two phalanges of the thumb supports it.

There are many triangles in the left hand in addition to two signs of the fish. These are good both for wealth and knowledge. The effect of the lines of the left hand is considered to be half that of the right hand lines.

The Heart Line is defective and one of its branches intersects or cuts across the Line of Saturn, the Head Line and the Line of Life and goes towards the Aggressive Mars. If you have a look at the lines of sexuality they are three in number and are inclined towards the Heart Line. The Line of Mars is indistinct and their is a grill on the developed Mount of Venus: the combined effect of all these signs is that there would be extra-marital relations and marital discord. If you look for confirmation you would find that the Line of Saturn in the left hand has another supplementary Line of Saturn emerging from the upper part of the Mount of Luna which meets the main Line of Saturn in the 40th year. If you look at the lines of sexuality and other signs you can say that the extra-marital relations should begin in the 30th year and continue upto the 40th year.

There are two forks in the Heart Line in the right hand and it ends in many forks. He should get a share in patrimony and also children. The vertical lines on the Mount of Venus near the base of the thumb show many children. But two are clear from both the hands and both the children would be helpful to their parents.

7-A, The Right Hand
A star between the mounts of Saturn and Apollo; the Line of Saturn is broken in the middle.

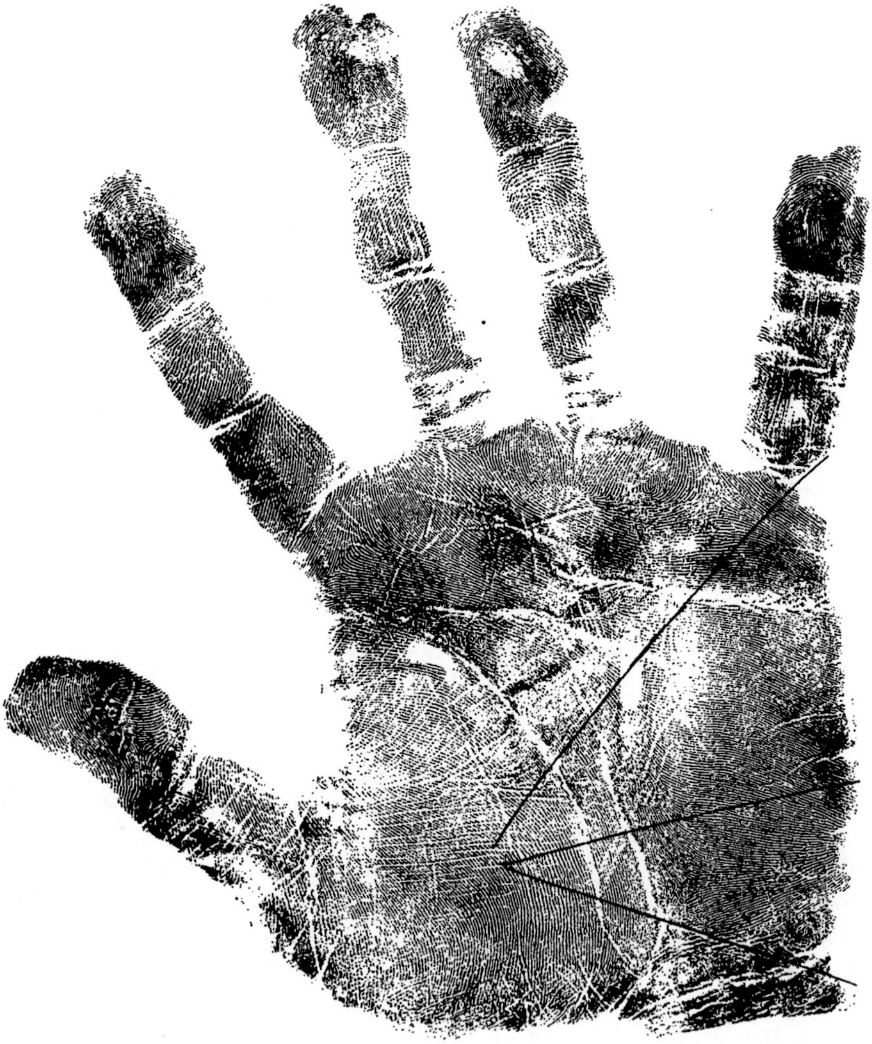

7-B, The Left Hand
A Saw toothed Line of Life of Saturn fragmented at many places.

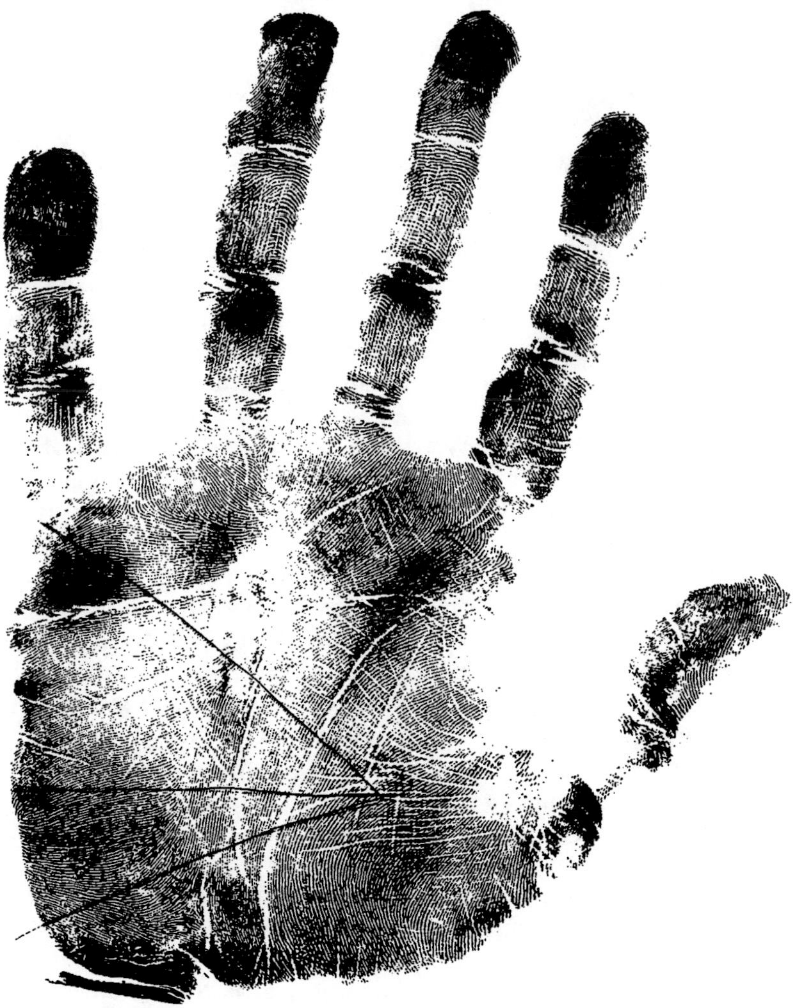

There is a depression in the Heart Line on the right palm. This is composed of segments. This person should get his blood pressure and the heart checked up regularly. The effect of these signs becomes apparent in the 60th year from the Line of Life. He should practise the digital posture designed to strengthen the heart.

The Ring of Solomon in both the hands shows tendency towards the occult. The man admitted that he is interested in spirituality, astrology and palmistry.

The upshot of the whole thing is that the hand shows possibilities of both wealth and knowledge, but is defective if one takes the marital life into account. If he wears an iron ring and also practises the digital postures he should benefit.

Handprint 7-A, B

The handprint belongs to a European male aged 31 years whose active hand is the left one.

The hand is both large and wide. The first phalange of the thumb is long, the fingers are knotty, the index finger is short and the third long. The fingers are inclined towards the middle finger. The mounts of Jupiter, Luna and the Aggressive and the Defensive Mars are under-developed. The mounts of Saturn and Mercury are over-developed. The mounts of Apollo and the Venus are normal in development. There is an island between the two phalanges of the thumb and a chain at its base. There are two straight lines of sexuality in the right hand. There is one such line in the left hand and that is inclined towards the Heart Line.

The large, wide palm points towards the fact that he is a man of action and is also able to go into the finer details of things. The first phalange of the thumb is longer than the second and the ring finger is longer than the index finger. Both these signs point towards a tendency to take risks. The Mount of Saturn is generally depressed but in this hand it is developed and because the fingers are inclined towards the middle one, the effect of Saturn is enhanced. The man is fond of solitude. The fingers are knotty, the Mount of Mercury is developed, the Mount of Jupiter under-developed. The index finger is short and the Heart Line is indistinct. All these signs point towards a tendency to put personal profit before principles: there is no sentimentality in the man.

An under-developed Mount of Luna and a developed Mount of Mercury shows a tendency for change of place. A sign of the fish on the palm shows the possibility of foreign travel. The combined effect of all these signs is that this youngman, born in Czechoslovakia, affiliated to a spiritual organisation goes about the world propagating its philosophy but the signs of the hand indicate that he is not basically spiritual.

We read the handprint taking his left hand as the main one.

On the inside of the Line of Life (that is towards the Mount of Venus and the Aggressive Mars) there are teeth like those of a saw and the segments of the Line of Mars overlap. A line of influence from the island on the Mount of Venus crosses the Line of Mars. The Heart Line in the right hand has islands, but the one on the left hand is broken. There are islands in the Head Line. The Line of Saturn is broken at many places but its segments overlap. These signs taken in conjunction with the fact that the line of sexuality in the left hand is inclined downwards, one can say that many women have come in contact with this youngman, but he is prone to severe relations with one the moment he comes in contact with the next. He has no sentimental attachments with anybody.

There is an island in the beginning of the Line of Life and the Line of Saturn is forked in the beginning. These signs show lack of guardianship of the parents till the age of 21. That is probably the reason why he has left home and the long third finger and the long first phalange of the thumb has helped him to succeed in his designs.

From the age of 21 to 29 years there is a sign of the fish which shows a tendency towards acquisition of knowledge and studies during that period. India, for him, is a foreign country. The Line of Saturn is broken in the year 29 and that shows change of residence. Also change of beloveds/lovers. The man has accepted both these things. From the age of 33 to 35 there is another change in the Line of Saturn. That is the answer to his question: whether he would go to Singapore. The answer is that the possibility would arise between the ages of 33 and 35.

At age 40, one Line of Saturn ends at the Head Line and re-emerges from another point on that line. That is an indication that his whole life style might change. He would give up the garb of spiritualism in that age and revert to his status as a lay man. He would marry and settle down at one place.

The left palm has a depression between the ages of 33 and 42, a similar depression in the right palm is between the ages of 32 and 40. The depression is under the Mount of Apollo. Looking at the depression in the left palm one can say that there is possibility of his getting ill-fame between the years 33 and 42. He must improve the Mount of Jupiter to ward off that possibility. Wearing a topaz might do the trick.

In the year 45 the Line of Saturn stops at the Heart Line. Slightly away from that point another line starts which goes to the base of the third finger. That means that the golden period of his life starts after 45.

In the right palm, the Heart Line starts from a point between the Mount of Jupiter and the Mount of Saturn and stops at the Mount of Apollo. This forms a star and a triangle. From there a segment of the Heart Line emerges and goes towards the Mount of Mercury. The star on the Mount of Apollo speaks of the possibility of diseases of the eye and hypertension. He should take to the digital posture calculated to strengthen the heart.

In the right hand the Line of Life becomes indistinct after 63; in the left it becomes indistinct after 70. It shows loss of vitality after the 62nd year. If he takes to the digital posture to strengthen the vitality of his body he can ward off the weakening of vital powers and can enjoy good health till 70.

In spite of the defective Head Line and the Line of Saturn, the island between the two phalanges of the thumb has given him financial security.

8-A, The Right Hand
A small island at the end of the Life of Life. Find another island in this palm.

8-B, The Left Hand
A typical example of a long palm.

The chain like line at the base of the thumb and the forks at the end of the Heart Line show that he has the capacity to father children. These signs would bear fruit after his marriage. The Heart Line has no branches, is indistinct and there are no lines of children on the Mount of Venus near the base of the thumb. That shows that there will not be any sentimental attachments with the children.

Handprint 8-A, B

The handprint belongs to a 28-year old, unmarried youngman working as a clerk in a firm.

The palm is long and the Mount of Venus is over-developed. The mount of Apollo and the Aggressive Mars are under-developed, with the other mounts being normal in development. In both the hands the line of sexuality is near the base of the little finger rather than near the Heart Line.

The main question he asks is about his marriage and career and his active hand is the right one.

The long palm speaks of his love for planning and tends to reduce his activities or the capacity to act. The line of sexuality is away from the Heart Line, nearer the little finger and his marriage therefore, is likely to occur in his 30th year. But one cannot make a prediction on the basis of this sign alone, but should look at the other lines too.

The main Line of Saturn emerges from the middle of the Mount of Luna at age 27. There was possibility of marriage in that year, but it did not materialise because there is a segment parallel to that line which runs with the Line of Saturn from 27th to 28th year. This segment speaks of his love affairs. He rejected the proposals of marriage made to him in that year. His beloved married somebody else which led to his being in a state of dejection for some time. Later on, he agreed to marry, but he could not get the right type of bride. This fact he has accepted as true.

Failure in love is evidenced from the gap in the Line of Saturn between the ages of 29 and 30. In his left hand their is an island in this line at that age which is formed by the three sides -- the Line of Life, the Line of Saturn and the Line of Mercury.

In the right hand, the Line of Saturn emerges at age 31 as a branch of the Line of Life. That is the time for marriage. In the year 32 another Line of Saturn emerges from the Line of Life. This line is distinct and well-defined which points to some special achievement. (NOTE: At the time this book went to the press the man came to see me again when his age was 32. He told me that he married in his 30th year and that his wife was expecting.) It is now clear that special achievement was his marriage/child.

After having answered this main question we go to the other lines. The Line of Life is thick at places and thin at others. It is not circular as it should be. The Head Line is short. These are signs of struggle and financial stringency. Even so things have improved after 32 because there are two Lines of Saturn in that age. One is the main Line of Saturn which emerges from the Mount of

Luna -- it stops a person from doing anything improper. The other is the Line of Saturn which emerges as a branch of the Line of Life. Till age 42 these two lines run parallel to each other. That shows that in spite of struggles the period between 32 and 42 would be a happy time.

The period between 42 and 50 is full of both struggles and achievements. Struggles are indicated by an axe line which runs parallel to the Line of Saturn and which makes an island in that age. From the Heart Line a branch moves towards the Mount of Apollo which signifies that the person would succeed after some struggle.

The Line of Saturn is distinct after 50 and there are vertical lines at the base of the finger. That is why there would not be any financial troubles in old age.

The Heart Line is defective, but the Girdle of Venus supports it. The Girdle acts as a parallel line to the Heart Line. The heart and the general health of the person would be good.

Let us see the number of children he is likely to have and his span of life. There are two distinct lines on the Mount of Venus near the base of the thumb which speak of two children who would be a source of happiness for the parents. The fact that the Mount of Venus is over-developed and the Heart Line is forked at the end, supports this view.

In the Line of Life there is an island between the ages of 60 and 65, which speak of loss of health in this period. It would be advisable for him to take care of his health from now onwards. He should use the digital postures calculated to strengthen one's vital force. He should also control his sexual urges. These remedies would ensure a healthy life till the age of 75.

Handprint 9-A, B

The handprint belongs to a famous 67-year old doctor whose active hand is the right one.

The hand is broad and heavy, the first phalange of the thumb is short and the little-finger is short and placed in a low setting. The Mount of Mercury is depressed, but the other mounts are normal. There is an incomplete line between the two phalanges of the thumb. There is a chain like line at the base of the thumb. The lines on the right palm are better as compared to those on the left one. That means that the man has improved his luck due to his own efforts. The evil effects of these signs are reduced because the hand is heavy. We read the hand keeping these things in view.

The Line of Life is thick and incomplete. There is an incomplete line between the two phalanges of the thumb. Both these signs speak of family complications. Having known this fact we turn to other signs.

The Line of Mars is just not there. That shows that the man has no sentimental attachments, nor does he expect any cooperation from any quarter. The Heart Line is thick and segmented, having emerged from the base of the middle finger. That shows that even to satisfy his sexuality he thinks only of his own pleasure. The depressions indicate that health might be adversely affected because of psychological traumas.

9-A, The Right Hand
The Line of Life in both the hands is short, but when this man came to consult me he was 67.

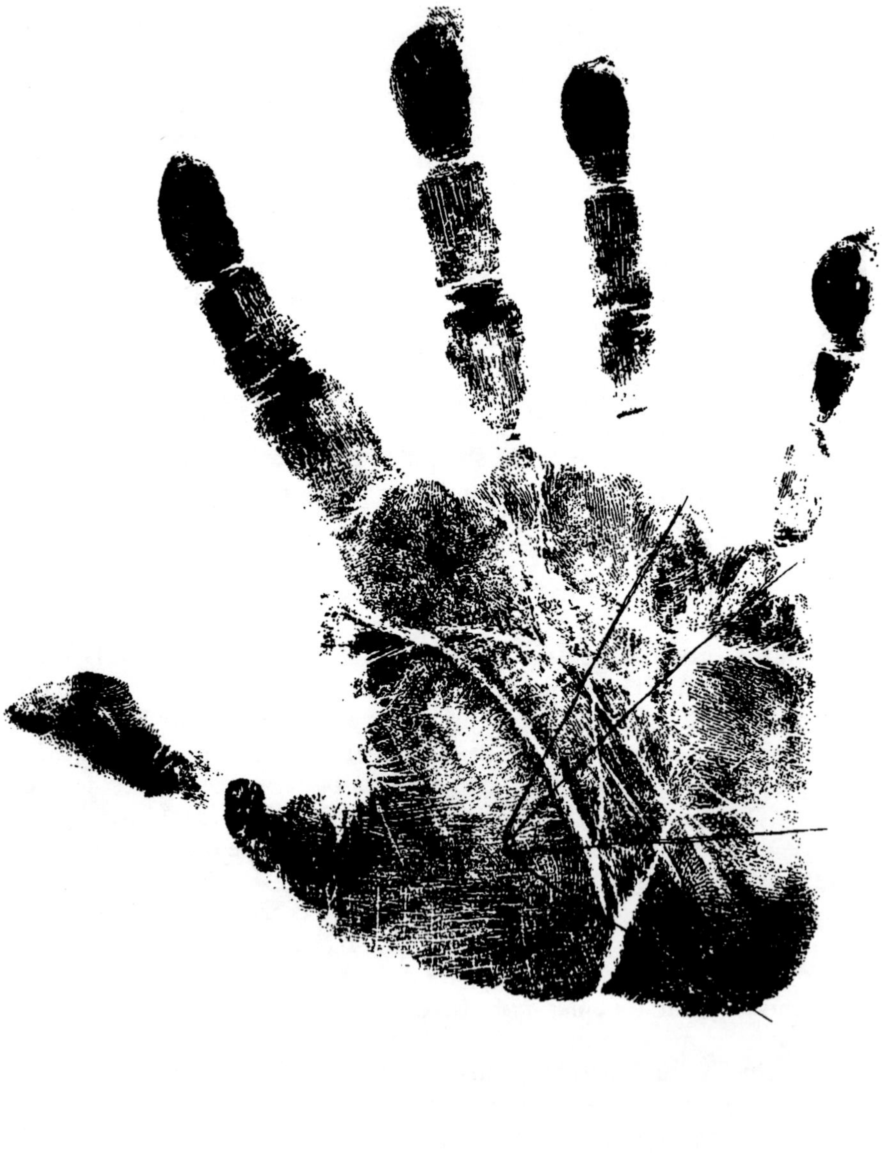

9-B, The Left Hand
Looking at the Line of Life in both the hands you can say that age is not apparent only from this line.

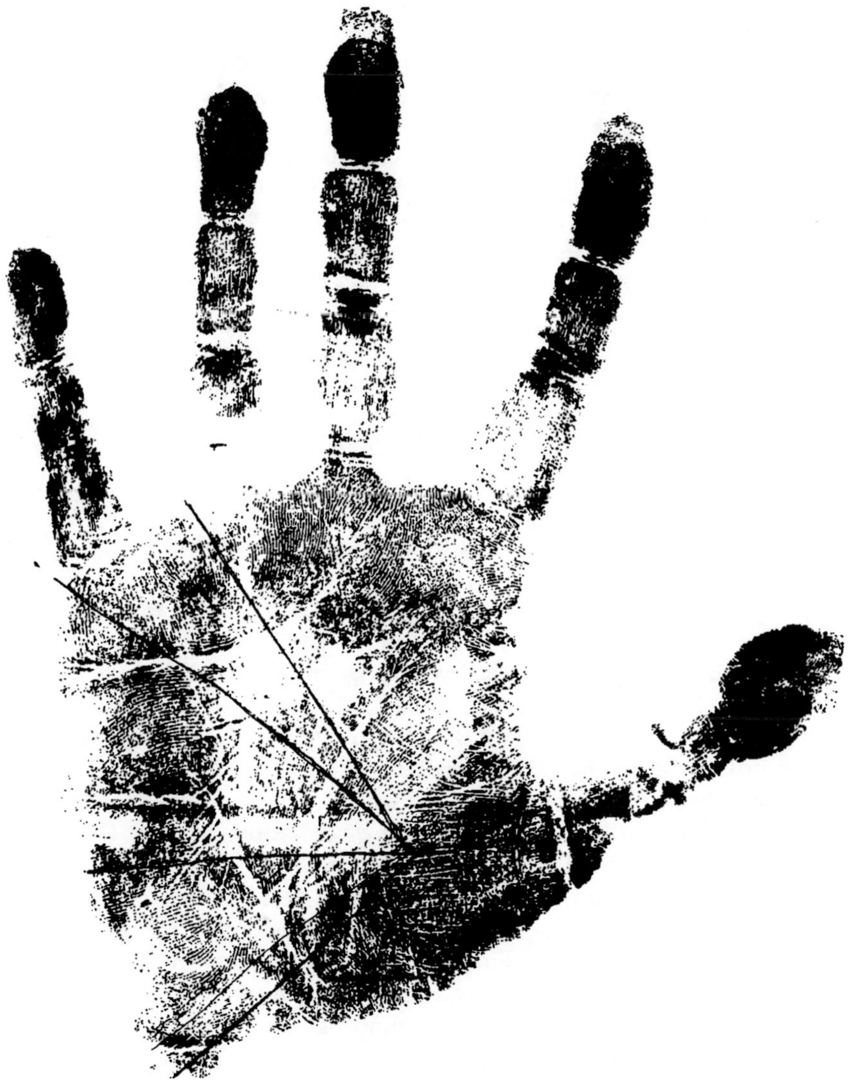

There are many Lines of Saturn in the right hand. The first of them emerges from the Line of Mercury at the age of 21. It is segmented and meets the Line of Life in his 28th year. At first sight it looks like a downward branch of the Line of Life. At 28 a clear and well-defined Line of Saturn emerges from the Line of Life. This man married at the age of 21, but the marriage was not successful. His medical practice started when he was 28.

An indistinct Line of Saturn has emerged from the Mount of Luna at the age of 27 and meets the other line of the same name (which emerged from the Line of Life) in his 36th year. This indicates a love affair which was surreptitious in the beginning but has become open at the age of 36 when his paramour started living in his home without having married him. He has got a bad name because of this. This fact is confirmed from the Line of the Sun in both the hand -- it is composed of fragments and is intersected by oblique/horizontal lines at many places. It shows financial gain, but also a bad name.

The Sun Line in the left hand is strange looking. At first sight it appears that a fork of the Head Line is inclined towards the Mount of Luna and is forming a sort of tassel. But, if you look closely, you would find that it is the Line of the Sun and has emerged from the Mount of Luna like a terraced line. It improves in his 35th year. That means that society has accepted his second involvement with another woman.

A short little finger in a low setting, undeveloped Mount of Mercury etc. show that the man is of a simple nature. It was not he, but his paramour who took the initiative. He is carrying on with her, nevertheless. And for this he has to face opposition from his legally-wedded wife, family and children. This has led to disintegration of his family life.

The hand is heavy; all the mounts except Mercury are normally developed and there is the sign of the fish in the middle of the palm formed by the Line of Mercury, the Line of Life and the two lines of Saturn. The Line of Life is circular which speaks of a comfortable financial situation.

The Line of Saturn and the Line of the Sun above the Heart Line are thin and distinct. It removes the fault of the short Line of Life. It signifies that he would have a comfortable old age, but, the Line of Life ends at age 60 in both the palms. It means only one thing: there would be a family crisis at that age. He tells me that he has three children by the first wife, which leads to quarrels. There is danger of a heart ailment in that age, evidenced by a depression in the Heart Line at that age. The horizontal line on the Mount of Luna speaks of possibility of diseases located in the middle of the body, especially the stomach.

A broken line of intuition has emerged from the Mount of Luna which ends at the Heart Line. It only signifies that the man has a rich imagination. A thick Line of Mercury emerges from the Mount of Venus in both the palms and continues upto 30 years without touching the Line of Life. Instead of being inimical to the Line of Life it supports it; in other words, it completes the incomplete Line of Life. From that one can conclude that the man would have a long life.

This view is supported by the fact that the Line of the Sun and of Saturn both reach the base of the fingers.

A chain at the base of the thumb, the Heart Line forked at the end and two lines on the Mount of Venus near the base of the thumb speak of two children, but they are thin and that means that there is little chance of happiness resulting from the fact of having two children.

He should use the digital posture designed to strengthen the heart and wear an emerald. It would offset the evil effects of the above hand signs.

Handprint 10-A, B

The handprint belongs to a youth of 28 years. It is a heavy hand of which the thumb is large, its second phalange is longer and there is a well-defined island between the phalanges. There is a string of islands clearly visible at the base of the thumb. Except the Mount of Luna all the mounts are developed. The fingers are knotty, the middle finger is inclined towards the third finger and vice versa. The line of sexuality is downwards and the active hand is the right one.

The hand is heavy and wide. Such a person is given to action and is lucky. The fact that the middle and the third fingers are inclined towards one another shows a vaccilating nature, but this effect is offset by a large thumb which signifies lots and lots of common sense. The fact that the second phalange of the thumb is longer speaks of the capacity to think in addition to being active. The lines on the right hand are better than those on the left. It means that there is a tendency towards the auspicious.

The challenging element in this hand is the fact that at first sight it appears that the Line of Life is short and the Line of Saturn has two forks in the beginning.

A Line of Saturn with two forks in the beginning signifies a life of want in childhood and also deprivation in the matter of love from parents. But since I know the person from childhood I was surprised because facts belie this conclusion. I studied the lines again and found my error.

In fact the Line of Saturn has merged with the Line of Life in the beginning. What appeared to be a fork of the Line of Saturn turning towards the Mount of Venus is in fact the last part of the Line of Life which encircles the Mount of Venus. And the Line of Saturn representing the age between 21 and 28 years is connected to the Line of Life through a fork of the latter line.

At the age of 28 years the Line of Saturn has a fork which connects it with the Line of Life. Later on it separates from the Line of Life and goes towards the Mount of Saturn. This means that upto the age of 21 the man led a wayward life, but later on till the age of 28 years he lived under the discipline of the family. After 28, he regains self-confidence, but because of the thickness of the Line of Saturn he does not succeed in leading an independent life. The time when success starts is the one when he becomes 32. At that point of time

10-A, The Right Hand
Notice in this palm the Line of Saturn which is thick, but which thins out later- a typical example.

10-B, The Left Hand
Is this Line of Life incomplete and the Line of Saturn forked in the beginning?

another Line of Saturn emerges from the Defensive Mars and goes towards the Mount of Saturn. Another Line of Saturn is thick till it reaches the Head Line. It crosses the Head Line in the 35th year and becomes thin. The first Line of Saturn ends at the Head Line in that year. The two Lines of Saturn, placed as they are, signify that when he reaches 32, he would enter business in partnership with an outsider and would also continue the family business till the age of 34. After 35 he would continue with the latter business and would sever his relations with the family business.

After the Heart Line a vertical line tends to reach a point in the middle of the base of the fingers (the third and the middle one). It signifies a combination of financial gain and success after 55.

There will not be any shortage of finances because there is an island between the two phalanges of the thumb and the Line of Life is circular.

Let us now look at the other lines. A fork of the Line of Life reaches the Mount of Jupiter which shows that his ambitions would be fulfilled and he would also get patrimony. We now look at the significance of the segment of the Line of Life which is a part of the Line of Saturn. We would apply the rule pertaining to the calculation of age from the Line of Life. Also we have to see its relevance to the Line of Mars. The Line of Mars is non-existent during the ages of 35 and 55 and the lines of sexuality incline towards the Heart Line. This line emerges again at 55 and supports the Line of Life till the age of 75. That means that there would be differences of opinion with the spouse between the years of 35 and 55. There would be a reconciliation later and the man would live to be 75.

I did not think it proper to tell the man about the quarrels between the ages of 35 and 55, but have told him that he would face family problems in this period, which would vanish later in life. The fact of a downward inclined line of sexuality and a line of Mars being in the middle probably signify that his wife might not live long or that she might not keep good health. The re-emergence of the Line of Mars after some time might also speak of a second marriage, but it is not good to make that forecast.

The Head Line is clear till the middle of the palm and later it becomes indistinct and goes to the Defensive Mars. Looking at the basic tendencies of the man one can say that the later portion of this line would also become distinct. The tendencies become apparent from the fact that the lines of the right palm are better than those of the left. The Head Line shows an excellent intellect and wealth.

A cross on the Mount of Luna points towards lack of mental peace and disorders of the stomach. Coming from the lower part of Mount of Luna, an oblique line reaches the middle of the palm and this signifies desire for travel. The time when this desire would be fulfilled would come after 35 when the Line of Saturn thins out.

The Heart Line is thin in the beginning and starts from below the Mount of Jupiter, a sign of a sympathetic nature. The latter portion of the line is thick and has islands over it. This is supported by the Line of Life between the ages of 35 and 55. It shows differences of opinion with the wife. He should take to the digital posture designed to strengthen the heart to remove this defect.

The branches of the Heart Line go to the Head Line which signifies greater pull of the mind. It means that the man is pragmatic. A parallel line over the Heart Line between the Line of Saturn and the Mount of Jupiter point towards a good financial position and also prestige. This time would come after 32.

A tassel at the end of the Heart Line and three clear islands at the base of the thumb show that he would have three sons. Two of them have been born and the third is a possibility. But, if he takes to family planning and does not want another child that would be a different matter.

The upshot of the whole thing is that this is the handprint of a man who progresses constantly. Between the years of 35 and 55 there might be a marital problem for some time which would vanish ultimately. If he takes to the practice of the digital posture to strengthen the heart he will be healthy till the age of 75.

Handprint 11-A, B

The handprint belongs to a young lady of 25 whose active hand is the right one. The question she asks is about when her marriage would take place.

The palm is long and the second phalange of the thumb is longer. There is a broken island between the two phalanges. There are one and a half islands on the line on the base of the thumb. The little finger is in a low setting and is long. The Mounts of Jupiter and Mercury are specially developed. The Aggressive Mars is under-developed and the other mounts are of normal development.

The palm being long and the second phalange of the thumb being longer than the first are both signs which show a weakening of resolve and an increase in mental activity. A long little finger and a developed Mount of Mercury show that she is clever. But the developed Mount of Jupiter adds an element of idealism, which would save her from taking to wicked ways.

There are many inauspicious signs in the left hand, e.g., there is an island in the beginning of the Head Line and another between the Line of Life and the Head Line. An island is formed by the Line of Life and the Line of Mars. Another island is formed by the beginning of the Line of Mercury, the end of the Line of Life and a line of influence. There is still another island at the end of the Head Line.

The lines on the right palm are better than those on the left. It means that there is a tendency towards the auspicious. The effect of the islands on the left palm is half of what it normally is. The last island between the Line of Life and the Line of Mars on the left palm is at the age of 28.

There is an island on the Line of Life on the right palm till the age of 21. There are signs that the troubles and problems would lessen after that period, but the effect of the islands on the left palm would persist till the age of 28.

11-A, The Right Hand
How different are the right and the left hands?

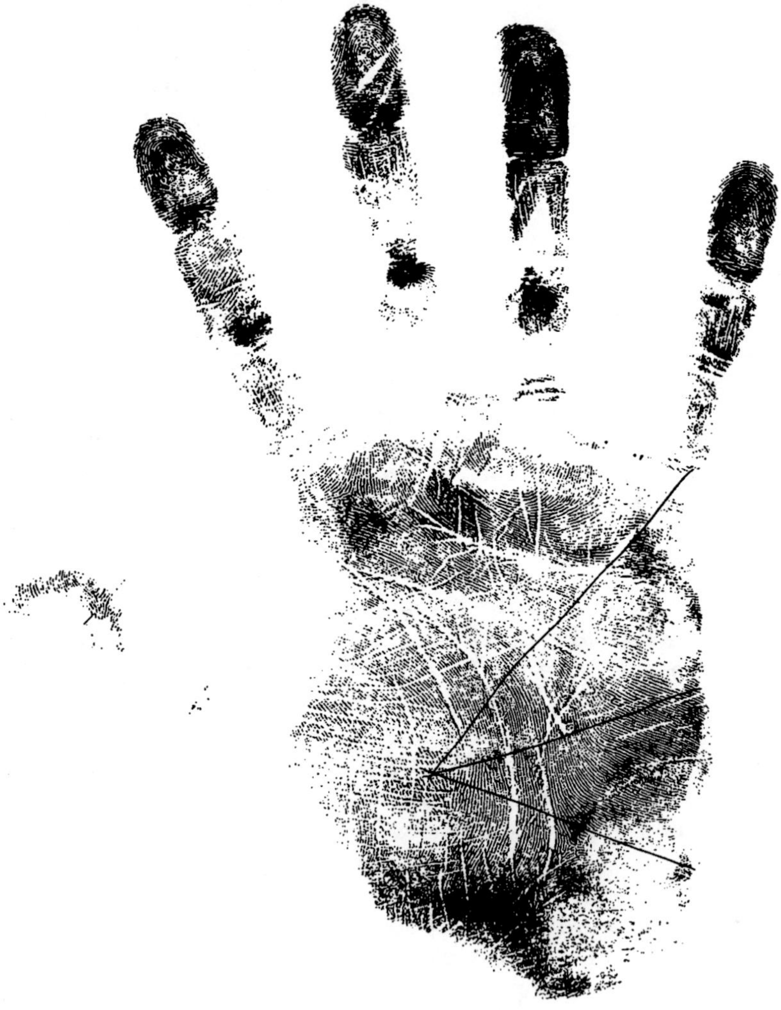

11-B, The Left Hand
Identify and count the number of islands in this palm.

Remedies to offset the effects of the island would have to be used. The girl is religious -- she would benefit if she worships Lord Shiva and his consort the Goddess Parvati and keeps fast on Mondays and during Navaratras. That would give her peace of mind and the inauspicious effects would be offset.

Let us now look at the right hand. The Line of Saturn has emerged in the 20th year of her life. At this age the girl took up a part time job in addition to her studies. The reason was that the social milieu in which she lives favours a working girl as a bride.

A line of influence emerges from the Line of Life and merges with the Line of Saturn at age 26. That means that marriage is a possibility in that year. This Line of Saturn ends in the 29th year but before that, in the 28th year, a line of influence goes towards the Mount of Mercury. This line reaches near a second Line of Saturn to form a triangle, branches out in two forks and ends. This second Line of Saturn starts from near the Defensive Mars in the 29th year. The line of influence going towards the Mount of Mercury form a triangle with the Line of Saturn in the year 29, which is a sure sign that the girl should marry. But, if she had taken remedial action the marriage could take place in the 26th year.

A branch of the second Line of Saturn goes towards the Mount of Apollo, which is a sure sign of success or some achievement. Another Line of Saturn has emerged at age 35 from the Line of Life which ends at the Head Line. The Line of Saturn from the Line of Life indicates a limited achievement, but the other Line of Saturn which has emerged from the Defensive Mars goes further and as it does, it gets support from the supplementary line. Above the Heart Line are two clear lines of Sun which will give success and fame at the age of 50. In fact the period when success and achievements would start commences from the 29th year.

The line of influence coming from the Aggressive Mars intersects the upward lines, but these lines, in addition to producing obstructions are also forming squares which would remove those obstructions. This means that all achievements would come after struggle.

The Head Line on the left hand is defective upto the age of 21. After that it is clear and straight and goes to the Defensive Mars. It indicates a pragmatic nature. The line of influence from the Aggressive Mars intersects it but it also forms squares and triangles. This may cause problems, but no evil would result.

The Heart Line is forked in the beginning and some of its branches are going towards the Head Line, but they do not touch it. That shows that the sentimental side of her nature is stronger but since it is inclined towards the Head Line, she would be pragmatic. Islands on the Heart Line speak of emotional traumas and she should undertake the exercise of digital postures designed to strengthen the heart. A small parallel segment over the Heart Line gives it support and would provide protection against emotional traumas. It is also auspicious from a financial point of view. The time when this girl is likely to have lots and lots of money would be the 34th and the 35th year, because it is at that time that the Line of the Sun emerges from the Line of Saturn.

The Line of Mars is becoming indistinct in the year 36. It signifies marital problems in that age. Another parallel line of Mars tends to support it which shows that there would be another person who would help the family. It is in this age that the Line of Sun emerges from the Line of the Saturn. It will tend to reduce the fault of the Line of Mars.

At the base of the thumb there are three vertical lines on the Mount of Venus and also one and a half islands at the same place mean that the girl is likely to have three children, out of whom one son and one daughter would help her till the end of her days.

The upshot of the whole thing is that the bad days would start ending from the year 26. After that there would constant progress and happiness. The pace of progress will increase after the year 35 and after the age of 50 most of her desires will be fulfilled.

The Line of Life on the right hand goes till the 70th year. The ascending lines reach the mounts of Saturn and the Sun. She would, therefore, live upto the 75th year. If remedies are taken recourse to, the benefits might start accruing from the year 29.

Handprint 12-A, B

This belongs to a boy of 17. This is the time in life when one has many questions to which he wants answers. We shall try to answer all of them.

The active hand is the right one and it is wide and heavy. There are vertical stripes on the nails, the thumb is short and there is an incomplete island between its two phalanges. There is a chain at the base of the thumb. The Mount of Venus is over-developed. In the fingerprints there are 6 whorls, two double loops, one closed loop and one loop. The Mount of Jupiter is under-developed, the other mounts being of normal development. In the right hand there are two long lines of sexuality which are looking downwards. In the left hand there are two such lines, the upper one is longer and downward looking and the lower one is short, but straight.

Two double loops in the fingerprints and the second phalange of the thumb being longer are signs of a person who is constantly in a dilemma. A short thumb indicates lack of commonsense and six whorls are signs of a person who must have his way. We should now look at the lines keeping these signs in mind.

The Line of Mercury, Saturn and the Head Line have, after many disturbances gone in the directions in which they should. This shows fluctuations and a state of indecision. Many ascending forks of the Line of life point towards the tendency to attempt many things. They also show lack of concentration on any particular task. All these signs are of a person who is indecisive. Vertical strips on the nails are rare in this age and they mean that the boy is suffering from tension.

Now for the information that he has himself supplied: there is a large family business and the family is waiting for him to complete his education and join

12-A, The Right Hand
Count the ascending branches of the Line of Life in both the hands.

12-B, The Left Hand
identify the Lines of Saturn, Mercury and the Sun in both the hands.

it. But the boy has other ideas. But he is not clear about what he should do.

Since it is the right hand which is active, we should, in the main, concentrate on it.

The Line of Life is circular and the hand is heavy. These two signs tend to convert the inauspicious into the auspicious. The line is forked at the end, one of the forks going towards the Mount of Luna. It shows foreign travel being a possibility. The time when he would undertake it would be the period when the Line of the Sun emerges.

The first segment of the Line of the Sun rises as a branch of the Line of Life. At first sight it looks like the Line of Mercury, but is, in fact, the Line of the Sun. It emerges at age 25. This is the time when the boy would marry. The Line of the Sun goes towards the Mount of Mercury and stops at age 29. Another segment of the line starts in the 30th year. This interregnum of one year is a year of dilemma. The dilemma is whether he should join the family business or strike on his own. He should take to remedial action to remove this dilemma. The remedy is that he should wear a topaz to strengthen the under-developed Mount of Jupiter. That would give him sagacity to solve this dilemma and the above faults would be removed.

The time when achievements and success start is the 30th year of his life, because in this age the ascending branches of the Line of Life are constantly emerging. The Line of Mercury which is parallel to the Line of the Sun emerges in the 32nd year. One segment of the Line of Mercury ends in the 33rd year and a new segment is starting which shows change of business. The Sun Line has vanished in this age which hinders progress. A new Line of Saturn emerges from the Head Line in the 36th year which is supporting the Line of Mercury. The latter line shows a tendency towards amassing wealth rather than gaining a good name. This Line of the Saturn meets the Heart Line and goes to the upper edge of the Mount of Saturn. It is a sign of wealth, but not of any tendency towards charity or benevolence towards one's fellowbeings. After the Head Line, the Line of the Sun is clear. That is a sign that all the dilemmas would vanish after 35. All his desires would be fulfilled after the age of 50. He would get not only wealth, but also fame, because after that age in addition to a clear Sun Line there are two parallel lines on the Mount of Mercury.

The Head Line has many branches. Some of them are going towards the Defensive Mars and others towards the Mount of Luna. But the main branch of the line inclines towards the Mount of Luna. Many forks of the Head Line point towards dilemmas. This period, as we have stated earlier, is between the 29th and the 30th year.

The Heart Line is like a twisted rope. It shows a bad psychological situation and emotional trauma. The Line of Mars is indistinct after the 34th year and this in conjuction with a downward Line of Sexuality means that after the 33rd year there would be discord in matrimonial relations or the health of the wife would be adversely affected.

The over-developed Mount of Venus and two clear lines of progeny on the mount near the base of the thumb indicate that two children would be born.

The Line of Life is long. Its upward branches have gone to the base of the fingers and that means that this person would live to be 80.

Horizontal lines on the Mount of Luna and the defective Heart Line indicate that his health might be indifferent, but who bothers about the possibility of ill-health when he is so young. This is the age when boys and girls see dreams and most of them are pleasant dreams. The heavy hand is auspicious. If he wears a topaz now he would be better able to deal with the dilemmas he would face between the ages of 29 and 30.

Handprint 13-A, B

This is the handprint of a young man of 30 whose active hand is the right one.

It is a firm hand. The colour of the nails is white and they have vertical stripes.

If you look at the fingerprints you would find double loops on both the thumbs. On the fingers there are six whorls and two loops. The nails are of normal size and there are vertical strips over them. The size of the thumb is also normal, with the first phalange being shorter and the second larger. There is a broken line at the junction of the two phalanges and a chain at the base of the thumb. The Aggressive Mars is under-developed, but the other mounts are of normal development. In the right palm there is one straight line of sexuality. In the left there are two forked lines and they look downwards.

A peculiarity of this hand is that instead of the Heart and the Head Line there is only one line. If this single line had been between the normal positions of these lines we could have called it the Simian line, but it is near the place where the Head Line should be and that is why it is the Head Line. In other words we can say that there is no Heart Line in the hand, which means that the person is not sentimental but one who would think of his own interest before he does anything.

Double loops in both the thumbs and the second phalange of the thumb being longer are the signs of a person who is always on the horns of a dilemma. There are six whorts on the fingers and the distance between the points of origin of the Head Line and the Line of Life is more than normal. These signs speak of a person who must have his way. In other words, a person who is indecisive, but wants others to act according to his wishes. This tendency comes in the way of success and is the cause of the lines being faulty.

According to what he himself told me, he has studied upto B.Com. and is working for a firm. He wants to get an M. Com. degree so that he could become a chartered accountant, but he fails every year. But he is determined to get through and get the degree.

His second wish is to leave the job and to start some business venture. He wanted me to tell him whether he should resign his job. We would study the

13-A, The Right Hand
There is no Heart Line in either hand.

13-B, The Left Hand
Look carefully at the Line of Life in both the hands and say whether it is forked at the end or is it something else?

hand signs in view of this query and would also find answers to other possible queries he might have in mind.

The Line of Life is forked in the beginning and is straight upto 21 years. In the left hand the Line of Life is circular in the beginning; in the 21st year one of its branches goes towards the Mount of Jupiter. Both these lines end at the Head Line. It means that there are trouble till the age of 21 from which point things have started improving.

In both the hands, the Line of Mercury starts from within the Line of Life which intersects this line at 55 and then stops. This type of Line of Mercury gives rise to an impression that the Line of Life is forked at the end. It ends, in fact, towards the Mount of Luna.

This could have two interpretations : First the man might travel abroad after the 42nd year because it is then that a line of influence from the Head Line goes to the Line of the Sun and the Line of Saturn gets rid of its fault at that point of time. But the Line of life going to the Mount of Luna has two forks at the end. It means that difficulties might arise during that journey and remedial action should be taken now.

The second interpretation of these signs is that the Line of Mercury intersects the Line of Life between the ages of 50 and 55. A health problem might arise during that period. The man should use the digital posture designed to strengthen the vital force from now onwards.

In the right hand a segment of a line has passed through the Defensive Mars and has gone towards the Line of Saturn. This happens in the 33rd year. This segment forms an incomplete island when it meets the Line of Saturn. This island would show its effect till the 42nd year. He should not undertake any new risks till the age of 42. He should continue doing what he is doing now and should give up the idea of getting an M. Com degree. His lines do not favour such a course of action.

In the left hand the Line of Saturn emerges from the Mount of Luna in the 30th year which is intersected by the lines of influence in the 32nd and the 34th year. A branch going from the Line of Life towards the Mount of Saturn emerges in the 32nd year which becomes indistinct as it goes further. There are prospects of gain in the 32nd year but the gain would not be permanent. This gain should be converted into a bank balance and should be preserved. No risk like a business venture should be undertaken before the 42nd year.

In the space between the Line of Life and the Head Line many lines intersect each other. These result in family troubles which will need a lot of sagacity to deal with. He should start wearing a topaz from now onwards.

In the right hand the branches of the Line of Life going towards the Aggressive Mars, help to strengthen the under-developed Aggressive Mars. The result is that the man never loses courage. A line of influence emerges from the Aggressive Mars and goes towards the Mount of Jupiter. It shows ambition, but, as we have already stated, the time when that ambition would be fulfilled is the 42nd year of life.

The period between the 42nd and the 50th year is the best period of life. In the 50th year a line of influence going towards the Mount of Apollo intersects the Line of Saturn and another parallel line overlaps the broken segment of the line. These three lines form two triangles under the Mount of Saturn, which signify wealth after the 50th year. But, since there is a cross too, difficulties and problems would arise. He must take care of his health in that age because the Line of Mercury intersects the Line of Life. This is the time when he should be careful about his health.

A fragmented oblique line on the Mount of Luna gives a clue towards the diseases to which the man might fall a prey. He must beware of disorders of the throat, the chest and the stomach. The fact that his nails are white in colour speaks of lack of haemoglobin in his blood which he should get examined and the dietary regimen suggested by his physician should be strictly followed. These precautions would remove this fault by the 55th year.

Vertical stripes on the nails speak of the tensions he is labouring under. He should do acts of charity like feeding the birds or helping the poor and should also pray to his favourite deity. If he does this he should have excellent health till the age of 75.

A chain at the base of the thumb and a long and a short line on the Mount of Venus in both the hands under the thumbs speak of many children but only one son and one daughter would be with him till the end of his days.

Handprint 14-A, B

This is the handprint of a 28-year old youth, who is a semi-skilled worker whose active hand is the right one.

The hand is hard, the nails are small with large stripes over them, the thumb is normal with the second phalange larger and the mounts of Jupiter and Apollo, together with the Aggressive Mars are under-developed. Mount of Mercury is developed and the other mounts are normal in development.

Persons with hard hands and small nails do not accept new ideas. The fact that the mounts of Jupiter and Apollo are under-developed and the Mount of Mercury is developed signifies that the man gives pride of place to his own self-interest and that social prestige or fame have no place in his scheme of things.

The main lines and the Line of Mars are thick. The Line of Life in the right hand is straight which, at first sight, appears to be the Line of Saturn and the Line of Life on the left palm is not only straight, but also short. These signs come in the way of the man getting full results from his endeavours. The incomplete Line of Life signifies not only financial but also family problems.

In the right palm the Line of Life has gone upto the Mount of Luna. In the hand of a rich man this could be the sign of travel abroad, but for a poor man, which this man is, even travelling from Bihar to Delhi is like travelling to foreign lands.

The Line of Mars is thick and has two branches which speaks of marital troubles. This line thins out after the 32nd year and remains away from the Line

14-A, The Right Hand
The Line of Life in this hand is likely to confuse one.

14-B, The Left Hand
All the main lines are thick, and the Line of Life is short.

15-A, The Right Hand
A good example of a hand with many lines.

15-B, The Left Hand
All the main lines except the Heart Line are thin.

of Life, which is a sign of another marriage or extra-marital relations.

There are many Lines of Saturn in this hand, but the first Line of Saturn in the right hand emerges from the Mount of Luna in the 22nd year. It vanishes in the 24th year and reappears in the 28th. The period from the 24th to the 28th year is not good either for finances or for the family. After the 28th year the line becomes distinct. In the 29th year the Line of the Sun emerges from the Line of Life and in the 30th a line of Saturn emerges from it. It means that the period after the 28th year is a time of constant gain.

The Line of Saturn which has emerged from the Line of Life disappears at age 40, but the other line which has emerged from the Mount of Luna continues. In the 42nd year the Sun Line emerges from the Head Line. All these signs offset the defects of the incomplete Line of Saturn, but full benefit of the Line of the Sun will not be available because the Mount of Apollo is depressed. It means that he would get the results of his endeavours but it would not be commensurate with the labour put in.

The Head Line and the Line of Life are combined for a long time; they separate at age 21. Till that age the person has suffered from a sense of inferiority. His brain has developed after that point of time. The Head Line being thick it is clear that financial difficulties would continue to chase the man.

The Heart Line is thick and long and has emerged from near the index finger. That means that the man has high expectations from his wife, family and friends and when they are not fulfilled he has a sense of dejection. The result is that the Heart Line has become faulty.

From the right hand you would see that the Line of Mercury has reached near the Line of Life to cross it at age 55 but has stopped short of it. This gives the impression that the Line of Life has two branches at the end. Let us look at the Line of Mercury in the left hand which crosses the Line of Life in the 50th year. It is inauspicious because after this the line of Mercury and other lines of influence form an island, which is injurious to health. He should practise the digital posture designed to strengthen the vital force so that he can keep healthy till the age of 65.

At the base of the thumb there are three lines of children -- two long and the other short. It means that he would have two sons and one daughter. He should wait till the 30th year for good times, should worship God and should wear a copper ring to strengthen the mounts of Jupiter and the Sun.

Handprint 15-A, B

It belongs to a 58-year old woman whose active hand is the left.

There are vertical strips on the nails, the first phalange of the thumb is long and the island between the two phalanges is broken. The Mount of Jupiter is over-developed, while the mounts of Venus and Aggressive Mars are under-developed. The other mounts are of normal development. There is a chain at the base of the thumb. The lines of sexuality in the right hand are short and forked.

There are two lines of sexuality in the left hand and they are inclined towards the Heart Line.

Too many lines in a hand indicate a personality whose mind is active on various channels. The fact that the first phalange of the thumb is longer indicates resoluteness. Vertical lines on the nails speak of tension and depression. In spite of the fact that lines on her hand are thin and auspicious, she is bereft of peace of mind and is under tensions. Let us go into some detail and find out the reason why.

One look at the hand and you feel that this is the hand of a very ambitious lady, because in both the hands the Line of Life has emerged from the Mount of Jupiter or its branches have gone to this mount. The mount itself is well-developed. All these signs speak of overweaning ambition. And excess of ambition brings disquiet.

A line of influence touches the Line of Saturn in the left hand at age 21. This acts as a bridge between this line and the Line of Life. Later there is another line of influence between the Line of Saturn and the Line of Life which continues till the 30th year. In the right hand the Line of Saturn starts with an island and the island has continued till the 26th year. All these signs speak of a life of want till the age of 21 and there was no happiness from the parents. For confirmation of this, notice the island and broken lines between the Head Line and the Line of Life during this period. Till the 26th year there have been problems of every kind and for 30 years she has been subjected to family pressures.

A line of influence emerges from the Mount of Luna at age 21 and meets the Line of Saturn in the 30th year. That means that the lady had a love affair, but because of the opposition from the family there have been obstructions to the fulfilment of her desire to join her paramour. But, being a very determined person she has married him in spite of the opposition from the family.

Except the Heart Line all other main lines are thin and deep. It was the fault in the Heart Line which created obstructions in her love affair : the fact that the Heart Line has started as a tassel under the Mount of Saturn shows that her love affair was based on selfish motives.

The Mount of Venus is undeveloped but the grill on it makes it as effective as a developed one. The line of sexuality is downward looking and the Line of Mars in the left hand is incomplete which means that her relation was never happy and that she carried on somehow or the other. There is self-interest involved in this because the financial position of her husband is better. She does not clearly accept this face, however. She has to pay for her ambition through depression and tension from which she suffers.

The Line of the Sun emerges from the Line of Saturn in the 32nd year. Because of a line of influence there is a triangle at the starting point of the Line of the Sun. It signifies success in relationships. In the 42nd year the Line of Saturn emerges from the Line of Life which nears the Heart Line and along with a line of influence reaches the Mount of Saturn. But an axe line also is found going along the Line of Saturn. This signifies financial gain after the 50th year

16-A, The Right Hand
Lines which are neither thick, nor thin.

16-B, The Left Hand
See the point of origin of the Line of Saturn. Is it forked? Or, is it something else?

but there are also problems. Near the fingers some lines make tassles which speak of lack of peace of mind after middle age. All these signs can be interpreted to mean that between 30 and 50 she had a happy life but later on there is a disturbance in the relations. The reason for this is that her marital life is not happy. It is because the Line of Mars has vanished from her left palm in her 50th year. But this line continues in her right hand. That is why her relations with the spouse have not broken up, but have continued somehow or the other.

There is an island in the Line of Life in the left hand after the 65th year. In the right palm the Line of Life stops at this age which shows loss of health. It may be due to a nervous breakdown which is evidenced by the mass of oblique lines on the palm. It may be good from a financial point of view but very bad for her peace of mind.

She should undertake exercises to watch her breath and regain her peace of mind. She should also engage in acts of charity and dedicate herself to her favourite deity. She should also use the digital postures designed to increase the vital force so that her health improves from now onwards and she can ward off the evil which is in store for her in her 65th year.

Handprint 16-A, B

It belongs to a youth of 19 whose active hand is the left one.

The hand is heavy, large and pliable. In the fingerprints there are 6 whorls one double loop, one closed loop and two normal loops. The thumb is short, the second phalange being larger. Between the phalanges of the thumb is an incomplete island. At the base is a large, but incomplete island. The fingers are thick and even when spread like a fan they tend to stay close to each other. The Defensive Mars is undeveloped while the mounts are of normal development. The line of sexuality in both the hands is near the little finger and not the Heart Line. He wants to know when he would get wealth.

Six whorls in the fingerprints and thick fingers which tend to stay close to each other in spite of their being spread and a short thumb are all signs of a person who does not easily change his views. But a soft skin and the large second phalange of the thumb tend to mollify the evil effect of these signs. Except the Defensive Mars all the mounts are of normal development. The heavy hand is also an auspicious sign which reduces the evil effect of the inauspicious lines. Thick fingers in a heavy hand and the short distance between them even when spread do not speak of a person who could engage in trade. Nor are they auspicious signs for a studious mind. But these signs are good for industry and production. When his efforts would bear fruit can be known from a study of the lines.

Taking the left hand as the main object of study we now see the lines.

The Line of Life is circular and ends towards the Mount of Luna which shows that there is a possibility of foreign travel. The time when this would be a possibility is the 32nd year, as we see from the Lines of the Sun. There is no Line of Mars in this hand which shows that the man does not want any cooperation from any quarter. It is possible that he would stand on his own feet.

The Line of Life which appears to have two branches at the end or in the beginning of the Line of Saturn is a very confusing sign. The Line of Saturn has emerged from near the wrist (from the lower end of the Mount of Venus) and after having crossed the Line of Life enters the area of Saturn in the 20th year. This Line of Saturn meets another which has emerged from the Mount of Luna. This meeting point of the two lines creates the impression that the Line of Life has two forks at the end and the Line of Saturn begins with two forks. In fact this is the Line of Saturn which has emerged from the Mount of Venus. Another Line of Saturn emerges from the Mount of Luna and this combination creates a confusion.

The Line of Saturn which has emerged from the Mount of Venus is an indication that this person would remain under the influence of his family till the 21st year. Afterwards, he would join the family business. But, in addition to that, he would have some part-time work. In the 26th year the part-time job would be converted into a full-time one.

Another Line of influence emerging from the Line of Life meets the Line of Saturn in the 30th year. The junction of all these lines looks like the sign of the fish between the Line of Life and the Line of Saturn. This sign is in the area of Saturn and that is why the rule for the calculation of age from Saturn applies here. It can be interpreted to mean that the time between the ages of 21 and 30 is the time of financial gain.

The Line of Saturn coming from the Mount of Venus meets the one coming from the Mount of Luna in the 26th year which signifies marriage of the youngman. The conclusion is supported by the line of sexuality which is nearer the little finger rather than the Heart Line, which indicates marriage after the 25th year.

Lines of the Sun are merging from the Line of Saturn in the 31st and the 32nd years. They form many triangles in conjuction with the Head Line. Above the Head Line too many lines of influence form triangles. This is a sign that after the 30th and the 35th year there would be many gains in the matter of finances and property. There would also be fluctuations because the lines of influence do not go to the end.

In left hand a Line of the Sun starts from the Head Line which is bisected by a line of influence in the 35th year. This line has come from the Aggressive Mars. This bisected by influence line. It is an indication of a love affair in that age, which might bring some disrepute, but because the Line of the Sun continues till the end this possibility of a bad name might be warded off.

The Heart Line is emerging from below the Mount of Saturn and except the beginning and the end of the Heart Line there is no fork or branch in between. There is a short Line of the Mars but it is indistinct. These signs speak of lack of responsibility in sexual relations. But, this is for the students to understand -- how much the client is to be told depends on their discretion and judgement.

17-A, The Right Hand
Look at the peculiarity of the Line of Life in both the hands and calculate the age till which the owner of his hand would live.

17-B, The Left Hand
Note the difference between the Heart Lines on the two hands.

The Heart Line has many forks in the beginning which shows that the man would get financial gain from his parents.

At the base of the thumb is a large island which is broken. At the end of the Heart Line there is only one fork. Near the base of the thumb there is one long and two short lines. All these lines of progeny indicate that in the final analysis the man would have only one child.

The Line of Life is thick after the 50th year : that is time when family problems are likely to crop up. After the 63rd year there is a short parallel line under the Line of Life which accompanies it till the end. This line tends to offset the inauspicious effects of the Line of Life. That means that after some trouble in the 65th year the man would live to be 75.

The gist of the whole thing is that from the point of view of finances and also health the man is lucky.

Handprint 17-A, B

The handprint belongs to a 40-year old businessman whose active hand is the right one.

The thumb is large. There are two lines between the two phalanges of the right thumb. Between the phalanges of the left thumb there is a broken island. On the base of the right thumb there are two large islands while there is one large island on the base of the left thumb. There is not much distance between the fingers when they are spread. The little finger is long and the mounts of Venus, Jupiter and the Aggressive Mars are under-developed. The mounts of the Sun and the Mercury are developed. The other mounts are of normal development. In the right hand the line of sexuality which is above the other one is long but downward looking. There are two straight lines of sexuality in the left hand. There are eight whorls and two closed loops in the fingerprints.

The man wants to give up his share in the family business in which his brothers are partners and wants to strike on his own in a different city. He wants to know whether he should do it or not.

Let us study the hand signs with this query in view. Later, we shall come to other matters. The Line of Life is straight in both the hands. In the right hand there is an axe line with the Line of Life which continues till the 28th year. In the 30th year the Line of Life has two branches, the smaller branch or fork looks towards Mars. The larger one looks towards Saturn. The large branch is clear till the 40th year and becomes indistinct later on. In the left palm a branch of the Line of Life touches the Line of Saturn.

A straight Line of Life, a Line of Life with an axe line -- both these conjunctions point towards family problems. Normally a small Line of Life indicates a short life, but, in fact, it is not so. Here keeping in view the query our client has made, the short Line of Life is an indication of change of place.

In the right palm there is a depression under the mounts of Sun and Saturn near the Line of Saturn. According to the rule applicable to the Line of Saturn the time would be between the 33rd and the 40th year. This is a period of serious difficulties but it is now coming to an end. That is why a change of place is a certainty. The effect of the depression is over after the 40th year and the branch of the Line of Life in the left palm has touched the Line of Saturn. The Line of Saturn gives support to the Line of Life and that means that the time of difficulties is almost over.

In the 30th year a line starts from the Defensive Mars and goes towards the mounts of Mercury and the Sun. A line ends between the 30th and the 40th year. Another line which starts from the area of Saturn earlier than that, covers it. This other line stops at the Heart Line. This is a sure sign of the change of business/place. But, what one has to find out is whether this change is for the good or has any evil consequences. The answer is that the change is all for the good because in the 40th year the evil effect of the depression in the palm is ending. Lines of influence which intersect the Line of Saturn and the Line of Mercury have their effect till the 40th year. After that there are no obstructions. The Sun Line is clear in the left palm after the age of 35.

Let us now interpret the other signs of the hand.

The Head Line starts from the Aggressive Mars which shows the amount of anger in the man. The eight whorls on the fingerprints and the short distance between the fingers when spread, points to a man of fixed views who does not change easily. The Head Line has (two branches) from the very beginning. It shows that in the beginning there is financial gain. It is due to patrimony in the form of ancestral property which, when sold, gives him a lot of money. This is the capital which has helped him to start a new venture in a different city.

In the Line of Saturn on the right palm there is an island between the ages of 20 and 23. One of the lines which forms this island goes towards the Mount of Luna which is a sign of mental disquiet. The broken island between the two phalanges of the thumb is not good for the man's finances, but there are many triangles near the Line of Saturn in the right hand. In the left, there is a large rectangle between the ages of 21 and 33. There are two triangles after that. All these signs are indicative of removal of all difficulties from a financial point of view. The Mount of Mercury is well-developed, the little finger is long and the Mount of Apollo is also well-developed. All these make for a comfortable financial position. The Mount of Jupiter is under-developed which in conjuction with the developed Mount of Mercury and a long little finger could lead the man astray and he could take to evil ways. But, he has beautiful Rings of Solomon in both the hands which seek to reduce the tendency towards self-centredness caused by the developed Mount of Mercury and a long little finger. This man will never make money out of anti-social things.

The lines of sexuality in the right hand look downwards which tend to cause discord between the husband and the wife. To know the time when this discord would raise its ugly head, look at the Line of Mars. It becomes indistinct at the age of 55. In the 65th year a new line of Mars starts from another point. These ten years are a difficult period from the point of health as well as marital life. Later on, the situation would improve. The cause of marital discord is the

18-A, The Right Hand
There is a difference between the Line of Life and the Line of Mars in the two hands.

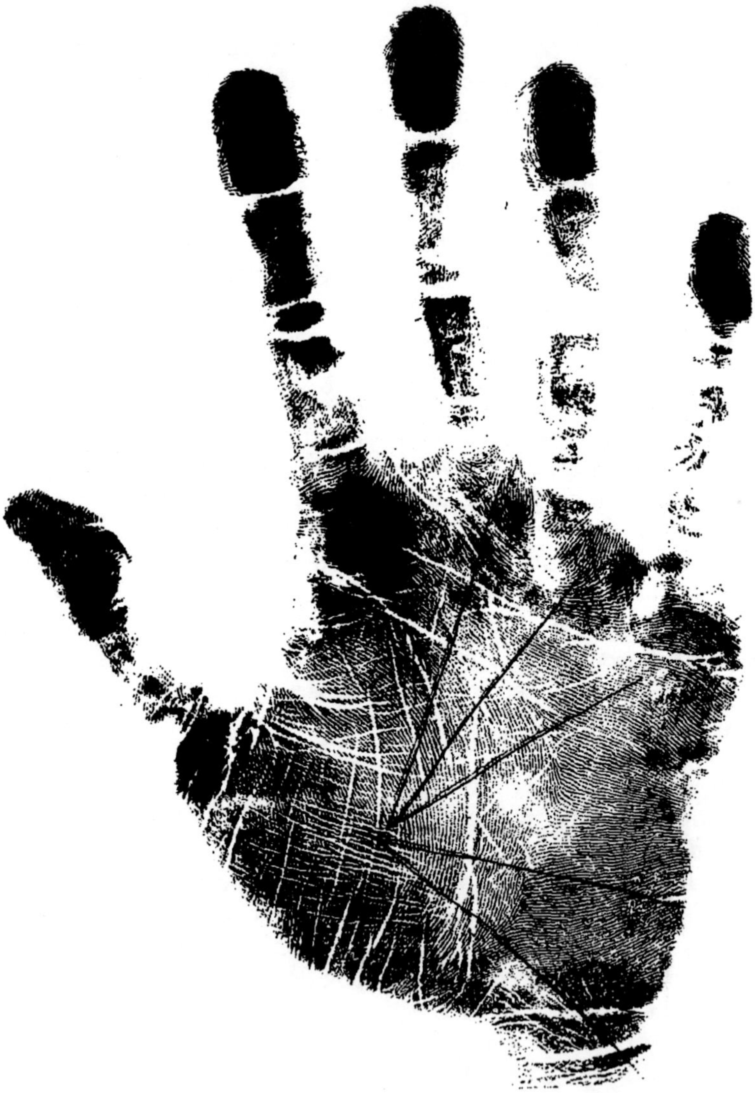

18-B, The Left Hand
The distorted shape of the mounts of Mercury and Apollo is due to corn like surfaces on the palms.

dictatorial nature of the man. It is caused by the Heart Line which in the left palm goes from one end to the other and is twisted like a rope. In the Right hand the Heart Line is short, but one arm of the Girdle of Venus supports it to give the man psychological strength. But, he must curb his dictatorial nature and also emotions so that he can understand the sentiments of his wife. He should wear a topaz which will help him to acquire the sense of proportion and discretion in marital affairs.

To get rid of the fault of the Line of Life he should undertake the exercise of digital postures designed to strengthen the heart so that he can live a happy life after the age of 55 and also to maintain good health.

At the base of the right thumb there are two large islands and at the base of the two thumbs two clear lines emanating from the Mount of Venus indicate that he would have two children who would be a source of happiness for him till the end of his days.

The remedies suggested above would give him strength and he can expect to be healthy and happy after 55. He should also wear a copper ring or a coral to remove the fault of an under-developed Mars.

Handprint 18-A, B

The handprint belongs to a 40-year old travel agent whose active hand is the right one.

The hand is hard and the fingers tend to stay close to each other even when they are spread. There are seven whorls in the fingerprints. The first phalange of the thumb is short. There are two broken lines between the two phalanges of the thumb and there are vertical stripes on the nails. The Mount of Jupiter, Defensive Mars and the Mount of Luna are undeveloped, the other mounts being normal in development. There is one line of sexuality in the right hand which is downward looking. In the left there is one line of sexuality which is straight. In the left hand there are hard spaces resembling corns on the Mount of Apollo and the Mount of Mercury which have been caused by driving a motor cycle and carrying a heavy bag.

The main question is about marital life and the time when he would get ahead in the world.

First we should look at the line of sexuality to know about his marital life. In the right palm it is downward looking. Later we will take a look at the Line of Life and the Line of Mars.

The Line of Life in the right hand is straight and finishes off in the 30th year. The Line of Mars too becomes indistinct in this year. Later it vanishes and reappears in the 65th year. The Line of Life is circular and long in the left hand but there is an elongated island till the age of 21. It shows family problems from the very beginning, but the active hand is the right one according to which there are many problems in the family and marital life. The other lines parallel to the Line of Mars provide support which give strength to the man.

The earlier part of the Line of Saturn is forked. It shows that the person was deprived of the love of parents in his childhood. A triangle adjacent to the Line of Saturn between the years 28 to 32 signifies financial gain during this period. But it is this period during which the Line of Mars stops and becomes indistinct. That is why marital problems have become more serious in this period. The man himself says that during that period he had secured a good job but members of his wife's family somehow managed to have him dismissed. Going into details he informed me that the family of his wife is better off financially than he is. Socially too that family is better than his own. He says that his wife's family, under whose influence the wife and his children are, cannot countenance the idea that he should rise above his present status and managed to have his services terminated whenever he is able to secure a good job.

The man may be right when he says that his wife's family is socially and financially better than his own but if that family comes in the way of his progress it is due to his own stubborn nature. The signs of such a nature are all there -- a hard hand, the fingers which stay close to each other even when spread and the multiplicity of whorls in his fingerprints. The Head Line in the left hand has started from the Aggressive Mars. All these signs show that the man is incapable of adapting himself to the circumstances and his wife is probably of a strong character who cannot abide by his stubbom nature. It is because of this that she goes and stays with her parents. But, then, every person justifies his own behaviour. One has, therefore, to point out these things indirectly. Alternatively, one must remain mum on this issue.

Whatever the reason his life is full of struggle till the age of 42, because the Line of Saturn is thick till the age of 35 after which it thins out. This thin Line of Saturn ends at the Head Line in the 42nd year. A new Line of Saturn emerges from another point on the Head Line in this year. From another point in the Head Line another thin Line of Saturn emerges. Both these lines are indicative of a beneficial change in that year. The man must rest content for the next two years and keep his peace.

The Heart Line in the left hand is thick and the one in the right hand has forks which are heading towards the Head Line. It tends to strengthen the Head Line and sentiments remain subdued. A line parallel to the Heart Line starts from the base of the index finger which strengthen the Heart Line again. That is how the fault of the Heart Line is removed and the Line of Life is also improved because its fault has been reduced to a great extent. Had this not been so the short Line of Life would have meant a short life. Looking at the Heart Line we can say that he will live a full life which might be more than 75 years because a segment of the Line of Mars makes up for the final part of the short Line of Life.

There does not appear to be any marital or family happiness in store for him. The only ray of hope for him is that the last obstacle he would face would be in his 42nd year. Afterwards it would be financial security, but in order to make that state of affairs permanent he must learn to compromise. The Mount of Jupiter should, for that purpose, be strengthened and for that wearing a topaz

19-A, The Right Hand
The junction of the Line of Luna and the Line of Meercury gives the false impression of a line of intuition.

19-B, The Left Hand
Notice the distance between the Line of Life and the Head Line.

is the right stone. If he cannot afford a topaz he should wear copper and undertake the exercise to watch one's breath. That would give him peace of mind. It would help him to develop a balanced state of mind.

Handprint 19-A, B

It is the handprint of a 37 year old woman entrepreneur whose active hand is the right one.

The thumb is large and there is a distinct island between the two phalanges of the right hand. In the left hand there is a string of islands and a chain at the base of the thumb. The index finger is short and the third finger long. The fingers are placed in the shape of an arch. When spread the fingers are not much distant from each other. The Mount of Mercury is well-developed and the Aggressive Mars is under-developed. The other mounts are normal in development.

The lady is in the garment export business and wants to expand it. Her question is whether the present is the right time to do so.

We would look at the lines of the palm, particularly those of the right palm, first with this query in view.

There is an island in the middle of the thumb. The mount of Mercury is developed and the fingers are placed in the shape of an arch. These are auspicious signs from the point of view of financial gain. To know which is the best time we cast a look on the lines.

The Sun Line arises after the 36th year and between the ages of 35 and 40 there is a triangle adjacent to the Line of Saturn. The Line of Mercury is improved after the 28th year. After 35 the Line of Mercury is clear and is inclined towards a point between the mounts of Mercury and Apollo. After the 42nd year a clear Line of Saturn has emerged. All these signs point towards profits from business. The time is ripe to expand the business but its good results would become apparent in the 42nd year, when a thin Line of Saturn emerges from the Head Line.

Let us now look at the hand from the point of view of student of palmistry. From the financial point of view this is a good hand but from the point of view of a family and marital life it is not good.

The line of sexuality is downward looking, the Line of Mars is fragmented and is constantly away from the Line of Life. It signifies distanced relations with the spouse or differences of opinion between them. The reasons will be apparent when we study the other signs.

The Line of Life and the Head Line have arisen at a distance from each other and there are many short lines between the two. The thick branch of the Heart Line meets the Head Line. The fingers appear to be close to each other in spite of their being spread. The thumb and the third finger are long. These are the signs of a woman with a strong personality. Had the husband been of a pliable nature, a compromise could have been reached, but, it appears that he too is a man of a strong character and stubborn. This has led to faults in the Line of

Mars and other lines. The Heart Line and the Head Line are thick. The Line of Life is comparatively thicker in the right palm, which also signifies a life of struggle and family troubles.

According to her own statement the woman lives separately from her husband for the past ten years, but no divorce has resulted. She is too busy to run her business to think of obtaining a divorce.

In the 21st year a line emerging from the Mount of Luna meets the Line of Saturn in the 25th year. From this meeting point till the age of 28 there is a multiplicity of lines which vitiate the Line of Saturn. From that year onwards the Line of Saturn improves a little bit when the Line of Mercury emerges from there which is inclined somewhat towards the Mount of Apollo. This shows that she married in her 21st year. The marital discord started in the 25th year and from the 28th year she started her own business.

Between the ages of 28 and 35 there is a triangle adjacent to the Line of Saturn which is indicative of financial gain. On the other side (the one towards the Line of Life) of the Line of Saturn on the right palm there is an island between the ages of 30 and 36. Between 35 and 42 there are two triangles. Near the Line of Saturn there is a sign of the fish or an elongated square between the Line of Saturn and the Line of Mercury. This means that between the ages of 28 and 42 while there has been gain from many sides there have been losses too. But, on the whole, there has been financial gain.

In the age of 23 a line of influence emerges out of the cross on the Mount of Luna and meets the Line of Mercury/Sun at age 32. This line of influence is intersected by oblique lines between the ages of 26 and 28. This could mean a partnership, a love affair or both. The lady says that it was a partnership. She is not clearly saying whether it was a love affair, but, I think that in the beginning it was a partnership. After some obstacles which appeared between the ages of 26 and 30, it has turned into a love affair. Probably it is because of this that there has been discord with her husband, because a line of influence from the Mount of Luna is there in the left hand too, but the time is different. I would, however, take it that the period indicated by the right palm is the right one.

A circular line emerging from the Mount of Luna meets the Line of Mercury which appears to be a line of intuition. But this has the effect of half a line of intuition, which is indicative of a business acumen, imaginativeness and common sense.

After the age of 35 the Line of Life is constantly thick. The incomplete, short lines of the Mount of Mars would not let the family relation remain sweet. There is danger that as there is financial gain there would be family problems too. The index finger or the Mount of Jupiter must be strengthened to ward off those problems, so that the effect of the Mount of Mercury -- selfishness -- could be mollified. Topaz would be the proper stone for her to wear.

On the base of the left thumb there are four lines of progeny. In the right hand there is one distinct line, which means that more children are possible, but

20-A, The Right Hand
The number of lines are limited
and they are t' ick.

20-B, The Left Hand
There is no Line of Saturn in the hand, but there is one in the right.

only one would support his/her mother. The lady says she has two daughters both of whom live with her.

The Line of Mercury intersects the thick Line of Life in the 63rd year, which indicates loss of health in this age. In order to know what diseases she is in danger of suffering from, look at the many crosses lines on the Mount of Luna. The Heart Line is like a thick rope and there are many influence lines making crosses on the palms. These signs show that she should beware of diseases of the nervous system, heart ailments and hypertension. She should use the digital postures to strengthen the vital force, the heart and the brain. That would save her from any health problems in the 63rd year.

The supplementary line above the Heart Line tends to reduce the fault of the Heart Line. The Line of Mercury intersects the Line of Life; even after that the Line of Life continues which shows a long life. She should use the above remedies to have a happy and long life.

Handprint 20-A, B

The handprint belongs to a 21-year old youth, whose active hand is the right one.

The hand is hard, the thumb long and its second phalange longer of the two. There are two short lines on the junction of the two phalanges of the thumb and a chain of islands at its base. The little finger is short and is in a low setting. The Mount of Venus is well-developed but the other mounts are of normal development. There is one line of sexuality in the right palm situated slightly above the middle portion of the Heart Line near the little finger. There are two lines of sexuality on the left palm; the upper one is long and the lower one short. There are nine whorls in the fingerprints.

Normally a person in this age group wants to know about his marriage and his career.

A person with a hard hand is not afraid of hard work and does not change his views lightly. The number of whorls in the fingerprints supports the view that he is of fixed ideas.

A long thumb is an indication of sagacity. The second phalange of the thumb being long shows that he is able to make plans, but because of the shortness of the first phalange, the plans do not come to fruition. The little finger is short and is placed in a low setting. Such a person is generally simple-minded and suffers from a sense of inferiority.

If the number of lines in a palm is limited, it becomes difficult to make any predictions. It also signifies that there will not be many ups and downs in life. Progress of such a person would always be slow.

The thick line indicates struggle, but a gain which is not commensurate with the efforts put in. Two broken lines between the phalanges of the thumb also support this view.

There is a Line of Saturn in the right hand, but it is missing in the left. This shows that the person is trying to rise above the social position of his family.

The question is when this desire of his would be fulfilled. Let us try to answer this question and find out when the good times would come.

The Line of Life is thick in the beginning and there are islands over it. His childhood has passed in want. The Line of Life in the right palm has become thin in the 35th year. This is the time when his fortunes would be in the ascendant. In the right palm a faint Line of Saturn has emerged in the 26th year and it has become distinct in the 35th year. Let us also look at the lines of sexuality in addition to this Line of Saturn which emerged in the 26th year. Those lines are a little above the middle of the palm. That means that there is a possibility of marriage in the 26th year and his fortunes would start improving from that time onwards. Greater improvement should come in the 35th year.

In the 35th year a line parallel to the indistinct Line of Saturn emerges from the Line of Life but it is not yet well-defined. One can hope that it would become distinct, because the tendency is towards improvement. The reason for this is that the lines on the right palm are better than those on the left. In the 35th year financial gain and better prospects in a job are indicated.

There being no Line of Mars means that there is no hope of any help or cooperation from any quarter and the man has to march forward on his own. The fact of his not being able to get any help from anybody is confirmed by the hardness of the hand, and the multiplicity of whorls in the fingerprints. These signs show a wayward nature of the man. The Heart Line is long in the right hand and short in the left one, but in the left palm there is a parallel line above the Heart Line which tends to reduce the fault of a short Heart Line. The Line of Life is also long and without any obstructions. A developed Mount of Venus is an indication of a considerable vital force : it shows that he has the capacity to ward off all kinds of diseases. It is possible that he would be healthy till the age of 75.

The Line of Life has two forks at the end, one of which goes towards the Mount of Luna. This shows a tendency for the man to settle at a place other than the one where he was born. He was born in Garhwal but has settled in Delhi which confirms the reading. But the man wants to go abroad. His desire would be fulfilled after 35.

A vertical line on the Mount of Apollo is an indication that the person might have all his desires fulfilled after the age of 60. But that time is far off. But by that time there is a possibility that many changes might take place. If he takes remedial action the fortunate time could be advanced.

There are two distinct islands at the base of the thumb and two clear lines on the Mount of Venus near the right thumb are a clear indication that he would have two children.

He must wear an iron ring to bring forward the happy times when he would be able to make progress. He should examine his palms immediately on waking and should pray to his favourite deity. That would give him peace of mind and the happy times would come nearer.

CHAPTER XVI

HAND LINES ARE SUBJECT TO CHANGE

In order to prove that the lines continue to change the author had included two handprints in the first chapter of his earlier work ALL THE SECRETS OF PALMISTRY. Both the handprints of the right Palm of the author, one taken in 1978 and the other in 1988. In the following pages are reproduced three handprints each of the two palms taken in three different years. That should convice you that handlines continue to change. In other words, certain remedies and hard work can change a person's luck or fortune.

A- Handprint of the right hand taken in 1978 at age 48.

B- The Left Hand- the lines of influence in the two hands are not many.

C- Handprint of the right hand
taken in 1988 at age 58.

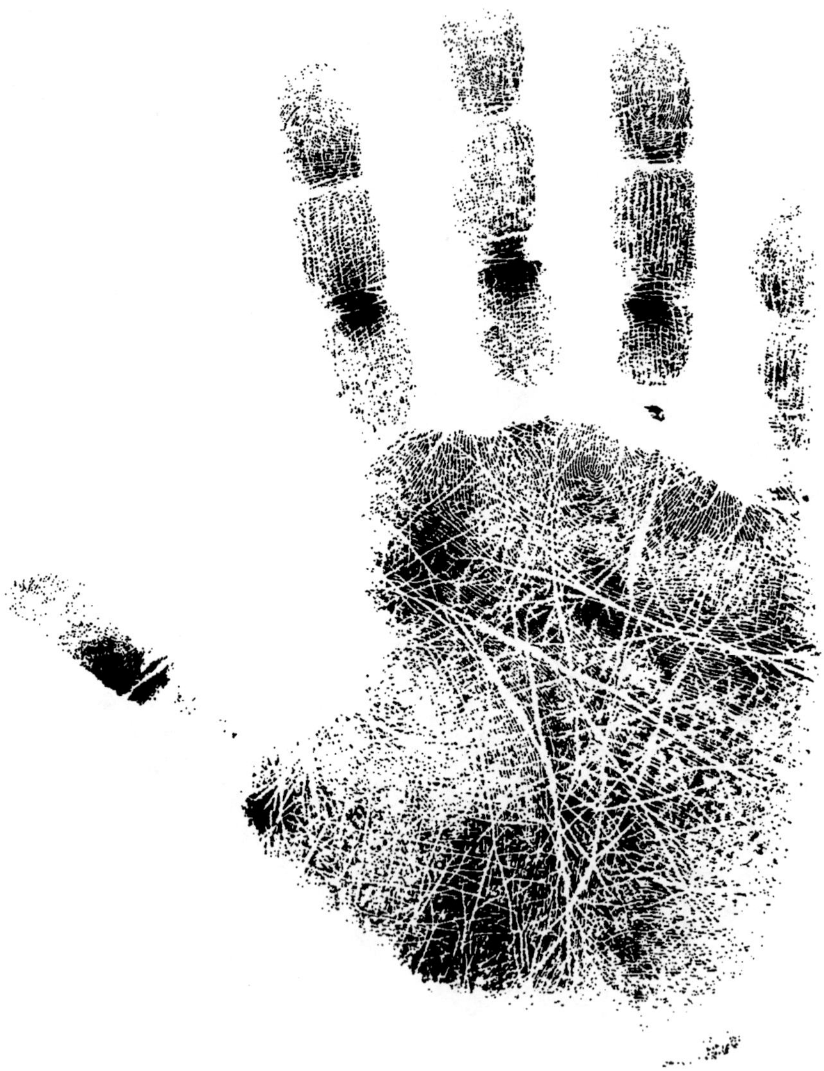

D- The Left Hand- the lines of influence in both the hands are so many that it is difficult to identify the main lines.

E- Handprint of the right hand taken in 1991 at age 61.

F- The Left Hand: the number of lines of influence has gone down and the main lines have become more distinct.